The Mexican Revolution

A Documentary History

The Mexican Revolution

A Documentary History

Edited and Translated, with an Introduction, by

Jürgen Buchenau and Timothy Henderson

Hackett Publishing Company, Inc.
Indianapolis/Cambridge

25 24 23 22   1 2 3 4 5 6 7

For further information, please address
    Hackett Publishing Company, Inc.
    P.O. Box 44937
    Indianapolis, Indiana 46244-0937

    www.hackettpublishing.com

Cover and interior designs by E. L. Wilson
Composition by Aptara, Inc.

Cataloging-in-Publication data can be accessed via the Library of Congress Online
Catalog. Library of Congress Control Number: 2022932816

ISBN-13: 978-1-64792-079-1 (pbk.)
ISBN-13: 978-1-64792-082-1 (PDF ebook)

The paper used in this publication meets the minimum requirements of American
National Standard for Information Sciences—Permanence of Paper for Printed
Library Materials, ANSI Z39.48–1984.

∞

CONTENTS

Contents

Contents

ACKNOWLEDGMENTS

This project was born during a lunch meeting during the 2016 meeting of the Southern Historical Association in St. Petersburg, Florida. We had gone to graduate school at UNC Chapel Hill together, lucky enough to study under Gilbert M. Joseph. Sharing our mentor's passion for the Mexican Revolution, both of us finished dissertations (and then published books) centered in large part on Mexico's revolutionary experience. We were interested in different regions and issues: Jürgen, in the border states and urban history, and Tim, in Puebla and agrarian history. We came together to compile this document reader because of our shared interest in letting historical witnesses speak. In this volume, we coauthored the Introduction; Tim edited Sections I–IV, spanning the period from the Old Regime to the Constitutionalist triumph in 1915; and Jürgen, Sections V–VIII, ranging from that triumph to World War II.

Aside from Gil, whose mentorship we have both treasured for the past three decades, we would like to acknowledge Rick Todhunter, who invited us to develop this collection of historical documents for Hackett Publishing. We also appreciate the help of Madison Green with two of the translations. Finally, we thank Duke University Press and the University of New Mexico Press for allowing the use of materials from two previous document readers: *The Mexico Reader: History, Culture, Politics*, edited by Gilbert M. Joseph and Timothy Henderson (Durham, NC: Duke University Press, 2003), and *Mexico OtherWise: Modern Mexico in the Eyes of Foreign Observers*, edited by Jürgen Buchenau (Albuquerque: University of New Mexico Press, 2005).

INTRODUCTION

The Mexican Revolution is arguably the key episode in the country's modern history. Perhaps its most notable aspect is its apparent lack of coherence and meaning. Although it was fertile in the production of slogans, heroes, and martyrs, it differed from, say, the French or Russian Revolutions in that it had no central premise or ideology. The revolution began with fighting between revolutionaries and the old regime, but quickly became a multifaceted fight of revolutionaries against other revolutionaries. It was often unclear precisely what each faction represented beyond a will to gain power. In fact, the revolution was so diverse and chaotic that historians have proposed different dates as its end point. Some view the Constitution of 1917 as the watershed between revolution and reconstruction, but most scholars have settled on the Plan of Agua Prieta of 1920—which inaugurated the last violent change of government to date. However, civil wars and major rebellions continued to wrack Mexico in the 1920s, and equally meaningful dates are 1929 (the foundation of the national revolutionary party), 1940 (the last year of the presidency of Lázaro Cárdenas, widely seen as the apogee of revolutionary reform), or 1946 (the transition to a civilian government not headed up by a participant in the revolution).

Nevertheless, the revolution became the touchstone of modern Mexican politics and culture. Images of the revolution's heroes—especially Pancho Villa and Emiliano Zapata—became ubiquitous. The political party created in an effort to tame the revolution's persistent passions would go on to govern Mexico until the year 2000, and for most of that time it justified its hold on power by referring to its supposed popular and revolutionary origins. The revolution's proudest achievements—the most sweeping agrarian reform ever carried out in Latin America up to that time; a constitution that expanded and protected the rights of all citizens; an expanded system of popular education; and new ideas in culture and the arts that glorified the theretofore-scorned contributions of indigenous peoples—turned out to be less impressive than advertised in the long run. These achievements nevertheless became key parts of the narrative of history, sometimes aiding and sometimes complicating the work of the country's leaders.

THE PORFIRIATO

The Mexican Revolution grew out of myriad popular manifestations of discontent engendered by the long dictatorship of Porfirio Díaz. Díaz, an army general who had distinguished himself in the war against the French Intervention (1861–1867), mounted an armed rebellion in 1876 that overthrew his predecessor, whom he accused of attempting to illegally prolong his tenure in office. The slogan of Díaz's rebellion—"effective suffrage, no reelection"—seemed genuine for a time, as Díaz surrendered the presidency from 1880 to 1884. But when he resumed office after that interregnum, it became clear that he had no intention of ever again abandoning power. His rule extended over three decades, a period known to historians as the Porfiriato (1876–1911).

The Porfiriato was a time of rapid and sweeping change. With the help of the army and a rural police force known as the *rurales*, Díaz was able to impose a level of stability that Mexico had not experienced in the half century since gaining independence from Spain. Díaz was also helped by a substantial quickening in the global economy, as railroads and steamships allowed trade to increase in both pace and volume. "Peripheral" nations like Mexico became integral to that global economy, mostly as suppliers of raw materials to the industrial countries. Mexico embarked on a feverish campaign of infrastructure improvement: railroads grew from around 500 miles at the start of the Porfiriato to over 15,000 miles by its end; telegraph lines went from 4,420 miles to nearly 20,000,000 miles; and roads and ports and postal service were likewise expanded and upgraded.

By some measures, the results were spectacular indeed. Mexico's exports quadrupled, while its gross domestic product nearly tripled. The government was able to finally repay foreign debts dating back to the early republic; foreign lenders, who had shunned Mexico for decades, now fell over one another to lend money; foreign investment flooded in, helping produce cotton fabrics, tobacco products, beer, soap, and other manufactured goods. The silver that Mexico had been exporting for more than three centuries was now joined by other minerals—copper, lead, zinc, and eventually petroleum—highly prized in the industrialized world. New commercial crops like sisal, cotton, coffee, tropical hardwoods, vanilla, cacao, and rubber found eager overseas markets.

The architects of this transformation were a group of Díaz's closest advisors known as the *"científicos"* (the scientific men), the most prominent of whom was Finance Minister José Yves Limantour. Taking inspiration from the ideology of positivism, the *científicos* scorned democratic politics in favor of technocratic expertise ("More administration, less politics" became a slogan of the Díaz regime). To their critics they were traitors who allied with Yankee imperialists against their own people; held Mexico's large indigenous population in racist contempt; belittled peasants and workers with elitist arrogance; and rigged the economy to serve their own interests rather than to benefit the people at large (doc. 1). Recent scholarship has suggested that these charges were oversimplified. The Díaz regime was wary of U.S. dominance and sought to balance investment from the United States with investment from Europe and Japan; and most *científico* policies were in line with those practiced throughout Latin America, and indeed throughout much of the nonindustrialized world, at the time. The ledger sheet seems to vindicate many of their policies, at least if modernization and economic growth are the key criteria.

Moreover, there were limits on the power and influence of the *científicos*. Díaz's political strategy made extensive use of "divide and rule" tactics. His support among the *científicos* was balanced by his other key base of support, the military. As these two groups vied for his favor, Díaz remained in control. At the state and local levels, Díaz sought to ensure his control by appointing loyalists to political office, though loyalty was often contingent upon the dictator's willingness to turn a blind eye to self-dealing. Not surprisingly, local authorities often bore the brunt of popular resentment.

The flaws in the design of this political apparatus became more glaringly apparent after 1900, when the economy slowed and Díaz turned seventy. Aging along with Díaz was his entire government, which, given Díaz's unwillingness to allow new players into the political game, was increasingly a full-fledged gerontocracy. Chief allies began to concern themselves with the matter of political succession, with the most important contenders being Limantour and the most prominent figure in the military faction, General Bernardo Reyes. When Díaz was pressured to ensure the succession by appointing a vice president, he displeased nearly everyone by choosing Ramón Corral, an obscure and unpopular figure aligned with the *científico* faction.

Economic growth, impressive though it may have been on paper, created many sources of discontent and resentment of the Díaz government. Railroads spurred the development of commercial agriculture, which increased land values and diverted attention away from the production of the basic foodstuffs that sustained the popular classes. Well-heeled individuals and companies found ways to increase their landholdings at the expense of peasant villages, leaving the rural population largely landless and dependent on miserable wages and abysmal working conditions on burgeoning haciendas and plantations. The henequen fields of Yucatán, the hardwood plantations of Chiapas, the tobacco plantations of Oaxaca (doc. 4)—all became synonymous with hyper-exploitation bordering on slavery. In the small state of Morelos, just south of Mexico City, Indian villages lost land to expanding plantations raising sugarcane for domestic urban markets, most of them owned by politically connected elites (doc. 2). Whole villages simply disappeared from the map. In the north, vast chunks of public lands were sold off, supposedly in the hope of encouraging immigration and development, but which in practice further enriched regime cronies. The situation worsened as the population increased and real wages declined.

Laborers in the mines and factories also had ample cause for discontent with the Díaz regime. In a notorious episode of 1906, copper miners in the Sonoran town of Cananea, just across the Arizona border, struck in protest against a U.S.-owned company's practice of paying its U.S. employees better wages than its Mexican ones. To put down the strike, the company and its political allies invited in a company of the Arizona Rangers, and the ensuing violence left at least twenty people dead (doc. 3). The Cananea strike was especially egregious for its highlighting the regime's anti-nationalist and anti-labor policies, but it was not an entirely isolated incident. Strikes also rocked the textile industry in Puebla and Veracruz, and those strikes were put down with a similar level of ruthlessness.

While peasants and workers bore the brunt of Porfirian economic development, complaints arose from every level of society. A younger generation of educated and ambitious middle-class men chafed at the lack of opportunity in both business and politics, for many businesses favored foreigners over Mexicans, and the political system was effectively closed to newcomers. Wealthy entrepreneurs charged that the regime's favoritism toward foreigners harmed their interests; and they had a point, for many of Mexico's most valuable assets and resources—the railroads, the banks, the plantations, the mines, the oil fields—were indeed foreign-owned, and foreign entrepreneurs were among the dictator's biggest fans (doc. 5). Some old-school liberals nursed an abiding hatred for the Catholic Church and resented the fact that Díaz had pursued an accommodation with the Church that restored some of privileges taken from it in the liberal Constitution of 1857. For some, Díaz's greatest sin was simply getting old and failing to adequately provide for a continuation of his regime after he was gone.

Still, there was relatively little in the way of organized opposition, and what did exist did not threaten the regime in any serious way. In 1900, disaffected liberals who felt that Díaz had veered too far from the Constitution of 1857 formed the Mexican Liberal Party (PLM), which published its political program in 1906 (doc. 6). As the PLM came increasingly under the sway of the brothers Ricardo and Enrique Flores Magón—who, like Porfirio Díaz, hailed from the impoverished and heavily indigenous southern state of Oaxaca—it grew more radical and disposed to advocate the violent overthrow of the dictatorship. Flores Magón wielded considerable influence through the pages of his newspaper, *Regeneración* (Regeneration), which circulated widely underground, but attempted uprisings in 1906 and 1908 came to naught.

In 1908, Díaz perhaps unintentionally initiated the destruction of his regime when he gave an interview to American journalist James Creelman (doc. 7), a major figure in the era of "yellow journalism." While much of the article was devoted to Creelman's boundless fawning over the dictator, the interview did produce some important news: Díaz declared that, at long last, the Mexican people were ready to assume the responsibilities of democracy. Accordingly, said Díaz, he would step down when his current term ended in 1910, at which time he would be eighty years old, and he would not run for reelection. He invited political parties to form and candidates to campaign.

Some seized upon that invitation to mount robust campaigns. One leading candidate was General Bernardo Reyes, who had served as governor of the state of

Nuevo León and later as Díaz's minister of war. Reyes, however, proved too much of a Díaz loyalist, such that Díaz was able to quickly remove him from contention by sending him on an overseas mission—a standard tactic for neutralizing potential rivals. Less amenable to this sort of thing was the other leading candidate, Francisco I. Madero.

Madero was the thirty-five-year-old scion of a wealthy family from the northern state of Coahuila. He had been educated in France and the United States, eventually taking a graduate degree in agronomy at the University of California at Berkeley. Short and balding, with a high-pitched voice and decidedly unorthodox beliefs (while in France he had converted to spiritism and spent much time communing with the spirits of deceased forebears) and practices (he was a strict teetotaler and devotee of homeopathic medicine), he seemed an unlikely hero for the times. He had been politically active since 1904, but he stepped up his political activities after reading the Creelman interview in 1908. He was able to fast-track a book into print—*The Presidential Succession of 1910*—in which he alternated praise for the dictator's achievements with condemnations for his abuses of power and of the constitution (doc. 8). Like Díaz had done more than three decades earlier, Madero called for "effective suffrage and no reelection," eventually forming the Anti-Reelectionist Party. Mounting Mexico's first modern political campaign, Madero traveled the country, holding rallies and giving speeches, and everywhere he was greeted with tremendous enthusiasm, despite the brutal repression that often followed his appearances.

As Madero's popularity grew, Díaz unsurprisingly revealed that his declarations to Creelman had been insincere, and he prepared to have himself elected to another six-year term. Madero was arrested while campaigning in the northern city of Monterrey, and his supporters were persecuted. With the help of supporters, Madero escaped from jail and fled to San Antonio, Texas.

The Madero Revolution

Madero's program was classic liberalism as envisaged by the Constitution of 1857: he wanted free and fair elections, no reelection, basic civil liberties, expanded education, tax reform, improvements in the conditions of workers and peasants, and a diminished role for the military. It was hardly revolutionary, which proved problematic: these, many believed, were not reformist but revolutionary times.

Madero entertained emissaries from all over the republic, hearing grievances and recommendations and making promises he could not possibly keep. His revolutionary "plan"—the Plan of San Luis Potosí (doc. 9)—concerned itself mostly with denouncing Porfirio Díaz and declaring his election null. Most importantly, though, it called for armed revolution to break out on November 20, 1910.

In fact, little happened on November 20, at least partly because two days before that date, authorities had uncovered a Maderista conspiracy in the city of Puebla, headed by a shoemaker and longtime liberal activist named Aquiles Serdán. The repression was swift and brutal: Serdán's home was surrounded by soldiers and police, and the ensuing shootout left most of the home's occupants dead (doc. 10).

Nevertheless, the revolution slowly gained steam, with significant rebel movements developing in the state of Chihuahua, led by muleskinner Pascual Orozco, and in the south, led by Emiliano Zapata. Even in this early stage, one of the key themes of the revolution was emerging, namely the divergent, and essentially local, aims of the various rebel groups. The northerners' fight was mostly against the abuses of local elites who monopolized the region's wealth and political power (doc. 11); the southerners fought to regain lands stolen from the villages by the sugar plantations. For the moment they shared a common enemy and nominal allegiance to Francisco Madero, but there was little basis for any meaningful and lasting alliance. Mexico's very diversity and complexity made the revolution a messy and chaotic affair.

Nevertheless, the Madero revolution gained ground. In April, rebel forces, acting in defiance of Madero's orders, attacked the border city of Ciudad Juárez and soundly defeated the federal garrison there. Díaz finally decided his situation was dire and agreed to negotiations that resulted in his reluctant resignation and departure into European exile (doc. 13). The Treaty of Ciudad Juárez (doc. 12) stated simply that Díaz and his vice president would resign and that Díaz's secretary of foreign affairs, a lawyer named Francisco León de la Barra, would serve as interim president until new elections could be held—elections that, it was generally assumed, Madero would win.

From the outset it was clear that Madero, though idealistic and well-intentioned, was not equipped for the role he had taken on. His blunders began immediately, long before he assumed the presidency in his own right. Moderate to a fault, he sought accommodation with the key elements of the vanquished dictatorship. Many of Díaz's legislators and governors remained in office; the federal army that had sustained Díaz in power remained largely intact; and de la Barra sided decisively with conservative elites against the more progressive elements of the revolution. Even some of Madero's earliest and most reliable supporters had serious doubts as to whether he was fit for the office he occupied (doc. 14).

The revolution was an improvised affair fought by amateurs who were undisciplined and nearly impossible to control. In one of the more shameful episodes of the early revolution, Maderista troops, nominally led by the president's brother, carried out a brutal, racist massacre of Chinese people in the northern city of Torreón (doc. 15). In fact, anti-Chinese racism was rampant in Mexico; even the Mexican Liberal Party's plan featured a clause banning immigration from China. In the south, Emiliano Zapata and his followers created headaches for Madero. In their first meeting in early June of 1910, Madero suggested that Zapata disarm and demo-bilize his followers. Zapata chafed at the suggestion, noting that the revolution's promises had yet to be fulfilled (doc. 16). Soon after, Interim President de la Barra sent federal troops into Morelos to harshly enforce Madero's orders. By the time Madero was formally inaugurated as president in November, Zapata had come to regard him as a bitter enemy. His Plan of Ayala disavowed Madero as president and called for immediate agrarian reform (doc. 18). Even so, Madero continued to adhere to a very conservative agrarian policy (doc. 20).

Other enemies were not long in appearing. General Bernardo Reyes, who had initially supported Madero, declared himself a frank enemy by the time of the inauguration (doc. 17). Soon after, Pascual Orozco, in a manifesto laden with exag-gerated and scurrilous charges, declared himself in open rebellion (doc. 21). The deposed dictator's nephew, Félix Díaz, got into the act, declaring his rebellion in the coastal city of Veracruz in October 1912 (doc. 22). The hostility came from every direction: from the press, which Madero had allowed a large amount of free-dom; from conservatives, who charged that Madero's government was incapable of maintaining public order and safeguarding private property; and even from his own erstwhile supporters, the progressives in Congress, who claimed that Madero was overly eager to compromise with reactionary forces (doc. 23).

All the while, Madero continued to rely on the dubious loyalty of the federal army, whose leadership tended to hold him in contempt and to wax nostalgic for the days of the dictatorship. When two of the army's leading lights—Generals Ber-nardo Reyes and Félix Díaz—were arrested for subversion and unwisely housed in prisons in Mexico City, Madero's days were numbered. In February 1913, cadets from the military academy broke them both out of prison, and for the first time, revolutionary violence visited the nation's capital. Reyes was killed attempting to take the National Palace on the rebellion's first day, leaving Félix Díaz in charge. The army's top officer, General Victoriano Huerta, had gained Madero's trust by dutifully carrying out vicious campaigns against the Zapatistas, Orozquistas, and others, but that trust was badly misplaced. During the "Decena Trágica" (doc. 25), as the uprising came to be called, Huerta switched sides at the urging of U.S. ambassador Henry Lane Wilson, arrested Madero and his vice president, and signed a pact with Félix Díaz to assume leadership (doc. 26). Soon after, Madero and his vice president were murdered, presumably on Huerta's orders.

The Huerta Interregnum (1913–1914)

Huerta quickly proved himself the dominant figure among the coup plotters, neu-tralizing his rival Díaz by dispatching him on an overseas diplomatic mission. While most Mexicans had become disillusioned with Madero, they did not support the coup, and Huerta made little effort to win hearts and minds, ignoring critics who pleaded for a more humane approach. He opted instead for a hardline military dictatorship. He disbanded Congress by force, stifled the press, drastically increased the size of the federal army through brutal conscription, and spent lavishly of Mexico's scant resources to import arms and munitions from overseas.

Like Madero before him, Huerta soon faced a plethora of enemies. Among the first to declare against him was a wealthy landowner named Venustiano Carranza, who hailed from Madero's home state of Coahuila. In March 1913 he issued the Plan of Guadalupe (doc. 27), a narrowly political document that did nothing beyond repudiating Huerta and declaring Carranza "first chief" of the "Constitutionalist" army. As in the fight against Porfirio Díaz, disparate factions joined forces to oppose a common enemy, but beyond that there was scant basis for cooperation. Zapata distrusted Carranza from the outset, as did another major figure in the fight: Francisco "Pancho" Villa, a former bandit turned revolutionary from the northern state of Chihuahua, who commanded a loyal following, and who rose to prominence in the fight against Huerta.

While Huerta armed Mexico to the teeth and forced recalcitrant recruits into his army—some of them barely school age—he faced more than a formidable array of domestic enemies. U.S. president Woodrow Wilson, who took office barely two weeks after Huerta seized power, vehemently opposed the Huerta government, his antipathy founded on the latter's violent route to power and his disdain for democratic and liberal institutions. In late 1913 and early 1914, the United States sealed the border and authorized the sale of arms to Huerta's opponents. At the same time, Secretary of State William Jennings Bryan sent a declaration to the world's embassies that the clear policy of the United States was the overthrow of Huerta, although he left unclear exactly how aggressively it was prepared to act in pursuit of that goal (doc. 28).

That issue became clearer in April, when Mexican soldiers in the port of Tampico arrested three sailors taking on supplies for the USS *Dolphin*. While the sailors were quickly released with apologies from all concerned, including Huerta himself, the squadron commander, Henry Mayo, declared the apologies insufficient and demanded a 21-gun salute to the U.S. flag, a demand that Huerta rejected. President Wilson seized upon the pretext to ask Congress for authorization to use armed force against Mexico (doc. 29), and in late April, U.S. forces invaded and occupied the port city of Veracruz at a cost of hundreds of Mexican casualties. They remained in control of that city for a full seven months. Wilson intended the invasion principally to intercept arms shipments to the Huerta regime, and to force it to divert forces from fighting domestic enemies to battling the invaders, thus bringing about its demise. Although Wilson justified his intervention in idealistic terms, Mexicans and Latin Americans in general were weary of U.S. bullying: not only was the invasion denounced by all factions in Mexico, but it provoked heated denunciations and anti-American demonstrations throughout Mexico and the hemisphere (doc. 30).

Huerta's enemies were able to capitalize on the U.S. invasion. In June, they won a series of battles culminating in the Battle of Zacatecas, wherein Villa's Division of the North routed the federal troops and followed up with mass executions of prisoners (doc. 33). It was the bloodiest battle of the entire revolution, and one of the most important. It not only ended any hope Huerta had for remaining in power, but it also marked the definitive destruction of the federal army. Huerta resigned the presidency on July 15, 1914, attributing to the United States the lion's share of the blame for his demise.

The War of the Factions (1914–1915)

For the second time since 1911, it appeared that the revolution had triumphed, though this time the victorious revolutionaries were far less idealistic and more radical than Madero had been. While Madero had put his faith in a naïve and idealistic notion of democracy and gradual reform, eagerly compromising with the Porfirian military and civilian elite, the winners of 1914 had no such illusions. The federal army was disbanded and many old regime elites fled into exile. The new revolutionaries tended to advocate radical reforms to improve the conditions of agricultural and industrial workers, though the zeal for such reforms varied among movements and their leaders.

But serious tensions had become evident among factions of the anti-Huerta alliance long before Huerta sailed off into exile. Now, with Huerta out of the picture, the prospects were dim that the most prominent revolutionary leaders— Venustiano Carranza, Pancho Villa, and Emiliano Zapata—would find a way to cooperate, and early efforts in that direction were not promising. In August, Zapata wrote to Woodrow Wilson to insist that the revolution was, first and foremost, about restoring land to the villages. Mexico's only hope for peace and progress, he claimed, lay in the nationwide acceptance of his Plan of Ayala, some- thing that Venustiano Carranza—himself a wealthy hacendado—would never do (doc. 34). Shortly after that, a pair of Carranza emissaries traveled to Morelos to confer with Zapata and encountered absolute intransigence. The "only basis for peace that the revolutionaries of the South admit," the emissaries reported, "is absolute submission of the Constitutionalists to the Plan of Ayala in all its parts." This, of course, was hardly something Carranza could agree to (doc. 35).

Nor was any love lost between Villa and Carranza, with Villa at one point threatening to execute General Álvaro Obregón, a rival for the military leader- ship of the revolution, whom Carranza considered an important counterweight to the Villistas (doc. 36). Villa and Zapata corresponded, making clear their shared antipathy toward Carranza (doc. 37). Nevertheless, in October the revolutionary factions accepted Carranza's invitation to meet in the neutral city of Aguascalientes to discuss how to move forward. The key objective, for Carranza, would be deciding who would serve as provisional president until national elections could be held. Given that Villa and Zapata were already on record repudiating Carranza for that role, the convention had no chance of succeeding in its supposed objective and became instead a forum for the Villistas and Zapatistas to air their demands and grievances. In the most infamous outburst of the convention, Antonio Díaz Soto y Gama, an anarchist intellectual who had made common cause with the Zapatistas, declared that the Mexican flag did not represent patriotism but instead the "clerical reaction"—a claim that many saw as treasonous enough to evoke jeers and the brandishing of loaded firearms (doc. 38). Despite the controversy, the Zapatistas dominated the convention, ensuring that their Plan of Ayala was accepted as the document that would guide the revolution. Seeing that the convention was not going his way, Carranza ordered his representatives to withdraw, and in short order civil war resumed, with one faction styling itself "Constitutionalist" (Carranza's faction) and the other, "Conventionist" (Villa and Zapata).

Carranza had several decided advantages. First, the revolution's most talented general, Álvaro Obregón, fought on his behalf. Second, when the factional fighting broke out, Carranza wisely abandoned Mexico City and set up operations in the city of Veracruz, where he could commandeer Mexico's all-important customs duties and import weapons and ammunition from overseas while also controlling the oil fields in the north of the state. He also sent another of his best generals—General Salvador Alvarado—to Yucatán, where Mexico's most lucrative commodity was produced. Henequen, the fiber drawn from an agave native to the peninsula, was used to bind sheaves of wheat in the U.S. Midwest, and in the early twentieth century, Yucatán was practically the only source. Alvarado made the marketing of the fiber into a state monopoly, which brought about a significant short-term windfall that greatly aided the Carrancistas' military efforts.

During the spring and summer of 1915, the Carrancistas focused on neutralizing the threat from Pancho Villa, whose favorite tactic—mass cavalry charges—proved suicidal against Obregón's machine guns. Villa's military skills were no match for those of Obregón, who won an impressive string of battles at Celaya, León, and Aguascalientes (doc. 41). By late summer, Villa's force had been reduced to a guerrilla band, able to mount hit-and-run actions but presenting no real threat to Carranza's dominance.

Although delaying any effort to deal with the Zapatistas militarily, Carranza was able to deal a decisive blow against the southerners through legislation. His Agrarian Law of January 6, 1915, decreed agrarian reform that was more radical than the Zapatistas' Plan of Ayala (doc. 40). Whereas the latter provided for stolen lands to be returned to the villages, Carranza's law promised to provide lands to any village that needed them, whether or not they could prove that those lands had been stolen from them. The lands were to be taken from the haciendas adjacent to the villages, and the government would indemnify the owners for their losses. Although soon enough it became apparent that Carranza was unenthusiastic about agrarian reform, and although the Zapatistas had been actively carrying out their own de facto agrarian reform in the areas they controlled, the law at least suggested that all hope for social reform might not be lost under a Carranza government. The Carrancistas also made a bid to win hearts and minds by punishing merchants who engaged in corrupt price gouging, leading Zapata's own generals to petition their chief to do the same. These moves, coupled with a generous offer of amnesty to any who could be enticed to desert the Zapatista cause, seriously damaged Zapata's movement. Worsening the situation still further, during the summer of 1915, Woodrow Wilson declared that the time had come for the United States to throw its weight behind someone he deemed capable of creating a stable government (doc. 42). By October, he had determined that man was Carranza, and he cut off arms shipments to all other factions.

By late 1915, then, the Carrancistas had won the war, but they presided precariously over a ruined country. The economy had collapsed and hunger was rampant; the Zapatistas, unable to challenge their foes frontally, launched raids of terror and sabotage that kept the city folk on edge (doc. 39).

THE EARLY TRIALS OF THE REVOLUTIONARY REGIME, 1915–1916

Due to the weakness of the central government, the time between the Constitutionalist victories at Celaya, León, and Aguascalientes and the formulation of a revolutionary constitution in February 1917 featured great regional disparities in revolutionary reforms. In some states, for example, in Oaxaca and Chiapas, counterrevolutionary factions held sway and ignored mandates from the federal government. In others, such as Jalisco, Sonora, and Yucatán, Carrancista proconsuls often exceeded their instructions, heading up early examples of what President Lázaro Cárdenas later called "laboratories of the revolution."

For instance, in Sonora, military governor Plutarco Elías Calles aimed at wide-reaching reforms. Taking a cue from the prohibition movement in the neighboring United States, his first decree as governor outlawed the production, distribution, and consumption of alcohol (doc. 43). Calles also expelled all priests, levied production taxes on the U.S.-owned copper industry, and began an ambitious public education program. A year later, Governor Adolfo de la Huerta instituted a Workers' Chamber, a parallel legislature that purported to represent the interests of mine and rural laborers.

In Yucatán, Governor Alvarado went even further. He reported to Carranza that the state's planter class loathed the revolution and all that it represented (doc. 44). Hence, Alvarado devoted much of his energies to the popular mobilization of Yucatán's rural laboring classes in *ligas de resistencia*, grassroots resistance leagues. A northerner, Alvarado did not feel beholden to the entrenched interests of Yucatecan elite men, advancing women's rights to an unprecedented degree in a revolution that one historian has called a "patriarchal event." Thus the governor convened the nation's first feminist congress, with Hermila Galindo, one of the foremost feminists in 1910s Mexico, in attendance (doc. 45).

Elsewhere, the enemies of the revolution kept organizing. The most infamous of these enemies was Félix Díaz, who plotted against Carranza from his bases in Oaxaca and Veracruz. While Díaz was the foremost face of the old regime in Mexico, even he understood the need for land reform, incorporating that goal into his platform (doc. 46). Farther north in Veracruz, the warlord Manuel Peláez—an old ally of Félix Díaz—served as a bulwark of the foreign-owned oil companies, preventing central government control of the Huasteca region until 1920. Although U.S. president Woodrow Wilson had conferred de facto recognition to the Carranza administration in October 1915, the survival of this administration remained an open question.

Similarly, the defeated Conventionists remained a factor. In April 1916, what called itself the Conventionist government, at this point dominated by the Zapatistas, issued a manifesto in Jojutla, Morelos. The plan reiterated demands for land reform and municipal autonomy, but also many of Carranza's own additions to the Plan of Guadalupe (doc. 47). As the Zapatistas settled into guerrilla warfare, the Carranza government failed to find an answer.

Seemingly a beaten faction, the Villistas caused new difficulties. On March 9, 1916, Villa's remaining band of 500 fighters crossed the U.S. border and sacked the town of Columbus, New Mexico, killing eight soldiers and ten civilians before retreating back to Chihuahua (doc. 49). Within a few days, the Wilson administration readied a "Punitive Expedition" to cross into Mexico and bring Villa to justice. Carranza did not mind a limited intervention, but as the expedition wound its way south, the first chief protested the action as a violation of Mexican sovereignty (docs. 50–51). The Punitive Expedition restored luster to Villa, bestowing upon him credentials as a patriot defending his country from the gringo invaders (doc. 52). It was not until after the ill-fated Zimmermann telegram (a German promise to restore to Mexico the lands lost to the United States in the 1830s and 1840s in exchange for a German-Mexican alliance) that the U.S. government withdrew *la punitiva*, aware that the troops would soon be needed to fight German forces in Europe (doc. 53). The Punitive Expedition became a proving ground for U.S. military leaders such as John J. "Black Jack" Pershing, who would soon thereafter direct the American Expeditionary Forces in France, and the young George

S. Patton, who later became famous as a U.S. commander in the European theater in World War II.

In this atmosphere, the Constitutionalist government could not fulfill its promises. The Carranza administration confronted an economy and society in shambles. While historians still debate the body count, the number of casualties was likely at least 500,000. An at least equal number of people were injured, malnourished, or left homeless, and hundreds of thousands had migrated to the United States. The fighting had devastated the rich farmland of the Bajío, the location of the critical battles between Villa and Obregón, and many other areas, leading to a severe food shortage. In addition, banditry was rampant, and paper money was practically worthless. Those areas of the economy that remained strong—for example, the oil wells protected by Peláez—thrived precisely because they had remained insulated from the revolution, helped also by high prices for strategic commodities during the world war. Under these circumstances, reform remained slow, and Carranza believed that he needed to accommodate entrepreneurs to stimulate the economy. Cracking down on labor, he dissolved the Casa del Obrero Mundial and limited the right to strike (doc. 48).

The Constitutional Revolution, 1917–1920

It was in such conditions that the victors undertook to write a new constitution. In September 1916, Carranza called for an elected constitutional convention and instructed the delegates to complete the task in two months. He circulated a draft in advance. This draft was based on the old liberal Constitution of 1857 but had several updates, incorporating Carranza's recent concessions to campesinos and workers. But the convention exceeded this blueprint and crafted the first constitution in the entire world guaranteeing social rights such as land, secular education, and the right to strike. The constitution also gave the government broad powers over the economy. Two articles were particularly noteworthy. Article 27 stipulated the land and subsoil as patrimony of the nation, restricted foreign ownership of agriculture and mineral resources, and provided a legal framework for expropriation and nationalization in order to carry out land reform. Article 123 guaranteed the rights of urban and rural workers, including collective bargaining, the right to strike, and an eight-hour workday. These social rights created high expectations for reform in the aftermath of the revolutionary fighting. The constitution also far exceeded the 1857 document in its anticlericalism, barring the political activity of clergy, Church ownership of real property, and outdoor religious celebrations (doc. 54).

Although the constitution thus realized many of the goals expressed by the revolutionary factions, it unsurprisingly failed to end political conflict. To begin with, implementation was difficult. To become effective, the constitutional articles required enabling legislation, legislation that could always be blocked by the *amparo* powers of the Supreme Court. Opinion about the constitution varied widely: some believed that the document realized the revolution's most cherished objectives, while others considered it an overreach, especially the articles regulating the Church and private investment. Many elite critics desired to return to the 1857 Constitution (doc. 55). Opposed to the fetters on foreign investment, the U.S. government pressured the Carranza government not to apply the provisions of Article 27 to existing foreign investments (doc. 56). Fortunately for Carranza, the Wilson administration was too preoccupied with the situation in wartime Europe to focus on Mexican economic nationalism, and for his part, Carranza used this opportunity to assert the right of each country to make its own laws (doc. 57). Finally, the central government still lacked political control outside the capital. In Sonora, the state government faced a major Yaqui rebellion, and the anticlerical policies of Jalisco governor Manuel Diéguez brought forth a powerful Catholic opposition. Clearly, reform would not happen by the stroke of a pen, and Mexicans disagreed about the nature of the needed reforms.

Nonetheless, conditions in Mexico improved during 1917. The restoration of a stable central government and the U.S. entry into World War I led to rapidly rising prices for Mexican commodities. Having hoarded gold coins during the "fiesta of bullets," affluent citizens began to spend them, and many cities and larger towns experienced a swift economic recovery, although one tempered by rising food prices, which especially affected the urban lower classes.

Conditions deteriorated the following year. The so-called Spanish flu reached Mexico in the fall of 1918. This worst pandemic of the century killed more than 60 million people worldwide and at least 300,000 in Mexico. The influenza particularly ravaged areas affected by war and famine. In addition, the end of World War I brought commodity prices back down to earth, and another downturn buffeted the economy soon thereafter.

In this atmosphere, Obregón, who had resigned from his position as secretary of war in May 1917, positioned himself for a run at the presidency. A few years after his successes against Villa, Obregón continued to enjoy strong support among the revolutionary military. Obregón enjoyed the reputation as an ally of the radicals at the constitutional convention. But this macho patriarch was also plagued by allegations of cruelty and marital infidelity (doc. 61). His image as the "undefeated caudillo of the revolution" was important in an era when female contributions to the revolution remained unappreciated; for example, the role of the *soldaderas*, one of whom was later immortalized in a vignette written by the contemporary novelist Nellie Campobello (doc. 58). Carranza resented the idea of someone whom he considered a rough, uncultured man running for president and plotted to prevent Obregón's success as early as January 1919, eighteen months before the scheduled elections.

Before the electoral campaign began in earnest, Zapata was assassinated in a cowardly ambush orchestrated by Colonel Jesús Guajardo, a retainer of the Carrancista general Pablo González. Faking defection from González's army, Guajardo got Zapata to agree to meet him in the hacienda of Chinameca, where his men killed Zapata on April 10, 1919 (doc. 59). Zapata's assassination sent shock waves through rural Mexico and made him a martyr for the revolution and the cause of land reform (doc. 60). It also made the Zapatistas look for allies outside their movement, which ultimately culminated in their support of Obregón.

In June 1919, Obregón made his candidacy official by means of a moderate political platform that reached out to those alienated by Carranza's policies, including foreign investors. He portrayed his candidacy for president as a sacrifice necessary for the nation (doc. 62). Carranza responded by cracking down on Obregón's supporters, and particularly Sonora governor Adolfo de la Huerta. When the president dispatched an army, de la Huerta, former governor Calles, and other Obregonistas resisted, promulgating on April 23, 1920, the Plan of Agua Prieta, which disavowed the Carranza government (doc. 63). Two weeks later, the rebels occupied Mexico City. When the train carrying Carranza and his entourage derailed en route to Veracruz, the president and his friends tried to advance on foot, and Carranza was murdered in the hamlet of Tlaxcalantongo on May 21, 1920. Thus ended the last violent overthrow of a Mexican government to date, which ushered in Sonoran rule and the beginnings of consolidation.

CONSOLIDATION, 1920–1928

Although the Sonoran takeover came with public acclaim, the new government of Interim President Adolfo de la Huerta faced the same problems that had plagued its predecessor, and one additional complication. Rebels remained in the field, food production continued to languish, and the economy remained sluggish. Moreover, the Wilson administration denied diplomatic recognition citing the fact that de la Huerta had come to power by the force of arms, but also to achieve leverage to secure U.S. property rights. After Obregón began a four-year term in December 1920, the U.S. government doubled down on its posture, especially after the inauguration of the Republican Warren G. Harding in March 1921. But de la Huerta succeeded in accomplishing something in six months that Carranza had failed to do in three years: come to an agreement with Pancho Villa and several other rebel leaders.

The Obregón administration therefore had some leeway in beginning the process of consolidation and showed itself adept at compromise. Obregón outlined plans to carry out a modest land reform, making small awards to all those eager to farm their own land and leaving the remainder in larger private agribusinesses such as his own chickpea emporium in Sonora (doc. 64). The proclamation pleased the formerly Zapatista *agraristas* in Congress, but it hardly constituted a full-throated commitment to Zapata's Plan of Ayala. On the other side, landowners such as the U.S.-born Rosalie Evans targeted by these modest land redistributions considered any agrarian reform a threat (doc. 65). Obregón also struck an agreement with the Holy See, inaugurated relations with the Soviet Union, and finally succeeded in securing U.S. diplomatic recognition in August 1923.

On the other side of the ledger, the Obregón administration used force to expand its power. For instance, in Laredo, Texas, Mexican government agents abducted and killed the Carrancista Lucio Blanco, a popular leader who had on his own accord expropriated a hacienda from Félix Díaz in 1913 and parceled out the land to rural workers. In 1922, the government also suppressed the revolt of General Francisco Murguía, another Carranza ally. At the same time, however, the federal army decommissioned tens of thousands of officers and enlisted men in an effort to reduce the military budget.

Meanwhile, some of the states that had exceeded Carranza's mandates for reform forged further ahead. The 1920s featured the emergence of the "socialist" Southeast, a group of states that included Yucatán, Campeche, Tabasco, and Chiapas. The tenure of Yucatán governor Felipe Carrillo Puerto featured the election of the first woman to public office, Rosa Torre González (doc. 66). Unfortunately, this election marked the exception rather than the rule, and broader voting rights for women remained elusive. Women were more successful in grassroots organizing outside the purview of formal politics. Witness, for example, the activism of María "Cuca" del Refugio García, an advocate for the rights of indigenous women, or the emergence of the Frente Único Pro Derechos de la Mujer (United Front for Women's Rights). Despite these efforts, the social mores of revolutionary Mexico remained patriarchal and conservative (doc. 70). The Unión de Damas Católicas de México (Union of Catholic Ladies of Mexico) included tens of thousands of members by the mid-1920s.

The summer of 1923 saw the unraveling of the tentative stability that three years of Sonoran rule had brought to Mexico. The assassination of Pancho Villa in July 1923 shocked the nation, especially once the complicity of the national government became clear (doc. 67). Obregón also fell out with Treasury Secretary de la Huerta, the leader who had struck an agreement with Villa during his interim presidency. These issues, a series of electoral disputes at the state level, and Obregón's efforts to impose Interior Secretary Plutarco Elías Calles as his successor brought forth another rebellion in December 1923, which de la Huerta reluctantly headed up a month after declaring his own candidacy for president (doc. 69). The de la Huerta Rebellion involved more than half of the military and failed only when the U.S. government lent decisive support to Obregón.

The expansion of rural education played a vital role in the building of the new state. The education campaign spearheaded by Secretary of Public Education José Vasconcelos spread not only literacy but also the Spanish language and the values of the revolutionary government. Hence it served as a homogenizing effort designed to win the hearts and minds of ordinary Mexicans, including many belonging to indigenous communities that attempted to hold on to their distinct cultures and ways of life. To help with this effort, Vasconcelos enlisted Chilean author Gabriela Mistral, who understood the critical role women could play in rural education (docs. 73 and 74).

New president Calles enjoyed the benefit of U.S. diplomatic recognition and decided to take on Mexico's foreign investors and the Catholic Church. When his government declared a moratorium on debt payment and prepared legislation to implement Article 27 with regard to the oil companies, U.S. secretary of state Frank B. Kellogg struck back in June 1925, declaring Mexico "on trial before the world" and implicitly threatening Calles that the United States would not again support the Mexican government against a rebellion, as it had just done (doc. 72). In response, Calles affirmed Mexico's right to make its own laws, a stance that won him popular support (doc. 73). Aside from this spat with the State Department, the Calles administration dedicated itself to improving physical and financial infrastructure, including a road building program and the foundation of the Banco de México as well as agricultural credit banks. Calles also doubled the pace of land reform compared to the Obregón years. He enjoyed the support of Mexico's main labor confederation, the Confederación Regional Obrera Mexicana (Regional Mexican Workers' Confederation, or CROM)—an alliance that co-opted this official labor movement into the government and marginalized other workers' organizations (doc. 74).

Perhaps the most-debated aspect of the Calles years was the conflict between church and state, which had been brewing for a decade but erupted in February 1926, after the archbishop of Mexico City reaffirmed his opposition to the anticlerical articles of the 1917 Constitution. The rapid growth of Catholic organizations frustrated Calles's attempt to remove the Church from public life, most notably through the so-called Calles Law, a reform to the penal code that imposed strict rules on the behavior of the clergy, set up a registration requirement, and forbade the wearing of clerical garb in public. The government also closed all monasteries, convents, and religious schools. The Mexican episcopate suspended religious services on July 31, 1926, and the Holy See responded via a sharply worded encyclical condemning the policies of the government and enjoining the faithful to protest via peaceful means (doc. 75). Finally, Catholics chose armed rebellion in the form of the Cristero Rebellion. While the intransigence of the high clergy had contributed to the problem, the Calles Law had galvanized Catholic opposition (doc. 76). For example, popular reaction to the removal of the local priest demonstrated the deep connection of the local clergy with the population (doc. 77). Based primarily in central and western Mexico, the Cristeros blended their support for the rights of the Church with a more general defense of their local and regional communities and opposition to land reform. Many of them were rural smallholders.

Meanwhile, Mexico faced three other major crises: a severe economic downturn caused by the collapse in commodity prices; the final Yaqui revolt in Sonora; and the succession crisis caused by Obregón's decision to run for another term in 1928 in violation of the revolutionary precept of "effective suffrage, no reelection." This decision raised fears that Obregón would never again relinquish power after the four-year reign of his ally, just as Porfirio Díaz had done in 1884. These fears grew after the execution of Obregón's principal rivals, Generals Francisco R. Serrano and Arnulfo Gómez, in the fall of 1927. However, on July 17, 1928, a Catholic fanatic assassinated Obregón just two weeks after his triumph in the presidential election.

Toward the "Institutional Revolution," 1928–1940

While many feared further chaos, the death of Obregón led to a crucial step toward institutionalization. As Calles gave his final address to Congress on September 1, 1928, a lot was at stake. Despite strong evidence that the Catholic gunman who killed Obregón had acted on his own accord (doc. 78), rumors implicated the government, and speculation ran rampant that Calles would continue his own term in office. Calles allayed these fears by declaring that he would never again serve as president and then called upon the nation to transition from the era of caudillos to one of institutions and laws (doc. 79). The declaration came at the height of the Cristero Rebellion, when the leadership of a Porfirian-era general had infused the rebellion with much-needed military leadership (doc. 80).

Within months of Calles's address, Congress settled on an interim president, the civilian Emilio Portes Gil, and the national political elite formed a ruling party named the Partido Nacional Revolucionario (National Revolutionary Party) that would rule in the name of "the Revolution" until the end of the millennium. Calles would serve an informal role in this new political system as "*jefe máximo*," or supreme chief, arbiter of political life behind the scenes. This scheme to preserve Calles's power under the guise of a ruling party brought about immediate opposition by the slain caudillo's former allies, and especially General José Gonzalo Escobar, who in March 1929 launched the last large-scale rebellion against the revolutionary regime (doc. 81). Within a few months, the government had defeated this rebellion and also put an end to the Cristero Rebellion via a negotiated solution involving the Mexican episcopate, but not the Cristero fighters.

Coinciding with the Great Depression, the new system hit the brakes on revolutionary reforms. Individual states still served as "laboratories of the revolution," particularly Tabasco under the leadership of Tomás Garrido Canabal (doc. 82). Moreover, women still demanded inclusion in the political process, and calls for women's suffrage continued gaining momentum (doc. 83). But Calles declared that the revolution had failed in the political realm, and that the agrarian reform had finished. From 1930 to 1932, Calles played an active role in undermining the elected administration of Pascual Ortiz Rubio, who had defeated José Vasconcelos in an election marred by widespread fraud; but during the presidency of his friend and ally Abelardo L. Rodríguez (1932–1934), he began fading into the background. Meanwhile, the continued pulse of the revolution showed itself in a number of instances: for example, the PNR's Six-Year Plan (1933), which promised a resumption of land distributions and an active role of the government in building an economy that benefited all citizens; and the growth of more radical labor confederations, especially the Confederación de Trabajadores Mexicanos (Confederation of Mexican Workers, or CTM).

Beginning in December 1934, the new president, Lázaro Cárdenas del Río, built upon these foundations to revive revolutionary reforms. Most importantly, he took land reform programs to new heights. In his very first year, he parceled out 2.5 million hectares, more than the entire Maximato combined. His land distributions attacked large agribusiness as a social and economic institution (doc. 84). Cárdenas also made a symbolic break with the past, opting to live in a residence at the bottom of Chapultepec Hill rather than in the castle, the opulent home of Mexican presidents since Emperor Maximilian. In contrast to Calles, whom many Mexicans considered corrupt and aloof, Cárdenas made it a point to be accessible to ordinary Mexicans (doc. 85). He also sought to eradicate graft in the national government. Calles and his allies did not go quietly, and in April 1936, Cárdenas sent the *jefe máximo* and three of his associates into exile in the United States.

Cardenismo built a new coalition with new partners. Instead of the CROM, Cárdenas relied on the CTM under the leadership of Vicente Lombardo Toledano, an avowed Marxist whose firebrand speeches assailed the capitalist class and demanded a new fatherland, one that existed for the workers (doc. 86). And instead of relying on the vintage Zapatistas, many of whom had turned to the political right, Cardenistas constructed the Confederación Nacional Campesina (National Campesino Council). Far from opening up the political system to anything resembling a multiparty democracy, Cardenismo further ensconced the new ruling party, now called the Partido de la Revolución Mexicana (Party of the Mexican Revolution), which relied on CTM and CNC support.

The enduring legacy of Cardenismo also rests upon the president's signature act while in office: the expropriation of the foreign-owned oil industry on March 18, 1938 (doc. 87). Citing the companies' multiple violations of Mexican laws and their defiance of court verdicts adverse to them, Cárdenas turned the oil industry into an asset of the nation (doc. 88). Even after late twentieth-century neoliberalism led to the privatization of most other state-owned companies, PEMEX (Petróleos Mexicanos) remained a vestige of economic nationalism. The popularity of this expropriation and land reform led observers to overlook the fact that the economy remained essentially capitalist.

Cardenismo had its detractors. Women expecting the franchise were disappointed when an effort to give them the vote failed on a technicality. Moreover, social mores remained slow to change (doc. 89). The Soviet exile Leon Trotsky chastised the regime for its failure to eradicate privately held agricultural property (doc. 90). And in 1940, when Cárdenas prepared to hand over power to someone from his inner circle, Secretary of National Defense Manuel Avila Camacho, he faced a revolt by General Juan Andreu Almazán, whose coalition amalgamated disgruntled Callistas and other critics from the right, who assailed Cardenismo as a Marxist scheme to collectivize the economy (doc. 91).

Although one can adopt different end points of the revolution as discussed above (1915, 1917, 1929, 1940, and 1946), the Avila Camacho administration marked an important transition. At the beginning of his rule, Avila Camacho announced "I am a believer," signaling the fact that the church-state conflict was over. As World War II engulfed the world, the conflict brought the U.S. and Mexican governments closer together, ending twenty-five years of difficulties dating to the 1917 Constitution. Most importantly, the 1940 election featured the last serious attempt to end the dominance of the ruling party (renamed the Partido Revolucionario Institucional, or Institutional Revolutionary Party, in 1946). Once an organic movement against an entrenched dictatorship, the revolution had congealed into a ruling party uninterested in significant further reform.

Timeline

1876

January — Porfirio Díaz launches rebellion that brings him to power.

1906

June 1 — Strike at Cananea Consolidated Copper Company in Sonora; Porfirian authorities and Arizona Rangers put down strike.

1908

March — Publication of James Creelman's interview with Porfirio Díaz.

Francisco I. Madero publishes *La sucesión presidencial de 1910*, launching his campaign for the presidency.

1910

June 6 — Arrest of Madero.

June 21 — Porfirio Díaz claims victory in fraudulent presidential election.

October 4 — Madero leaves Mexico for San Antonio, Texas; issues the Plan of San Luis Potosí calling for revolution to break out on November 20, 1910.

November 18 — Police attack and kill Aquiles Serdán and his supporters in the city of Puebla.

1911

May 8 — Rebel forces win Battle of Ciudad Juárez.

May 15 — Maderista troops massacre the Chinese population at Torreón.

May 21 — Signing of Treaty of Ciudad Juárez.

May 25 — Porfirio Díaz resigns the presidency; Francisco León de la Barra becomes interim president.

June 8 — Emiliano Zapata and Madero meet for the first time.

November 9 — Madero is elected president.

November 16 — Bernardo Reyes declares rebellion against Madero's government in Tamaulipas.

November 25 — The Zapatistas issue the Plan of Ayala, declaring themselves in rebellion against Madero.

1912

March 25   Pascual Orozco issues his Plan Orozquista, declaring rebellion against Madero.

October 16   Félix Díaz declares rebellion in Veracruz.

1913

February 9–18   The "Decena Trágica," or Tragic Ten Days, occur.

                          Félix Díaz and Victoriano Huerta overthrow Madero with assistance from U.S. ambassador Henry Lane Wilson; Huerta assumes the presidency.

February 19   Murder of Madero and Vice President José María Pino Suárez.

March 26   Carranza issues his Plan of Guadalupe, disavowing Huerta.

1914

April 9   Arrest of U.S. sailors in port of Tampico provides U.S. president Woodrow Wilson a pretext to intervene against Huerta.

April 21   U.S. troops occupy Veracruz.

June 23   Battle of Zacatecas is a major victory for Villa's forces.

July 15   Huerta resigns the presidency.

August 27   Carranza's emissaries unsuccessfully meet with the Zapatistas.

October 10–November 9   Sovereign Revolutionary Convention in Aguascalientes results in Villa-Zapata alliance against Carranza; beginning of war between the factions.

1915

January 6   Carranza issues agrarian law.

April–June   Obregonistas defeat Villistas in central Mexico.

October   United States extends diplomatic recognition to Carranza.

1916

March 9   Pancho Villa attacks the town of Columbus, New Mexico.

March 16   Wilson administration sends the Punitive Expedition into Chihuahua to capture Villa.

1917

February 5   Promulgation of revolutionary Constitution.

February 7   Wilson withdraws the Punitive Expedition.

1919

April 10   Assassination of Zapata.

1920

April 23   Plan of Agua Prieta disavows Carranza.

May 21   Assassination of Carranza.

November 30   Inauguration of President Álvaro Obregón.

1923

July 20   Assassination of Villa.

December 7   Beginning of de la Huerta Rebellion.

1924

November 30   Inauguration of President Plutarco Elías Calles.

1926

Fall   Cristero Rebellion begins.

1928

July 17   Assassination of Obregón.

December   Formation of Partido Nacional Revolucionario.

1929

March–June   Escobar Rebellion.

1934

November 30   Inauguration of President Lázaro Cárdenas.

1938

March 18   Cárdenas expropriates foreign oil properties.

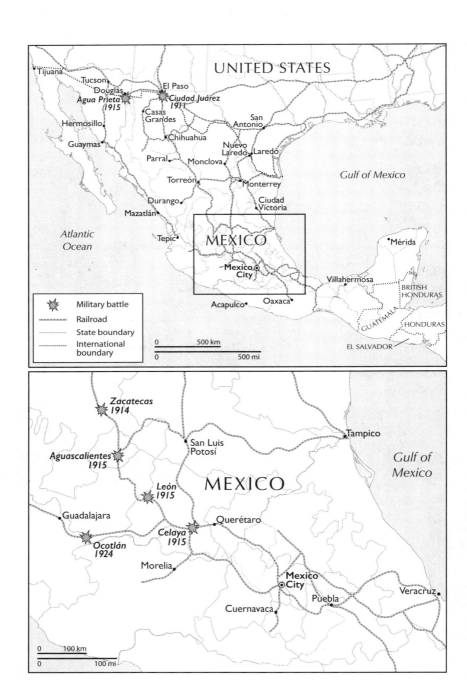

I. The Porfiriato, 1876–1910

Although the injustices that plagued Mexico during the late nineteenth and early twentieth centuries were severe and widely acknowledged, the prospect of revolution struck most observers as remote. "I consider general revolution to be out of the question," wrote a German diplomat in 1910, "as does public opinion and the press." Peasants complained of land theft and hyper exploitation (doc. 2); in some rural areas, labor conditions differed little from slavery (doc. 4); factory workers suffered low pay, brutal conditions, and discrimination; middle-class folk chafed at the lack of opportunity and the abuse of civil and political rights. Even so, most observers believed that the dictator was fully in control, despite his advancing age (he turned eighty in 1910). His closest advisors were wealthy technocrats who claimed that science bolstered the dictator's claim to power (doc. 1). He had the full support of the army and law enforcement, enabling him to deal quickly and severely with any outbreak of unrest (doc. 3). What's more, Mexican society was sharply divided by region, class, and ethnicity: the prospect that the people would unite to carry out a revolutionary project seemed far-fetched. There were dissident voices, of course, but their sporadic attempts at rebellion were easily put down.

Certainly Díaz himself had few doubts about his mastery of the situation. In 1908, he spoke to American journalist James Creelman, adopting a posture of world-weariness as he announced his intention to retire from public life in 1910 when his current term would end (doc. 7). Candidates rose up to challenge him. By far the leading candidate was the scion of a wealthy northern landowning family named Francisco I. Madero, who would soon become known as Mexico's "Apostle of Democracy." Madero published a book called *The Presidential Succession of 1910* in which he addressed Mexico's many problems, the most serious of which, in his judgment, was the lack of democracy (doc. 8). He waged an energetic and undeniably popular campaign, despite harassment from the dictator's minions. His political party, which went by the unwieldy name Anti-Reelectionist Party, put forth its program in April 1910. Shortly after that Madero was imprisoned while Porfirio Díaz and his handpicked vice president, Ramón Corral, claimed triumph after a blatantly rigged election. Madero, released on bail, fled to San Antonio, Texas, finally convinced that change would only come as a result of armed revolution. In his Plan of San Luis Potosí, he called for that revolution to break out on November 20 (doc. 9).

Document 1. What Is the *Científico* Party?[1]

Luis Cabrera (1876–1954) is widely seen as one of the most influential intellectuals of the revolutionary period. In this prerevolutionary writing, published in the newspaper El Partido Democrático *in 1909, he takes aim at the group of Díaz's advisors who provided the official ideology of the Porfirian regime, the so-called* cientificos. *Heavily influenced by European positivism, the* cientificos *claimed to privilege hard science over feeble notions of democracy and social justice, arguing that government is best managed by disinterested experts like themselves. While later scholarship has suggested that Cabrera's portrayal of the* cientificos *as cynical enablers of U.S. economic dominance is overstated, many of his criticisms hit the mark, and he certainly gives readers a strong sense of how the* cientificos *were viewed by large swaths of the Mexican public.*

[The *científico* party] has taken the pompous named "*científico*" because it claims that its conduct is based in science; and even though it has dazzled many with this name, it should be noted that the party has taken from science only those postulates that accord with its interests.

The científicos have studied sociology, and as a result they have begun to preach a dangerous cosmopolitanism, totally contrary to the idea of the Fatherland. Sociology has taught them that the borders of nations are outdated barriers that egoism places in the way of human progress. . . . They believe in the gospel of the superiority of Anglo-Saxons and preach contempt for, and advocate the destruction of, the race they deem incapable of evolving, that is, the indigenous race. They explain Anglo-Saxon expansion scientifically and profess the doctrine of the "manifest destiny" of the Latin American race.

These are the lessons that the científicos have taken from their study of sociology. I condemn any science that wants to do away with the idea of the Fatherland!

The científicos have studied political science. They know how to divide others while remaining cohesive themselves. They understand the psychology of the masses, and they practice it in their newspapers, where they prove themselves to be admirable sophists and polemicists. . . .

Their deep study of political science has taught them that virtue is nothing more than a product of the historical moment, and in accordance with these theories they have replaced the science of justice with the art of influencing; they have converted the courts into their tools, ensuring that justice is nothing more than whatever most effectively advances their interests and proves the most dangerous weapon against their enemies. They have made any act that attacks their interests into a crime.

---

1. Gerald L. McGowan, ed., *La Revolución a través de sus documentos* (Mexico City: Universidad Nacional Autónoma de México, 1987), 2:34–49. Originally in *El Partido Democrático*, July 24, 1909. Translated by Tim Henderson.

They call the democratic awakening of the people a "revolution," and any popular demonstration a "riot"; they call democratic leaders "agitators" and "mutineers," disdainfully characterizing them as "obscure people without prestige." And finally, they have perfected a system of muzzling and eliminating—if not corrupting—the independent press, which allows them to maintain a monopoly on journalism. . . .

They are advocates of voting restriction. Incredibly, they have managed to convince some well-meaning democrats that the most efficacious means of achieving democratic practices is to restrict the vote, and that the people must abstain from practicing democracy as long as they are not sufficiently adept at it.

In international policy they are partisans of Yankee imperialism; they admire Roosevelt's "wise" interpretation of the Monroe Doctrine and consider his blatant theft of Panama an act of genius. They attend all the international conferences to show off their science. . . . They fervently collaborate in the search for international peace, not disapproving of the intervention of strong peoples into the domestic affairs of weak ones. It is they who have put us in such a weak position with respect to Central America. They are the authors of a policy of cowardice and servility that makes us look, in the eyes of the Latin American Continent, like a satellite of the North and traitors to our race.

These are the lessons that the científicos have taken from their study of political science. I condemn science, for it is the greatest enemy of the freedom and independence of peoples!

The científicos have studied the science of political economy. From their profound studies they have deduced that high capitalization, which is what they hypocritically call monopoly, is a system of production that is superior to free trade, and in practice they have sought the means to implant monopolies and "trusts" in ways that are strictly constitutional. The streetcars, electrical power, yarns and fabrics, printing paper, meat, bread, tortillas, and even pulque, have been monopolized. On the governing boards of the monopolizing syndicates there is never lacking the name of some científico banker, functionary, merchant or lawyer.

They have figured out how to channel the prodigious daily flow of capital into their own businesses, and they are clever enough that ninety-nine per cent of the economic progress of the country benefits their interests exclusively. They have a hand in the best businesses, they own shares in the newest banks, they own the best-traded stocks in London, Paris or New York, and they are the first to take advantage of lucrative official concessions.

In the field of labor, the científicos have learned and practiced the theory that the worker only has the right to receive charity from capital, and that he has no standing before the entrepreneur. Above all, they have discovered that, to maintain public order, the worker must fulfill his contract with the boss. They preach to the workers in a pompous tone about the dangers of organizing and the advantages of resignation, putting them on their guard against the agitators who would exploit them. They have convinced General Díaz that strikes disturb the public peace even more than rebellions, and above all that Mexican rifles must be placed at the service of the administrators of the great industrial centers like Puebla or Orizaba.

But the thing that brings the most honor to the científico group is the fact that they have figured out how to closely link their interests with those of foreigners, contending that any attack on científico interests has repercussions to the North and imperils our national sovereignty.

These are the lessons that the científicos have taken from their study of political economy. I condemn science, which is the greatest enemy of the progress and the independence of the Fatherland!

Above all, the científicos have studied finance.

They claim to be masters in this area, and indeed they are. We acknowledge their supremacy, not because of the disdainful superiority with which they preach to the ignorant people from the columns of their newspapers, nor because they carry in their blood an inheritance of great intelligence: it is because they have turned our government into a financier government.

Governments exist to achieve the aggrandizement of their nations, to educate their people, to defend their territory, and above all, to make justice effective, that is, to promote harmony among the governed.

Money and finances are not a means of achieving these goals. Just as a man who makes the acquisition of money the goal of this life is called miserly and despicable, so the government that believes its principal function is not justice but the movement of wealth, is called a financier government, and such a government does not fulfill its duties.

Military governments have always been seen as the most dangerous kind of government; but financier governments are worse, because financiers cannot be patriots, neither through their education nor their race. . . .

The científicos apply science to the resolution of our national questions, and for that purpose they have studied every one of the sciences; all of them except one, which they ignore entirely. . . .

The science of patriotism.

Document 2. Morelos Before the Revolution[2]

The daughter of a British tea merchant, Rosa King was born in India in 1865. She emigrated to Mexico City with her husband, Norman, in 1905, where the couple lived until Norman's unexpected death in 1909. At that point, left nearly penniless, Rosa moved to the town of Cuernavaca, Morelos, where she proved herself an astute businesswoman. She opened first a tea shop and later a hotel that would play host to some of Mexico's most celebrated personalities. Unfortunately, Ms. King had settled in a region that would soon become the epicenter of Mexico's agrarian revolution, where Emiliano Zapata led an uprising of Indian peasant villagers who had been displaced by burgeoning sugar plantations. In this excerpt from her 1935 memoir, she begins to glimpse the coming conflagration and to understand its causes.

Occasionally, but very rarely, in my search for curios, I would come on something that antedated the Spanish Conquest and harked back to the time when these Indians had been a free people and a nation controlling their valley. One of my most valued treasures was an old bull's horn, and one day a professor from one of the colleges in the Eastern United States, who was a student of the Conquest, spied this and picked it up with reverence.

"Do you know what this is?" he asked.

I said that I knew it was a very old ceremonial horn that had been used, as was also a drum made of a hollow log of some precious wood like mahogany, to call the tribes together in time of war.

"For an important assembly," corrected the professor, and added quietly, "I heard the blast of one of these not long ago."

"Good heavens!" I said, thoroughly impressed, for I had not known they were still in use. An American youngster who had been examining the inlaid butt of an antiquated Spanish pistol turned frankly around to listen.

"I have come down to Mexico," said the professor, "to study early Spanish documents; and not long ago I appealed to the patriarch of one of your neighboring Indian villages, whose name I have promised to keep secret, to let me look at the sixteenth-century parchments that prove the title of the village to its land; a title based, as you know, on the decree of Charles V, who was ashamed of the greed of his grandees and returned certain lands to the tribes for their use and that of their descendants. Only the patriarch, the *cacique*, knows where the documents are hidden, and he was most reluctant to bring them out lest some harm come to them. It seems the villages hereabouts have been having trouble defending their lands from *hacendados*, who want them for sugar cane."

---

2. Rosa King, *Tempest Over Mexico: A Personal Chronicle* (Boston: Little, Brown, 1935; repr. 1940), 39–44.

"Yes, that is so," I nodded, "the governor has told me about it"; for, because I was a foreigner, and did not even speak the language, Don Pablo[3] sometimes spoke more frankly to me than he might have otherwise. "It is a great trial to Don Pablo," I went on. "The *hacendados* perpetually want more land for planting sugar cane, but since practically all the land in the state is already parceled out among them, there is nothing left but the scanty patches belonging to the Indian villages. When the *hacendados* try to buy these fields, the Indians refuse to sell. Money means little to them, but they know that so long as they have the *milpa* which fed their father and their father's father, they can grow what they need to eat."

"Very sensible of them, too," commented the professor.

"But the *hacendados* do not understand, or wish to understand, that point of view. When the time comes for planting, they want land in a hurry; so they seize the Indians' *milpas* by force and deposit the purchase money in the banks, to the Indians' account. They consider this honorably ends the matter, but the Indians, naturally, do not think so. They won't touch the money. They want their land."

"And they should have it," said the professor. "The patriarch eventually consented to call the people of his village together,—they were called with a blast from just such a bull's horn as this, Mrs. King,—and they gave him their permission and authorization to show me the documents. I studied them carefully and the legality of the title is unquestionable."

"Perhaps," I said sadly, "but that doesn't seem to help the Indians. I believe they have even appealed to Don Porfirio, but they continue to lose their *milpas*. It seems a wicked thing to me, this taking the land by force from those who work it with their hands and love it. Some day, I think, there will be an upheaval here."

The younger American had been drinking in our conversation. Now he struck in earnestly, "It may come sooner than you think!" He was an eager, sensitive-looking boy. "Our newspapers have been carrying rumors of unrest in Mexico for the last year or two."

"Your newspapers!" I said, smiling a little. "Ours are written here on the spot, and they talk of nothing but peace and progress."

"The dictator muzzles them!" came back the boy. He put down the pistol and came closer. "No, really, Mrs. King, you have an election coming on, and Don Porfirio isn't going to have everything his own way this time. I studied Spanish at school, and as our train came down from the North I used to get off at the stations and talk to the people. They're tired of Porfirio Díaz!"

---

3. Pablo Escandón (1856–1926) was the scion of a wealthy sugar planting family of Morelos. Educated in England, he became governor of the state in 1909. As a member of the superelite *científico* faction, he was uniquely ill-suited for this post. He fled to the United States in March 1911 to escape the revolutionary violence. He would later return to back the dictatorship of Victoriano Huerta (see Section III).

His gravity was appealing. I said, to let him down as gently as possible: "Of course people are tired of Porfirio Díaz, after thirty years. Many of them have been tired of him for quite a while. Why, only the other day, a gentleman for whom I have the greatest respect and liking put up his hand here in my tearoom and solemnly swore that he would aid in his downfall. But such talk has been going on for years, and nothing ever comes of it."

The professor said kindly to the boy, "Don't take too seriously the campaign speeches of this Madero, who has been set up as Díaz' opponent in the coming election. There has to be an opponent, to make the thing look right, but Madero is only a straw man for the dictator to knock down."

"Oh, I don't think so!" said the boy ingenuously. "This Madero is different. I've been reading some pamphlets they gave me, and he tells the people all about the rights and liberties they ought to have, and how there should be justice for all and better living conditions for the working classes!"

The professor and I glanced at each other. Even the boy, I think, realized how the phrases sounded. . . .

The professor was smiling. He had been standing in the doorway all the while, still fingering the bull's horn, and now he said smoothly, "Conditions have been much the same here for nearly four hundred years. So long as the *politicos* continue to hurl abuses at each other in perfect *castellano*, I think we may conclude that all is well in your charming country, and you need have no fear, Mrs. King. But," and he paused impressively, "when the blast of the bull's horn and the drum call of the hollow log sound again in the soul of the people, as they will one day, then there will be no peace and no safety. Then there will be a revolution!"

Document 3. An Eyewitness Account of the Events at Cananea[4]

The American-owned Cananea Consolidated Copper Company, which was located about twenty miles south of the Arizona border in the Mexican state of Sonora, had the custom of paying its American employees significantly more than its Mexican ones, and justifying the discrepancy in blatantly racist terms. In June 1906, the Mexican mine workers, aided and abetted by Mexican dissidents based in St. Louis, Missouri, launched a strike to protest that practice; the strike turned violent, and it was brutally suppressed.

The events at Cananea soon became notorious, for they seemed to draw together several of the most common criticisms of the Díaz regime: the economic dominance of

---

4. First published in *El Progreso Latino*, August 28, 1906, 239–41, and September 7, 1906, 260–61. Reprinted in McGowan, *La Revolución Mexicana a través de sus documentos*, 1:270–81. Translated by Tim Henderson.

foreigners, the brutal exploitation of labor, and the willingness to resort to state violence. Most infamously, the panicky governor of Sonora arranged for a group of around two hundred American volunteers and Arizona Rangers to cross the border and participate in quelling the uprising—a clear violation of the laws of both countries. The sight of armed Americans threatening Mexicans on Mexican soil provoked lasting outrage against the Díaz dictatorship.

In this excerpt, Leopoldo Rodríguez Calderón (1870–1933), a journalist and educator, provides a stirring eyewitness account of the events.

As one might expect, the higher wages and prerogatives enjoyed by foreigners—principally Americans—caused discontent among the Mexican miners of Cananea and was the reason they went on strike. They asked Mr. Greene,[5] president of the mining company, to reduce their workday to eight hours and to pay them five pesos per day, which is what the American miners were paid. They also asked him to replace some American foremen who hated Mexicans and abused the poor workers they supervised. Mr. Greene answered that he could not grant their request because the Company was undergoing a crisis owing to the bad state of trade and the low price of metals. He added that the wages he paid Mexican workers seemed fine to him.

Mr. Green's first two reasons were lamentably true, for the low price of metals had caused the Company's shares to decline significantly. Also, some inspectors sent from New York found a deficit of about a half million pesos in the Company's accounts. The third reason, however, exasperated the Mexican miners, because the Americans were paid better wages despite the bad economy and the declining value of metals.

Peacefully, and believing in good faith that their good conduct would oblige the Company to improve their situation, the miners decided to strike. They did so with the full knowledge of the local authorities, for they made no effort to keep their meetings secret. Dr. Filiberto V. Barroso, the Municipal President, knew well in advance what the miners were planning, and he telegraphed that information to Governor Izábal.[6] He was ordered to stall the movement's leaders, for the Governor was planning to go to Cananea at any time.

---

5. William C. Greene (1852–1911) was an American entrepreneur who discovered rich copper deposits in Northern Mexico and founded the Greene Consolidated Copper Company in 1899 to exploit them. By 1905 he was among the world's wealthiest men.

6. Governor Rafael Izábal (1854–1910) was a member of what the inhabitants of the state knew as the "Sonoran Triumvirate"; a group of three corrupt Porfirian leaders close to the *científicos* who dominated the governorship in the 1890s and 1900s. One of these three was the vice president of the republic, Ramón Corral.

Nevertheless, on the night of May 31st, during a shift change, the miners and other workers declared that the strike was on. They blocked any newcomers from filling the jobs in the mines and workshops they had abandoned. In the early morning hours of June 1, no fewer than two thousand workers gathered in the workshops and mines. All morning they roamed through the various departments of the business, recruiting more Mexican workers and swelling the ranks of the strikers. Their leaders were high-ranking workers who carried two banners. One was the national flag of Mexico; the other was white with two inscriptions, one side saying, "five pesos" and the other "eight hours."

The entire population of Cananea watched from their balconies and windows as the strikers wound through the rugged city streets at the foot of the beautiful mountains that crown the western edge of the village.

For years the region had seen plumes of thick white smoke issuing from the tall and majestic chimneys of the foundries. But on that day, a little after 11 in the morning, the foundries stopped sending up those plumes, creating a somewhat mournful atmosphere for the city's inhabitants.

At around 3:30 on that warm and serene afternoon, everyone in the higher part of the city commonly called "The Mesa" learned that a group of strikers, now numbering over 3,000, was climbing in perfect order up the hill that leads to the Avenida Chihuahua, with the lumberyard at the top of the hill. . . . The strikers went to the lumberyard to recruit the Mexican workers there, for it was the only part of the company that they had not yet visited. . . . The strikers stopped some fifty meters from the main door, and the ones who carried the banners wanted to ask Mr. Metcalf and the other bosses of the lumberyard for permission to take out the Mexican workers. Ignacio Cabrera, the bookkeeper of that department, upon learning what the strikers wanted, told Mr. Metcalf that he should open the doors and give them what they asked since they were being peaceful. Mr. Metcalf answered that he would not open the door to anyone and that instead he was going to rid himself of this nuisance by dousing the strikers with water from one of the large fire hoses that he had on hand. Cabrera again advised Mr. Metcalf and the rest of the lumberyard employees . . . that they should not resist. Just then Mr. Metcalf sprayed a small group of workers with water, completely drenching the two banners they carried. Those workers then approached the building, shouting their pleas that the "gringo" who had doused their banners come out, and they began to throw stones at the place where the water had come from. The reply was a detonation. The bullet hit one of the strikers and sent him to the ground in a pool of blood. The crowd then forced Mr. Cabrera and Mr. Fort to open the doors, and many strikers, most of them young, stormed through to find the Mexican workers inside the warehouses. Upon seeing their companion shot dead, and having no weapons to repel Mr. Metcalf's aggression, the rest of the strikers pelted the building with a hail of stones, hitting Mr. Metcalf in the face. Mr. Metcalf, hearing the noise made by the strikers who had entered the building and who were now climbing the stairs and running through the first-floor rooms, jumped through a window onto the street. He wielded a .30-40 Winchester rifle with two cartridge belts full of bullets across his chest. He sat cross-legged and shot another round, killing another striker. The strikers attacked him with stones. Mr. Metcalf managed to get up and hide in a passageway of the lumberyard, but the strikers chased him and killed him with stones about 200 meters from the window he had jumped out of. Another of the three Metcalf brothers, William, armed with a rifle identical to his brother's, ran down the stairs toward a recently built bridge that serves as a conduit to move lumber between departments. He fired several rounds into the crowd which, mad with vengeance, pursued him at about 600 meters. Four young strikers confronted him. He killed three of them and injured the finger of the other, but the lone survivor managed to kill him with his own weapon. Four corpses now lay on the ground by the bridge. Suddenly the main building erupted in flames. Some say that several street kids who had joined the strikers broke some lamps that they had found on the tables, soaking the books and desks with gasoline and then lighting a match. The building and the warehouses were destroyed, and three individuals who had hidden inside were killed. Their incinerated bones were found the next day lying in symmetrical heaps.

Before Mr. Metcalf jumped out the window, two automobiles arrived at the scene carrying Mr. Greene, Mr. Dwight, and some other high-level employees of the business. They were escorted by twenty Americans, all armed with magnificent rifles. Upon hearing the first shot and seeing stones thrown at the building, they turned tail and came to a halt in front of the home of Mr. Gorious, an employee of "La Moda," a clothing warehouse whose owners were French. . . .

When the strikers arrived in front of the Municipal Palace, a strong blast of rifle fire sounded from the intersection where Mr. Greene was stopped. A group of peaceful citizens, drawn by curiosity to where the strikers were, were mowed down by the Americans who accompanied Mr. Greene. Five people died right there. Another was gravely wounded in the stomach, and a child was hit in the thigh; both died the next day. . . .

These killings greatly angered the Mexican people. Antonio Murrieta, a meat seller, abandoned his car and ran to the Police Headquarters, pleading that the people should be given weapons to defend themselves from being miserably murdered. He was immediately locked in the jail by order of Judge Isidro Castañedo, who then mounted a horse and, pistol in hand, rode around the plaza attacking groups of strikers who had come to the Town Hall asking for arms. Many citizens who energetically protested the acts of the Americans were jailed, while the Americans went unmolested.

The Municipal President and the Judge were in the Telegraph Office informing the Governor of what had occurred. At the same time, Mr. Pablo Rubio replaced the guard at the Town Hall and the jail with a group of fourteen armed Americans selected from the thirty that had villainously murdered defenseless people a moment earlier. . . .

Although he lacked any official capacity, Judge Castañedo ordered the police to disband any groups of citizens they found gathered, and anyone who resisted *should be killed like a dog.* . . .

By nine o'clock that night all was quiet. The streets were filled with mounted gendarmes. The only buildings with lights on were the Company offices and the home of Mr. Greene. It is thought that these places housed over a thousand Americans with rifles and large amounts of ammunition. It was said that the previous night a boxcar filled with arms and ammunition had arrived at Cananea from Bisbee and Douglas, and a young railroad employee claimed to have helped move those weapons from the boxcar to automobiles that went to the home of Mr. Greene. Mr. Greene's home was well fortified, for in all the windows and dormers were Americans preparing for an assault. . . .

At 9 o'clock in the morning, news arrived in the city that Governor Izábal would soon arrive by special train with Mexican forces to disarm the Americans. . . . Nearly all of the municipal and State employees and many local merchants, both Mexican and American, gathered at the Railroad Station, some out of curiosity and others out of duty, to greet the Governor and the Mexican forces that they believed were accompanying him. Upon hearing the whistle of the locomotive at around 10:30, everyone tried to find a comfortable place in the southern part of the little Station house so they would not miss anything. The train arrived with six passenger cars. When the Governor emerged . . . he was hailed with hurrahs and shouts of enthusiasm from the Americans, for five of the railroad cars were filled with Americans, all armed. Among them were 275 soldiers of the rural forces of the District of Arizona under the command of Coronel Rinning [*sic*].[7]

It is impossible to describe in words the profound sorrow felt by the honorable and patriotic citizens upon seeing their national territory trod by American soldiers.

Everyone had protest on their lips and sorrow in their hearts upon finding themselves helpless before so many armed Americans. And their moral leaders were a group of prominent Mexicans, including the State Governor himself.

There was no lack of harsh phrases proffered by those who were unable to contain their indignation, and those individuals were immediately arrested and jailed in dark dungeons. . . . Dr. Luis G. González announced loudly that he would rather be Malaysian or Chinese or whatever, than to be Mexican after what he had just

---

7. Thomas Rynning (1866–1941) was a U.S. Army officer who fought Indians in the western United States, served in the Spanish-American War, and in 1902 became a captain of the Arizona Rangers.

seen in the Station. He avoided being jailed because he left that same afternoon for Tucson on private business.

That same day the American press, which hides nothing, published several telegrams in which Governor Izábal asked the U.S. Government for forces to protect American interests and establish order at Cananea. In addition, several photographs were taken at Bisbee of groups of soldiers that in Naco, Arizona, formed by Mr. Izábal, being made to swear allegiance to the Mexican flag, so they were suddenly Mexicanized (!) and sent to Cananea.

Document 4. The Contract Slaves of Valle Nacional[8]

John Kenneth Turner (1879–1948) was an American muckraker who, having been apprised of the horrors of the Díaz regime by exiled dissidents Ricardo Flores Magón, Juan Sarabia, and others, determined to expose those horrors by traveling in Mexico, claiming to be a wealthy tobacco merchant and thereby gaining the trust of planters who, in his telling, presided over a system of labor exploitation that differed little from outright slavery. His reports were serialized in The American Magazine *starting in 1909, and published as the book* Barbarous Mexico *in 1910. The book was a thoroughgoing exposé of the abuses of the Díaz regime. Turner did not pretend to be impartial—when the revolution broke out, he abandoned journalism for activism, running guns to the revolutionaries—and critics have charged that his reporting is characterized by lurid exaggeration. There is no denying, however, that it served to darken the reputation of Díaz among the American public, which is what Turner set out to do.*

In the following excerpt, Turner recounts the conditions of labor on the tobacco plantations of northern Oaxaca, some of the most brutal in Mexico.

Valle Nacional is undoubtedly the worst slave hole in Mexico. Probably it is the worst in the world. . . . In the Valle Nacional all of the slaves, all but a very few—perhaps five per cent—pass back to earth within a space of seven or eight months.

This statement is almost unbelievable. I would not have believed it; possibly not even after I had seen the whole process of working them and beating them and starving them to death, were it not the fact that the masters themselves told me that it was true. And there are fifteen thousand of these Valle Nacional slaves—fifteen thousand new ones every year!

"By the sixth or seventh month they begin to die off like flies at the first winter frost, and after that they're not worth keeping. The cheapest thing to do is let them die; there are plenty more where they came from."

---

8. John Kenneth Turner, *Barbarous Mexico* (Chicago: Charles H. Kerr, 1910), 67–81.

Document 4. The Contract Slaves of Valle Nacional

Word for word, this is the statement made to me by Antonio Pla, general manager of one-third the tobacco lands in the Valle Nacional. . . .

"They die; they all die. The bosses never let them go until they're dying."

Thus declared one of the police officers of the town of Valle Nacional, which is situated in the center of the valley and is supported by it.

And everywhere over and over again I was told the same thing. . . .

The secret of the extreme conditions of Valle Nacional is mainly geographical. Valle Nacional is a deep gorge from two to five miles wide and twenty miles long tucked away among almost impassable mountains in the extreme northwestern corner of the state of Oaxaca. Its mouth is fifty miles up the Papaloapan river from El Hule, the nearest railroad station, yet it is through El Hule that every human being passes in going to or coming from the valley. There is no other practical route in, no other one out. The magnificent tropical mountains which wall in the valley are covered with an impenetrable jungle made still more impassable by jaguars, pumas and gigantic snakes. Moreover, there is no wagon road to Valle Nacional; only a river and a bridle path—a bridle path which carries one now through the jungle, now along precipitous cliffs where the rider must dismount and crawl, leading his horse behind him, now across the deep, swirling current of the river. . . .

It is a tobacco country, the most noted in Mexico, and the production is carried on by about thirty large plantations owned and operated almost exclusively by Spaniards. Between El Hule and the head of the valley are four towns . . . all provided with policemen to hunt runaway slaves, not one of whom can get out of the valley without passing the towns . . . [E]very runaway slave brings a reward of $10 to the man or policeman who catches and returns him to his owner. . . .

A *jefe politico* is a civil officer who rules political districts corresponding to our counties. He is appointed by the president or by the governor of his state and is also mayor, or *presidente*, of the principal town or city in his district. . . . The methods employed by the *jefe politico* working alone are very simple. Instead of sending petty prisoners to terms in jail he sells them into slavery in Valle Nacional. And as he pockets the money himself, he naturally arrests as many persons as he can. . . .

The *jefe politico* of each of the four largest cities in southern Mexico, so I was told by [people] whose veracity in the matter I have no reason to question, pays an annual rental of $10,000 per year for his office. The office would be worth no such amount were it not for the spoils of the slave trade and other little grifts which are indulged by the holder. . . . They send their victims over the road in gangs of from ten to one hundred or even more. They get a special government rate from the railroads, send along government-salaried *rurales* to guard them; hence the selling price of $45 to $50 per slave is nearly all clear profit. . . .

In this partnership of the government and the labor agent—popularly known as an *enganchador* (snarer)—the function of the labor agent is to snare the laborer, the function of the government to stand behind him, help him, give him low transportation rates and free guard service, and finally, to take a share of the profits.

The methods employed by the labor agent in snaring the laborer are many and various. One is to open an employment office and advertise for workers who are to be given high wages, a comfortable home and plenty of freedom somewhere in the south of Mexico. Free transportation is offered. These inducements always cause a certain number to take the bait, especially men with families who want to move with their families to a more prosperous clime. The husband and father is given an advance fee of $5 and the whole family is locked up in a room as securely barred as a jail.

After a day or two, as they are joined by others, they come to have misgivings. Perhaps they ask to be let out, and then they find that they are indeed prisoners. They are told that they are in debt and will be held until they work out their debt. A few days later the door opens and they file out. They find that the *rurales* are all about them. They are marched through a back street to a railroad station, where they are put upon the train. They try to get away, but it is no use; they are prisoners. In a few days they are in Valle Nacional.

[Another] method employed by the labor agent is outright kidnapping. I have heard of many cases of the kidnapping of women and of men. Hundreds of half-drunken men are picked up about the *pulque*[9] shops of Mexico City every season, put under lock and key, and later hurried off to Valle Nacional. Children, also, are regularly kidnapped for the Valle Nacional trade. The official records of Mexico City say that during the year ending September 1, 1908, 360 little boys between the ages of six and twelve disappeared on the streets. Some of these have later been located in Valle Nacional. . . .

Every slave is guarded night and day. At night he is locked up in a dormitory resembling a jail. In addition to its slaves, each and every plantation has its *man-dador*, or superintendent, its *cabos*, who combine the function of overseer and guard; and several free laborers to run the errands of the ranch and help round up the runaways in case of a slave stampede.

The jails are large barn-like buildings, constructed strongly of young trees set upright and wired together with many strands of barbed wire fencing. The windows are iron barred, the floors dirt. There is no furniture except sometimes long, rude benches which serve as beds. The mattresses are thin grass mats. In such a hole sleep all the slaves, men, women and children, the number ranging, according to the size of the plantation, from seventy to four hundred. They are packed in like sardines in a box, crowded together like cattle in a freight car. . . . And on not a single ranch did I find a separate dormitory for the women or the children. Women of modesty and virtue are sent to Valle Nacional every week and are shoved into a

---

9. Pulque is the fermented juice of the maguey plant, which was the preferred intoxicant of Mexico's poor.

sleeping room with scores and even hundreds of others, most of them men, the door is locked on them and they are left to the mercy of the men. . . .

One-fifth of the slaves of Valle Nacional are women; one-third are boys under fifteen. The boys work in the fields with the men. They cost less, they last well, and at some parts of the work, such as planting the tobacco, they are more active and hence more useful. Boys as young as six sometimes are seen in the field planting tobacco. Women are worked in the field, too, especially during the harvest time, but their chief work is as household drudges. They serve the master and the mistress, if there is a mistress, and they grind the corn and cook the food of the male slaves. . . . I asked the president of Valle Nacional why the planters did not purchase cheap mills for grinding the corn, or why they did not combine and buy a mill among them, instead of breaking several hundred backs yearly in the work. "Women are cheaper than machines," was the reply.

Document 5. Porfirio Díaz, Friend of the Worker[10]

Not surprisingly, some of Porfirio Díaz's most ardent admirers were not Mexicans, but foreigners who benefited greatly from his generosity toward foreign entrepreneurs and investors. One such admirer was Edward L. Doheny (1856–1935). Doheny was among the pioneers of the petroleum industry. He was largely responsible for causing an oil boom in Southern California in the early 1900s, after which he turned his attention to developing the oil industry in Mexico's Tampico region. By the early 1920s he was among the world's richest tycoons. During the 1920s his reputation was damaged by accusations that he had paid bribes to Interior Secretary Albert B. Fall, though he was never convicted.

The following excerpt is from testimony Doheny gave before the U.S. Senate in 1919, in hearings ironically convened by his later partner in crime, Albert B. Fall. Fall detested the government of Venustiano Carranza, which had the support of the Woodrow Wilson administration. The hearings aimed to portray Mexico in the worst possible light, and to weaken both the Wilson and Carranza administrations. Doheny obligingly waxed nostalgic for the prerevolutionary regime of Porfirio Díaz.

10. Testimony of Edward L. Doheny, United States Cong., Senate Comm. on Foreign Relations, *Investigation of Mexican Affairs. Preliminary report and hearings of the Committee on Foreign Relations, United States Senate, pursuant to S. res. 106, directing the Committee on Foreign Relations to investigate the matter of outrages on citizens of the United States in Mexico* (Washington, D.C.: Government Printing Office, 1920), 1:224–25.

I think it would be throwing some light upon the situation here if you knew that from the very beginning of our industry there, we were deeply interested in the question of our relations to the laboring classes of Mexico.

It is needless to say that I myself was quite familiar with the fact that a great many of the people of Mexico, who worked for wages, had for a great many centuries been employed under conditions which are entirely foreign to those of our own country; and without desiring to criticize the laws and customs of Mexico, I am compelled, however, to admit that the system which obtained there was not altogether to the disadvantage of the laborer or peon; that there were many features of it which were to his advantage, and many others, again, which were abused so as to operate greatly to his disadvantage, but never, except in very rare instances, to the extent detailed by the letters of John Kenneth Turner, published in the American Magazine, and in which Mr. Turner picked out the very sorest spot in Mexico to describe as a sample of the conditions there. Mr. Turner's description of the conditions in Mexico, relating what he saw in the Valle Nacional, are much more exaggerated and, consequently, much more unfair, than many of the statements made in the famous book which was published before the Civil War and which had so much to do with inflaming the minds of the people of the North against the people of the South in our own country. I refer to the book of Mrs. Harriet Beecher Stowe, which has been dramatized and presented to all the people of the United States so many times under the name of "Uncle Tom's Cabin."

The people of the Southern States never had one-hundredth part as much cause to complain of the exaggerations stated in that book as have the fair-minded and well-meaning and humane hacendados of Mexico to complain of the publication to the world of the conditions in one of the sorest spots in that country as being typical of the entire conditions there.

In 1903 or 1902—I am not certain now which year—there was held in the City of Mexico a Pan American conference at which there were in attendance a great many men from the United States and from several Central and South American States.

I happened to be in the City of Mexico at that time with friends from Pittsburgh, St. Louis, and Los Angeles, and, not wishing to intrude upon the President of Mexico at a time when there were so many other strangers there demanding his attention, I merely sent word of my presence and desire to pay my respects, through the medium of a messenger, so that I could make a record which I have kept up ever since of always having called upon the chief executive of the nation whenever I visited the capital.

Gen. Diaz, however, sent for me and the party who were with me. . . . He told us of his early hopes with regard to the bettering of conditions of his own people, and in the midst of his conversation about the futility of his endeavor to alleviate the working conditions of his own people he stopped, choked up with emotion, and the tears rolled down his cheeks. He begged our forbearance, and later proceeded to apologize for his emotion by saying that he never contemplated the failure of his design in bringing good conditions to the working people of Mexico without being overcome as we had seen him.

The men who were with me were hard-headed men, coal producers of Pittsburgh, iron men from Pittsburgh and St. Louis, a farmer from Nebraska, and prospectors from California. Every one of us believed, and every one of them who were with me and who are still alive, believes that Gen. Diaz's heart was as close to that of the laboring man of Mexico as any other Mexican who has ever lived there before or since.

He told us that the way to treat the Mexican peon was to treat him as a friend, not as a mercenary; that he should be made to believe that the place where he worked was his home. If a small piece of land and a house to live in could be assigned to him as his own he would be contented, but as a mercenary he did not make a good laborer.

He told us that we must be patient with the ignorance and the lack of initiative in the Mexican workman. He called our attention to the fact that they could not learn by instruction, that they must be taught by precept, by example; that they were very imitative, that anything they saw others do they could learn to do, and do well; that they would be faithful to those whom they worked for if they were treated well. He told us that his greatest desire for our prosperity in Mexico was the example which our workmen would present to the Mexican workmen of how to work, how to live, and how to progress.

We left that meeting feeling that as long as we treated the Mexican laborers well in Mexico we would have the friendship of the chief executive. This afterwards proved to be true.

Document 6. The Program of the Liberal Party, 1906[11]

The Mexican Liberal Party (PLM) was organized in early 1901 by a mining engineer named Camilo Arriaga. It was soon joined by the famed Flores Magón brothers—Ricardo, Enrique, and Jesús—radical journalists who pushed the organization steadily leftward and popularized their cause in the pages of their newspapers Regeneración *and* El Hijo de Ahuizote. *The leaders of the movement, after multiple arrests and imprisonments, fled into exile in the United States, first settling in San Antonio and later in St. Louis. The Program of the Liberal Party was published in St. Louis, and*

11. Severo Iglesias, ed., *La Revolución Mexicana: Documentos* (Morelia: Universidad de Michoacán de San Nicolás de Hidalgo, 2010), 33–64. Translated by Tim Henderson.

it displayed the evolution of the movement under the leadership of the Flores Magón brothers. Whereas in its earliest incarnation the Liberal Party aimed mostly to support the traditional precepts embodied in Mexico's 1857 Constitution, the sweeping 1906 program addressed education, agrarian reform, capital punishment, labor condition, the Catholic Church, and the status of immigrants. The party had become frankly revolutionary, though its attempted uprisings were easily crushed by the Díaz regime.

The Liberal Party, dispersed by the dictatorship's persecutions, for so long weak and almost dying, has managed to revive itself, and is now organizing rapidly. The Liberal Party fights the despotism currently reining in our fatherland, and it will surely triumph in the end. We believe that the time has come to solemnly declare to the Mexican people the goals that it aims to realize once it is able to guide the nation's destiny. . . .

PROGRAM OF THE LIBERAL PARTY

Constitutional Reforms

1. The presidential term shall be reduced [from six] to four years.
2. The reelection of presidents and state governors shall be ended. These officials will be eligible for reelection only after two terms have elapsed following the one they served.
3. The Vice President shall be prohibited from performing legislative functions or from holding any other elective position; his position is conferred by the executive.
4. Obligatory military service shall be ended, and a National Guard established. Those who serve permanently in the military will do so freely and voluntarily.
5. Articles 6 and 7 of the Constitution shall be reformed and regulated to eliminate the restrictions that privacy and public peace impose upon freedom of speech and of the press; the only punishable offenses will be ones involving fraud, blackmail, and violations of the law in matters of morality.
6. The death penalty shall be abolished, except for traitors to the Fatherland.
7. Public officeholders will be held accountable, and severe prison sentences will be imposed on violators. . . .

Improvement and Development of Education

10. The number of primary schools shall be increased in such measure as to compensate for the educational establishments closed because they belong to the Clergy.
11. Instruction in all schools of the Republic, be they state or private, will be entirely secular. Directors who fail to adjust to this precept will be held responsible.

12. Education shall be obligatory until the age of fourteen years. The government shall have the duty to protect, as far as possible, children who might lose the benefits of education due to their poverty.
13. Primary school teachers shall be paid good salaries.
14. All schools of the Republic will be required to teach the rudiments of the arts, trades, and military education. Special attention shall be paid to civic instruction, which is currently so badly neglected.

Foreigners

15. Foreigners wishing to acquire real estate in Mexico shall renounce the nationality of their birth and become Mexican citizens.
16. Immigration from China shall be prohibited.

Restrictions on the Abuses of the Catholic Clergy

17. Churches are considered commercial enterprises, and as such they are obligated to keep accounts and pay the taxes they owe.
18. The real estate holdings that the Clergy controls in the capacity of "straw man" will be nationalized in accordance with the law.
19. Penalties for infractions of the Reform Laws shall be increased.
20. The schools run by the Clergy will be closed.

Capital and Labor

21. The maximum workday shall be eight hours, and the minimum wage will be determined according to the following formula: For most of the country, where the wages paid are less than one peso, the minimum wage shall be raised to one peso; in those regions where the cost of living is so high that this would be insufficient to keep the worker out of poverty, the wage shall be more than one peso.
22. Domestic service and housework shall be regulated.
23. Measures shall be adopted to ensure that employers do not use piece work to evade the laws on minimum wages and length of workday.
24. The employment of children under fourteen years of age shall be absolutely prohibited.
25. The owners of mines, factories, workshops, etc., shall be required to maintain good hygienic conditions on their properties, and to ensure the safety of workers operating in dangerous places.
26. Employers or landowners shall be required to provide hygienic accommodations for workers when the nature of the work demands that they be housed.
27. Employers will be required to pay indemnities for work-related accidents.

28. All debts currently owed by farm workers to their employers shall be canceled.

29. Measures shall be adopted to prevent landowners from abusing sharecroppers.

30. Owners of lands or houses shall be required to indemnify the renters of their properties for making necessary improvements.

31. Employers shall be prohibited, under severe penalties, from the following practices: Paying their workers in anything other than cash; imposing fines on workers; discounting wages; delaying payment of wages for more than one week; or dismissing a worker without immediately paying all wages earned. Company stores (*tiendas de raya*) shall be abolished.

32. Foreigners must be a minority of the workers and employees in all businesses and enterprises. Mexican workers shall not be paid less than foreign workers when doing the same kind of labor in the same establishment, nor shall Mexicans be paid in a different manner than foreigners.

33. Sundays shall be a mandatory day of rest.

Lands

34. The owners of land must use their properties productively; any lands left unproductive shall be seized by the State and used in accordance with the following articles: . . .

36. The State will grant land to anyone who asks for it, on the sole condition that they dedicate it to agricultural production and not sell it. The maximum size of the land that the State can cede to a person will be determined.

37. In order to ensure that lands not be granted only to those few persons who have the elements needed to cultivate them, but also to the poor who lack such elements, the State will create or develop an agricultural bank that will make loans to poor farmers, repayable in installments.

Taxes

38. The tax on moral capital and the poll tax shall be abolished, and the Government shall study the best means of decreasing the tax on stamps to the point where it is completely abolished.

39. All taxes on capital under $100 shall be suppressed. Churches and other business shall be exempted from the privilege, for they are harmful and undeserving of the guarantees given to useful enterprises.

40. Taxes on usury, luxury items, and vices shall be increased, while those on articles of prime necessity shall be reduced. The rich shall not be allowed to adjust rates with the Government so as to pay less than the taxes imposed upon them by the law. . . .

General Points

43. Civil equality shall be established for the children of the same parent, and the differences currently established by law between legitimate and illegitimate children shall be suppressed.

44. When possible, penitentiary colonies shall be established to take the place of prisons and penitentiaries in which criminals currently suffer punishment.

45. Political bosses shall be suppressed.

46. Municipalities that have been suppressed shall be reorganized, and municipal power shall be strengthened.

47. Measures shall be taken to suppress or restrain usury, pauperism, and the lack of basic needs.

48. The indigenous race shall be protected.

49. Ties of union with other Latin American countries shall be established.

50. Upon the triumph of the Liberal Party, the goods of the wealthy officials of the current dictatorship shall be confiscated, and the profits shall be used to the carry out the restoration of lands to the Yaqui, Maya, and other Indian tribes, communities, or individuals—lands of which they were deprived—and to service the national debt.

51. The first national congress that convenes after the fall of the dictatorship will annul all the reforms made to our Constitution by the government of Porfirio Díaz; reform the Constitution as much as necessary to put this program in force; promulgate the laws necessary to achieve this end; regulate the articles of the Constitution and other laws; study all those questions it deems vital to the Fatherland, whether or not they are covered in the present program; and enforce the points recorded here, especially in matters of labor and land. . . .

Special Clause

52. The Organizing Committee of the Liberal Party shall, as soon as possible, contact foreign governments, informing them in the name of the Party that . . . it will not recognize any debt contracted in any form or on any pretext by the Dictatorship, or any current loans, or belatedly recognizing any past obligations of no legal standing. . . .

Reform, Liberty, and Justice
Saint Louis, Missouri, July 1, 1906

Document 7. President Díaz, Hero of the Americas[12]

James Creelman (1859–1915) was a major figure in the era of "yellow journalism." The flamboyant reporter covered the Indian Wars in the western United States; the Sino-Japanese War of 1894; and the Spanish-American War of 1898, wherein—as much participant as journalistic observer—he was wounded in action. He became infatuated with Mexico's dictator, interviewing him in 1908 for an article published in the popular Pearson's Magazine. While much of the article consists of gushing praise of the dictator, the article generated some news that helped to change the course of history. Porfirio Díaz announced to Creelman that the Mexican people, having benefited from his leadership, were ready to practice democracy, and that he would step down from the presidency when his term ended in 1910. Historians continue to speculate about Díaz's motives. Perhaps he was sincere but later had a change of heart; or perhaps he intended to get his enemies to show themselves. Whatever his intent, there were some who took his words seriously and launched their campaigns for the presidency, only to have Díaz thwart them, retaining the presidency after a rigged election. These, it turned out, were major developments leading to the outbreak of revolution in 1910. Creelman, for his part, would go on to publish a hagiographic biography of Díaz in 1912.

There is not a more romantic or heroic figure in all the world, nor one more intensely watched by both friends and foes of democracy, than the soldier-statesman, whose adventurous youth pales the pages of Dumas, and whose iron rule has converted the warring, ignorant, superstitious and impoverished masses of Mexico, oppressed by centuries of Spanish cruelty and greed, into a strong, steady, peaceful, debt-paying and progressive nation.

For twenty-seven years he has governed the Mexican Republic with such power that national elections have become mere formalities. He might easily have set a crown upon his head.

Yet to-day, in the supremacy of his career, this astonishing man—foremost figure of the American hemisphere and unreadable mystery to students of human government—announces that he will insist on retiring from the Presidency at the end of his present term, so that he may see his successor peacefully established and that, with his assistance, the people of the Mexican Republic may show the world that they have entered serenely and preparedly upon the last complete phase of their liberties, that the nation is emerging from ignorance and revolutionary passion, and that it can choose and change presidents without weakness or war. . . .

"It is a mistake to suppose that the future of democracy in Mexico has been endangered by the long continuance in office of one President," he said quietly.

---

12. James Creelman, "President Díaz, Hero of the Americas," *Pearson's Magazine*, March 1908, 231–77.

"I can say sincerely that office has not corrupted my political ideals and that I believe democracy to be the one true, just principle of government, although in practice it is possible only to highly developed peoples." . . .

"Here in Mexico we have had different conditions. I received this Government from the hands of a victorious army at a time when the people were divided and unprepared for the exercise of the extreme principles of democratic government. To have thrown upon the masses the whole responsibility of government at once would have produced conditions that might have discredited the cause of free government.

"Yet, although I got power at first from the army, an election was held as soon as possible and then my authority came from the people. I have tried to leave the Presidency several times, but it has been pressed upon me and I remained in office for the sake of the nation which trusted me. The fact that the price of Mexican securities dropped eleven points when I was ill at Cuernavaca indicates the kind of evidence that persuaded me to overcome my personal inclination to retire to private life.

"We preserved the republican and democratic form of government. We defended the theory and kept it intact. Yet we adopted a patriarchal policy in the actual administration of the nation's affairs, guiding and restraining popular tendencies, with full faith that an enforced peace would allow education, industry and commerce to develop elements of stability and unity in a naturally intelligent, gentle and affectionate people.

"I have waited patiently for the day when the people of the Mexican Republic would be prepared to choose and change their government at every election without danger of armed revolutions and without injury to the national credit or interference with national progress. I believe that day has come." . . .

"General Diaz," I interrupted, "you have had an unprecedented experience in the history of republics. For thirty years the destinies of this nation have been in your hands, to mold them as you will; but men die, while nations must continue to live. Do you believe that Mexico can continue to exist in peace as a republic? Are you satisfied that its future is assured under free institutions?"

It was worthwhile to have come from New York to Chapultepec Castle to see the hero's face at that moment. Strength, patriotism, warriorship, prophethood seemed suddenly to shine in his brown eyes.

"The future of Mexico is assured," he said in a clear voice. "The principles of democracy have not been planted very deep in our people, I fear. But the nation has grown and it loves liberty. Our difficulty has been that the people do not concern themselves enough about public matters for a democracy. The individual Mexican as a rule thinks much about his own rights and is always ready to assert them. But he does not think so much about the rights of others. He thinks of his privileges, but not of his duties. Capacity for self-restraint is the basis of democratic government, and self-restraint is possible only to those who recognize the rights of their neighbors.

"The Indians, who are more than half of our population, care little for politics. They are accustomed to look to those in authority for leadership instead of thinking for themselves. That is a tendency they inherited from the Spaniards, who taught them to refrain from meddling in public affairs and rely on the Government for guidance.

"Yet I firmly believe that the principles of democracy have grown and will grow in Mexico."

"But you have no opposition party in the Republic, Mr. President. How can free institutions flourish when there is no opposition to keep the majority, or governing party, in check?"

"It is true there is no opposition party. I have so many friends in the republic that my enemies seem unwilling to identify themselves with so small a minority. I appreciate the kindness of my friends and the confidence of my country; but such absolute confidence imposes responsibilities and duties that tire me more and more.

"No matter what my friends and supporters say, I retire when my present term of office ends, and I shall not serve again. I shall be eighty years old then.

"My country has relied on me and it has been kind to me. My friends have praised my merits and overlooked my faults. But they may not be willing to deal so generously with my successor and he may need my advice and support; therefore I desire to be alive when he assumes office so that I may help him."

He folded his arms over his deep chest and spoke with great emphasis.

"I welcome an opposition party in the Mexican Republic," he said. "If it appears, I will regard it as a blessing, not as an evil. And if it can develop power, not to exploit but to govern, I will stand by it, support it, advise it and forget myself in the successful inauguration of complete democratic government in the country.

"It is enough for me that I have seen Mexico rise among the peaceful and useful nations. I have no desire to continue in the Presidency. This nation is ready for her ultimate life of freedom. At the age of seventy-seven years I am satisfied with robust health. That is one thing which neither law nor force can create. I would not exchange it for all the millions of your American oil kings." . . .

"And which do you regard as the greatest force for peace, the army or the school-house?" I asked.

The soldier's face flushed slightly and the splendid white head was held a little higher.

"You speak of the present time?"

"Yes."

"The schoolhouse. There can be no doubt of that. I want to see education throughout the Republic carried on by the national Government. I hope to see it before I die. It is important that all citizens of a republic should receive the same training, so that their ideals and methods may be harmonized and the national unity intensified. When men read alike and think alike they are more likely to act alike."

"And you believe that the vast Indian population of Mexico is capable of high development?"

"I do. The Indians are gentle and they are grateful, all except for the Yacquis [*sic*] and some of the Mayas. They have the traditions of an ancient civilization of their own. They are to be found among the lawyers, engineers, physicians, army officers and other professional men."

Over the city drifted the smoke of many factories.

"It is better than cannon smoke," I said.

"Yes," he replied, "and yet there are times when cannon smoke is not such a bad thing. The toiling poor of my country have risen up to support me, but I cannot forget what my comrades in arms and their children have been to me in my severest ordeals."

There were actually tears in the veteran's eyes.

Document 8. Madero's Warning[13]

Porfirio Díaz may not have been altogether sincere when, in his interview with James Creelman, he invited political parties to form and to field candidates. But there were indeed some who decided to test his sincerity. One leading presidential candidate was General Bernardo Reyes, but his candidacy ended when Díaz ordered him overseas on a supposed diplomatic mission, which was in fact an involuntary exile. Another leading candidate was Francisco I. Madero, the scion of a wealthy landowning family from the northern state of Coahuila. In early 1909, Madero published a book entitled The Presidential Succession of 1910. The book was hardly revolutionary: it spoke critically, yet respectfully, of the dictator and outlined what Madero saw as Mexico's most pressing problems. The following excerpt appears toward the end of the book. Both plaintive and vaguely threatening, the book evidently struck the right tone, for it became a best seller, and Madero was christened the "Apostle of Democracy." His campaign was greeted with delirious enthusiasm.

Although all indications are that General Díaz plans to perpetuate his absolutist policy and that we must resolve to fight him, we should not lose all hope of changing his course. If patriotism is not completely dead among Mexicans; if we can organize effectively, making the nation's voice strong and vigorous; then perhaps General

13. Francisco I. Madero, *Obras completas de Francisco I. Madero: La sucesión presidencial en 1910* (Mexico City: Clio, 1999), 260–61. Translated by Tim Henderson.

Díaz will be moved, and the more sensitive fibers of his soul will vibrate when he hears the sonorous voice of the fatherland speaking to him thus:

> Until now, under the pretext of bringing stability to the government, transforming the Mexican's turbulent spirit, and stifling unhealthy ambitions, you have placed yourself above the law and forgotten your most solemn duties, sustaining yourself in power, which you have used arbitrarily.
>
> But now your work is done: You have given your government a stability that is dangerous due to its long duration; the spirit of your fellow citizens has gone from turbulent to servile; and you've killed all ambitions—not just the unhealthy ones, but also with those with the best intentions.
>
> What do you hope to achieve by trying to perpetuate such a dangerous regime?
>
> Up until now all your faults can be forgiven, your acts satisfactorily explained by history, if only you show your good faith by fulfilling your promises and resolving, in the final years of your life, to place yourself under the rule of law, respecting it sincerely and declaring yourself its protector.
>
> In this way you can brilliantly consummate your work of pacification; you have brought the republic to an enviable height; your name will be honored by your fellow citizens, venerated by future generations, and you will be remembered as one of history's greatest figures.
>
> However, if sterile vanity leads you to demonstrate that you are more powerful than the people; if you insist on prolonging this era of despotism; and if, rather than declare yourself the representative of our most precious interests, you stubbornly defend those of your own inner circle: then you will have undermined the success of your work. The nation's aspirations, finding all channels blocked, will overflow, inundating everything in their path. You should tremble, for I will declare you a bad son, and you will go down in history as an ambitious and fortunate soldier who, with immense elements at his disposal, could be nothing but a vulgar tyrant who never fulfilled his most solemn promises, whose contempt for the law caused him to lose all prestige; and whose personal ambition reduced his fellow citizens to servitude, and the republic to decadence.

Document 9. Plan of San Luis Potosí[14]

Francisco Madero had steadfastly clung to the notion of peaceful change, resisting the many calls for the violent overthrow of the Díaz dictatorship. He and other Anti-Reelectionist leaders were arrested in the summer of 1910, and he was in prison in the city of San Luis Potosí when, on June 21, Porfirio Díaz and Vice President Ramón Corral claimed reelection. Released on bail, he made his way to San Antonio, Texas, where the Plan of San Luis Potosí was written (it was backdated to October 5, the last day Madero was in San Luis Potosí, in order to avoid problems with U.S. authorities). The plan declared the presidential election invalid and called for an armed uprising to break out on November 20. While it addressed some of the social issues that motivated many revolutionaries, it clearly emphasized political reforms.

Peoples, in their constant efforts to see the triumph of the ideals of liberty and justice, are forced at certain historical moments to make great sacrifices.

Our beloved country has reached one of those moments. A tyranny, which we Mexicans have not suffered since we won our independence, is so oppressive as to be intolerable. We are offered peace in exchange for tyranny, but that peace is shameful for the Mexican people because it is not based on law, but on force; because its objective is not the aggrandizement and prosperity of the nation, but the enrichment of a small group who, abusing their influence, have converted public offices into fountains of exclusively personal benefits, unscrupulously exploiting lucrative concessions and contracts.

The legislative and judicial powers are completely subordinated to the executive; the division of powers, the sovereignty of the States, the freedom of the city councils, and the rights of citizens exist only in writing in our great charter; but in fact, it may almost be said that martial law prevails in Mexico. The administration of justice, rather than protecting the weak, merely legalizes the strong in their plundering; judges, instead of representing justice, are agents of the executive, whose interests they faithfully serve; the Congress has no will apart from that of the dictator. The State Governors are named by him, and they in turn designate and impose the municipal authorities in the same way.

From this it follows that the whole administrative, judicial, and legislative machinery obeys a single will, the caprice of General Porfirio Díaz, who during his long administration has shown that his principal motive is to maintain himself in power at all cost.

For many years the Republic has been profoundly discontented with this system of government; but General Díaz, with great cunning and perseverance, has

---

14. Javier Garcíadiego, ed., *La Revolución Mexicana: Crónicas, documentos, planes y testimonios* (Mexico City: UNAM, 2008), 95–107. Translated by Tim Henderson.

succeeded in annihilating all independent elements, so that it was not possible to organize any sort of movement to take from him the power of which he made such ill use. . . .

Therefore, and in representation of the national will, I declare the last election illegal and, the Republic being accordingly without rulers, provisionally assume the Presidency of the Republic until the people designate their rulers pursuant to the law. To attain this end, it is necessary to eject from power the audacious usurpers whose only legal title involves a scandalous and immoral fraud.

In all honesty I declare that it would be weakness on my part and a betrayal of the people, who have placed their confidence in me, not to put myself before my fellow citizens, who anxiously call me from all parts of the country, to compel General Díaz by force of arms, to respect the national will.

The current Government, although it originated in the violence and fraud that the People have suffered for so long, may retain certain legal titles in relation to other countries until the 30th day of next month when its powers will expire: but a government rooted in fraud can no longer retain power, or at least must face the better part of the Nation protesting with weapons in hand against that usurpation, I have decreed that on SUNDAY, November 20, from six in the evening, all the populations of the Republic will rise in arms under the following plan:

1) The elections that took place in June and July of this year for President and Vice-President, as well as for Supreme Court Magistrates, Deputies and Senators, are hereby declared null and void.

2) The Government of General Díaz is disavowed, as are all other authorities whose power should be based on the popular vote; for in addition to not having been elected by the people, they have lost all claim to legality by committing . . . the most scandalous electoral fraud in Mexico's history.

3) To avoid insofar as possible the upheavals inherent in all revolutionary movements, we declare all the laws and their respective regulations promulgated by the current administration shall remain in force, except for those that manifestly go against the principles proclaimed in this Plan. Likewise excepted are the laws, court decisions, and decrees that have sanctioned the accounts and management of funds of all the officials of the Porfirist administration in all its branches; for as soon as the revolution triumphs we will begin to form commissions to investigate and determine what responsibilities the officials of the Federation, States and Municipalities have incurred.

In all cases, contracts made by the Porfirist administration with foreign governments and corporations will be respected until the 20th of next month.

Abusing the law of idle lands, many small landowners, mostly indigenous, have been despoiled of the lands, whether through agreements of the Secretary of Development or rulings by the tribunals of the Republic. It is entirely just to restore to their original owners those lands that have been arbitrarily stolen from them; all such dispositions and rulings are subject to revision; and those who acquired them immorally, or their heirs, must return them to their rightful owners; they will also be required to pay an indemnity for damages suffered. Only when such lands have passed to a third person before the promulgation of this Plan, the old owners will receive indemnity from those who benefited from the despoilment.

4) In addition to the Constitution and the prevailing laws, we declare that the supreme law of the Republic is the principle of No-Reelection of the President and Vice-President of the Republic, State Governors and Municipal Presidents, while the constitutional reforms are being made.

5) I assume the office of Provisional President of the United Mexican States, with the powers necessary to make war upon the usurper Government of General Díaz.

As soon as the capital and more than half of the states are in the hands of the people's forces, the Provisional President will convoke extraordinary general elections for the following month, and he will surrender the power to the winner as soon as the election's results are known.

6) The Provisional President, before surrendering power, will inform the Congress of the use that has been made of the powers conferred upon him in this plan.

7) On the 20th of November, from six o'clock in the evening, all citizens of the Republic will take up arms to overthrow the authorities who currently govern them. . . .

8) When the authorities put up armed resistance, we will be obliged by the force of arms to respect the popular will; but in this case the laws of war will be rigorously observed, with special attention to the prohibitions on expanding bullets and the shooting of prisoners. We also call attention to the duty of all Mexicans to respect the persons and interests of foreigners.

9) The authorities who resist the realization of this plan will be imprisoned so that they can be judged by the courts when the revolution has ended. As soon as each city or town recovers its liberty, the principal chief of arms will be recognized as the legitimate provisional authority, with power to delegate his function to any other citizen who will be confirmed or removed by the provisional Governor.

One of the first measures of the provisional Government will be to free all political prisoners. . . .

TRANSITORY. A) The leaders of the voluntary forces will assume the rank that corresponds to the number of forces under their command. In cases of joint operations by military and volunteer forces, the commander will be the leader of highest rank; if both leaders have the same rank, the command will fall to the military leader.

Civilian leaders of all ranks will enjoy said rank while the war lasts, and once it ends, those appointments, at the solicitude of interested parties, will be reviewed by the Secretary of War who will ratify or reject their rank according to the merits.

B) All leaders, civilian and military, will maintain the strictest discipline with their troops. The Provisional Government will hold them responsible for any excesses committed by the forces under their command, unless it is proved that it was impossible for them to contain their soldiers and that they have given the guilty parties the punishment they deserve.

The severest penalties will be applied to the soldiers who sack a town or who kill defenseless prisoners.

C) If the forces and authorities that support General Díaz shoot prisoners of war, the same will not done as a reprisal with those of his forces who fall into our hands. Instead, civilian or military authorities who serve General Díaz will be shot by firing squad within 24 hours following a summary judgment if it is determined that, once the revolution began, they shot any of our soldiers, or ordered or transmitted such an order.

The highest authorities will not be exempt from this penalty; the only exception will be General Díaz and his ministers, who, in case they ordered or permitted such shootings, will suffer the same penalty, but only after they have been judged by the courts once the revolution has ended.

If General Díaz orders that the laws of war be respected and he treats the prisoners who fall into his hands humanely, his life will be spared; but in any case he will be tried in the courts for how he managed the fortunes of the Nation and how he has complied with the law.

D) It is an indispensable requirement of the laws of war that belligerent troops wear a distinctive uniform, but since it would be difficult to uniform the many forces of the people who are going to take part in the fight, we will adopt as the symbol of all liberating forces, whether volunteer or military, a tricolored ribbon worn on the hat or the arm.

FELLOW CITIZENS: If I call upon you to take up arms and defeat the government of General Díaz, it is not only for the outrage that he committed during the last elections, but it is also to save the nation from a dark future that awaits if we continue under his dictatorship and under the government of the heinous científico oligarchy, who, without scruples and in great haste, are seizing and squandering our national resources, and if permitted to continue in power, in a very short span of time will have completed their work: they will have brought the people to ignominy and debased them; they will have sucked up all of the people's wealth and left them in the most absolute misery; they will have caused the bankruptcy of our finances and the dishonor of our nation, which—weak, impoverished and in chains—will find itself unable to defend its borders, its honor, and its institutions.

As for me, I have a tranquil conscience and no one can accuse me of promoting the revolution for personal ends, for the nation is well aware that I did everything possible to arrive at a peaceful agreement, and that I was willing to renounce my candidacy if General Díaz had permitted the Nation to designate even the

Vice-President. But, dominated by incomprehensible pride, he refused to listen to the Nation and preferred to precipitate a revolution rather than concede one iota, before returning to the people any of their rights, before complying with the promises he made at Noria and Tuxtepec.

He himself justified the present revolution when he said: *"No citizen shall impose and perpetuate himself in the exercise of power, and this will be the final revolution."*

If General Díaz had put the interests of the Nation ahead of the sordid interests of himself and his counselors and made some concessions to the people, he would have avoided this revolution. But since he has not done that . . . so much the better! The changes will be quicker and more radical, for the Mexican people, instead of crying like cowards, will boldly accept the challenge. And since General Díaz uses brute force to impose an ignominious yoke on them, the people have recourse to the same force in order to shake off that yoke, to throw this evil man from power and to reconquer their liberty.

Fellow Citizens: Do not vacillate for a moment: take up arms, overthrow the usurpers, recover your rights as free men, and remember that our ancestors bequeathed to us a glorious inheritance that we cannot taint. Be like they were: Invincible in war, magnanimous in victory.

EFFECTIVE SUFFRAGE. NO REELECTION.

San Luis Potosí, October 5, 1910

II. The Madero Revolution, 1910–1913

Having determined that peaceful methods were ineffective, Francisco I. Madero's Plan of San Luis Potosí called for revolutionary violence to break out on November 20, 1910. The first real violence of the revolution took place before that date, however. A shoemaker and ardent Maderista from the city of Puebla in central Mexico named Aquiles Serdán had been gathering weapons and plotting an uprising, but the plot was discovered. Police and soldiers surrounded his home on November 18, leading to a bloody firefight in which Serdán and his closest supporters were killed (doc. 10). Throughout the country, people suddenly found themselves forced to make a wrenching decision: continue their lives as usual or join the revolution (doc. 11). The revolution gained steam very slowly, but by the spring of 1911 the momentum had shifted decisively to the rebels, who, under the bold leadership of Pancho Villa and Pascual Orozco, took the strategically crucial city of Ciudad Juárez on the northern border. The loss of that engagement finally persuaded Porfirio Díaz to negotiate with the rebels, leading to his resignation at the end of May (doc. 13).

While some Mexicans were soon decrying Madero as a tyrant worse than Díaz, a more common (and more charitable) view is that he was ill-suited by temperament and by his privileged upbringing to control the dangerous forces he set in motion (doc. 14). Whether anyone in Mexico would not have been overmatched by those circumstances is a valid question, for the revolution unleashed frightening passions that would have been nearly impossible for anyone to control. Maderista troops, gripped by xenophobic hatred, massacred Chinese immigrants in northern Mexico (doc. 15); peasants from southern Mexico, guided by land hunger, were at first dismayed then angered by Madero's refusal to honor their demands and his dalliance with frank enemies of agrarian reform (docs. 19–20). Rebellions soon broke out in various parts of Mexico, led by people with confusing and contradictory agendas (docs. 17, 18, 21, 22). Madero was too revolutionary for some and not nearly revolutionary enough for others (doc. 23).

By early 1913, anti-Maderista forces were, it seemed, ascendant everywhere, and the revolution he launched would soon take some surprising and horrific turns.

Document 10. Brutal Repression in Puebla[1]

One of Madero's staunchest supporters was a thirty-four-year-old shoemaker from the central Mexican city of Puebla named Aquiles Serdán. Serdán was descended from a long line of political activists. He read Madero's book and determined that Madero "incarnates our aspirations." He was arrested for political activity in 1909 and subsequently left for San Antonio where he helped to write the Plan of San Luis Potosí, which called for revolution to break out on November 20, 1910. Serdán returned to Puebla and began stockpiling firearms in anticipation of the uprising. His efforts were discovered, however. When police arrived to search his home on November 18, he and his supporters decided to resist, leading to a fearsome firefight in which Serdán's brothers were killed and he was forced into hiding, only to later be discovered and executed. The home's defenders managed to inflict a heavy toll on the attackers and provided the revolution with its first martyrs, but in all it was an inauspicious beginning to the revolution. The following account was written by an anonymous participant in the events for the newspaper El Demócrata Mexicano.*

Aquiles and his brother Máximo tirelessly put out their highly risky propaganda, in which they shrewdly mocked the secret police who spied on them, catechized workers, found determined collaborators, distributed arms and ammunition, and even sustained, for a while, a set number of individuals who were ready to take up arms as soon as they were told. The police of Mexico who captured Sr. Cosío Robelo and discovered the important plans which guided the armed movement, precipitated developments. The police of Puebla organized a major raid. On the day before the unforgettable 18th of November, I went to the Serdán workshop in the morning. Upon leaving it, I met with my friend and collaborator Francisco Yépez, who pointed out the need to gather at the home of our leader, don Aquiles, to await developments. We did so, and at nightfall we received a warning that the police were approaching to pay us a little visit. . . . Aquiles decided we should resist with everything we had before abandoning the arms and ammunition that he had stored in his house. Also, he had a blind confidence that "his dear workers," as he affectionately called them, would rally quickly to his aid. The entire night of the 17th we spent on watch, weapons in hand and keeping a constant vigil. On the morning of the 18th, hardly had we eaten a frugal breakfast when Miguel Cabrera[2] arrived at the house, along with his second-in-command, Fregoso, and several henchmen. The rest is well known: a very accurate bullet took Cabrera down, and several of us fell upon Fregoso

---

1. "Represión Brutal en Puebla," *El Demócrata Mexicano,* July 16, 1911. Reprinted in Gerald L. McGowan, ed., *La Revolución Mexicana a través de sus documentos* (Mexico City: Universidad Nacional Autónoma de México, 1987), 3:39–43. Translated by Tim Henderson.
2. The notorious police chief of Puebla.

trying to finish him off. Don Aquiles impeded us, ordering that we should subdue Fregoso and take him to a secure site. Some of us insisted that the mercy shown by our leader was very dangerous in such moments, but his undeniable nobility obliged him to spare the life of Modesto Fregoso, who, trembling convulsively, barely murmured "take me, don't kill me, now is not the time." Immediately we took up our positions and prepared for the fight. There were fourteen of us, with the majority led by Máximo Serdán, and we positioned ourselves along the rooftops. Don Aquiles, during the greater part of the fight, was on the top floor of the house, listening closely, waiting always for the reinforcements that never arrived. . . . Máximo fought like a lion; his courage astonished us; his presence multiplied in the sites of greatest danger, where the bullets fell like an interminable rain. I consider Máximo Serdán a great hero, like the prototypical valiant and patriotic Mexican.

"Do you know the rumor that ran through the city, that the house had a hundred defenders?"

"Ah! If that were the case, the city would be ours! Sure, weapons are important, but we lack men. Carmelita Serdán, the heroic sister of Aquiles and Máximo, invited the people to join the defenders, but only three people responded to her ardent pleas by entering the house."

"There were only seventeen of you?"

"Yes, only seventeen, and of those the majority were killed, leaving only six. But those who died sold their lives dearly! And how much havoc we caused, those of us who were lucky enough to be respected by the bullets! Our extremely numerous attackers, composed of forces from the Federation of the State and of the Police, blasted away without rhyme or reason: you can see for yourself the bullet holes in the home of don Aquiles and in those of his neighbors, some of which are several meters from the site of the siege. By contrast, nearly every one of our shots hit its target, and our carbines never rested. From my perspective, those who most distinguished themselves for their assurance and fortitude were Máximo Serdán and Manuel Velázquez; and for their ardent courage, everyone. When after long hours during which we held our enemies at bay, we thought we were lost before the overwhelming mass of attackers. Máximo could easily have saved himself, but his tremendous valor and honor would not allow him to abandon his post, and finally he fell with a terrible shot to the head. That was the last I witnessed of the fight, for I dragged myself out by my fists, my hands and knees bloody, and I slid along the rooftops until I could escape through a house on Mesones Street, hiding in an abandoned hen house. From there I was turned over to my pursuers by one of the clueless Spaniards who later told me he was the owner of a farm and his dependent, whose name was Campos, called to several rural police saying, 'Here's one of those bandits!' I don't know how I managed to escape from that situation alive. Several times I was at the point of being shot by firing squad and I was constantly treated with real fury, with savage cruelty. At last I was taken to the Commissariat, then

I was sent to jail and sometime later to the Penitentiary. Several times during my detention the police insisted they would shoot me, for I had a rope tied around my neck and was taken to a patio to be prepared for execution."

"They say that you were surely treated with excessive harshness."

"You cannot imagine the extent of the cruelty of our enemies. In the Commissariat I was held in a humid and infected area for three days with nothing to eat or drink when, gripped by an implacable thirst, I cried out for a drink of water, one of the infamous jailers answered: 'Ask Madero for a drink of water,' and 'maybe Madero will bring you something to eat.' Someone should tell those vile tyrants that don Francisco I. Madero very soon will do away with their tyranny, and free us from the steely claws of Caesar and his executioners!"

Document 11. Joining the Revolution[3]

In late 1910 and early 1911, throughout Mexico, people of every status and occupation had to make the wrenching choice of whether to join the revolution or to support the dictatorship. Among those struggling to make that decision was Máximo Castillo of the northern state of Chihuahua. At forty-six, Castillo was older than the average recruit, though his hard life had predisposed him to favor radical change. He was born into rural poverty, worked as a small farmer, miner, and itinerant farm laborer. After years of poverty and frustration, Castillo left his home and family in 1907 to seek work in the United States. There he was struck by the dramatic contrast between the prosperity he witnessed and the misery of his homeland, and he concluded that the root of the problem was bad government. He returned home just as the Madero revolution was gaining steam. He would go on to serve briefly as Madero's bodyguard before becoming disillusioned with the slow pace of reform and joining the anti-Madero rebellion led by Pascual Orozco (see doc. 21). In 1914, he went to the United States, where he was arrested and charged with causing a train disaster that killed some seventy people, including many Americans. Though he vehemently and credibly denied involvement, he was held in an American prison for two years. He died in 1919 at the age of fifty-five.

Finally, after my long expedition, I returned to my blessed home. It was a happy moment when I saw my three loved ones: my wife and my two children.

---

3. Máximo Castillo, *Máximo Castillo and the Mexican Revolution*, ed. Jesús Vargas Valdés, trans. Ana-Isabel Aliaga-Buchenau (Baton Rouge: Louisiana State University Press, 2016), 88–92.

After passing a pleasurable day with my family, I went for a walk in the streets. I encountered my friend José Sáenz. After talking for a good while, I asked him what was new, and he answered me:

—There is a lot that you don't know: an anti-reelectionist club has been formed.

—"And what is up with this club?" I asked.

—Its goal is to make propaganda to go to war with dictator Díaz. If you would like, go to the club so that you can find out what it is all about.

I answered:

—No, I will not go to the meeting . . . I am very cowardly, and I am afraid of going to prison. I do not want to share the fate of Juan Sarabia[4] and his comrades. There will be a denunciation; they will apprehend us while we are defenseless; and we will be off to [the infamous prison of] San Juan de Ulúa. It is better to wait until after the elections. If there is no political resolution (and I do not think there will be), and if it is necessary to take up arms, I will be ready and then we will talk . . . See you later.

I said good-bye to my friend without worry. The next day, I met with another friend of mine, José de la Luz Fourzán. He held a book in his hand. I asked him:

—What book is that?

—It is the history of the presidents, written by don Francisco I. Madero. If you would like, take it with you so you can read it.

I answered: "With pleasure."

I read the book carefully, paying attention to all of the chapters. The book inspired me with great enthusiasm. I was frustrated because the day did not appear near when I could go and fight for my poor brothers and destroy the dictator who had held us in the cruelest servitude for so many years, since we did not even have the freedom to elect our own officeholders. I thought that we might have the liberty to elect a government that would look out for its people in the upcoming elections—a government that would give us the freedom to elect whomever we wanted so that it could govern us and make us truly free. Although I thought that such task was difficult, I wondered what would happen if we really tried. . . .

I impatiently bided my time until the elections. We went to cast our votes at the voting booths, and events unfolded just as I had foreseen. After a short while, the authorities threw those of us in jail who had lined up to fill out our ballots, for the sole crime of not filling out those ballots in favor of General Díaz's candidate.

Tremulous with impatience, I wanted the revolution to start immediately in order to exact revenge for the abuses of the bad authorities. I thus lived in continuous despair, looking for the moment in which we could face off with those who oppressed the people. On occasion, I saw in my imagination those enormous fields

---

4. Juan Sarabia (1882–1920) was a journalist and founder of the Mexican Liberal Party (see doc. 6). He spent the years 1907–1911 in the prison of San Juan de Ulúa in Veracruz.

that I had seen during the expedition to the United States during the previous year. In my mind, I could already see the poor with their small plots of land, very pretty little homes, and my fatherland in full bloom and beautiful.

Many poor neighbors lived close to my house. We were appalled to see the squalor in which they lived: they appeared ragged, almost naked, and hungry. No matter how hard they worked, there was not enough to eat. Moved by the impulse of humanity, and whenever we could, my daughter and I made sure to give them alms and our leftover food, as well as the clothes and shoes that we discarded. At times, we went too far in helping them, as we gave them our only change of clothes, but I maintained a steadfast faith that one day the situation would improve, and that we would all live in better conditions.

I thus lived through two long years until the desired day finally came. At noon on November 9, 1910, my friend José Sáenz came to my house and told me:

—My friend, the hour of bullets has already come. . . . We are going to see if you will keep the promise that you made. I told Herrera. He will bring you up to date on what is happening. . . . [H]e is waiting for you at his house.

—With much pleasure, I will go there right away.

At three in the afternoon, I went to Mr. Herrera's house. His wife told me that I would find him in the Plaza Hidalgo. I went to the square and found him there. I greeted him and told him:

—Here I am, at your command.

—Well, comrade, Mr. José Sáenz has told me that you are willing to help us defeat the Díaz dictatorship, which has deprived us of our liberty for so many years.

—Yes, sir; give me your orders.

—Well, do you have a room we could use?

—Yes, sir.

—Can you go to the gunpowder plant at Ocampo, bring a case of gunpowder and take it to your house?

—Yes, sir.

—Tomorrow night, we will meet at your house with several people to plan the beginning of our work, and so that you can get to know several of our comrades as well as Mr. Madero's Plan of San Luis, under which we will fight.

The Plan of San Luis was read [aloud], and [the group] assigned a few tasks to its members. My commission entailed leaving post haste for Santa María de Cuevas, on the way to Santa Isabel, in order to raise [a contingent] among our supporters, and to return to Sierra Azul on November 19, near Chuviscar. We agreed to attack Chihuahua City that same day.

On November 11, 1910, I did not know how to inform my family about the great commitment that I had assumed. I finally decided and told my wife:

—My dear wife, I will rise up in arms to join the revolution. I am already committed, and I will need to leave on the 14th to raise the people of Santa María de Cuevas.

My wife replied:

—I will never allow you to go to war. . . . How is it that you want to leave my children and me? If you are killed, what will we do by ourselves?

My wife said these words with her eyes drowned in tears. When I heard them, my chest constricted so that I could not talk for several minutes. At last, I answered her:

—See, my dear, war is now necessary, and I have to contribute my insignificant services to defeat this fiend who has kept us under his feet for so many years without giving us the freedom to speak out against his offenses.

She interrupted me:

—Let others go and offer their services; you won't go!

At that moment, my two children unexpectedly entered the room where my wife and I were having this conversation. Félix asked his mother:

—Why are you crying? What is happening between you and my daddy?

—Because your daddy says that he is going to war.

—Yes, my son; I have already made my promise, and I have to leave.

—And why do you need to go fight in the revolution? We have enough to eat and wear; let others go who need to do so. Why do you have to sacrifice yourself?

—Yes, my son, we have enough to eat, but . . . how many poor people do not even have a slice of bread? We have to sacrifice ourselves to meet the needs of those unfortunate people, our brothers.

He answered me:

—Let others go; my sister and I need you.

—See, my son, this Mr. Madero is a millionaire and does not need anything, and even so, he will sacrifice himself for the good of the people.

—Allow me to tell you that this is not true about this man; he will sacrifice himself for the presidency, which will give him enormous riches.

—Look, my son, he is offering to return the lands that have been taken from the poor. . . . If that is so, it will be good for our people and our fatherland, and we have to help him.

—Papá, don't believe that. These men are not sacrificing themselves for the poor; instead, he will sacrifice the people for his own benefit.

—Son, I have already committed myself.

I made a few more comments, but it was impossible to convince them. Finally, my children told me:

—Do what you want, but we don't agree with you if you insist on joining the revolution. . . . [W]e will stay, shedding abundant tears.

They said these words to me; but finally, when they knew that there was no other way, they realized that they could not prevent me from going to fulfill my word of honor, and that I was already committed to the cause. It was not possible to assuage my wife, but there was nothing else that I could do.

Document 12. The Treaty of Ciudad Juárez[5]

*Following the debacle of Puebla, where Maderista leader Aquiles Serdán and his sup-
porters were killed by police on November 18, 1910, Madero's revolution lost much of its
momentum. Madero stayed in the United States until February 1911. In April, his forces
laid siege to Ciudad Juárez, Chihuahua, across the border from El Paso, Texas. Madero,
concerned that the battle might lead to casualties on the U.S. side of the border, ordered
his forces to lift the siege, but commanders Pascual Orozco and Pancho Villa ignored
him and soon defeated the federal forces. The resulting treaty was brief and has been the
object of much criticism, for, while it secured the resignation of Porfirio Díaz, it left most
of his government and military intact. Installed as interim president was Francisco León
de la Barra, a conservative who had served in various diplomatic posts during the Díaz
government. The treaty angered some Madero supporters by failing to mention any of the
social reforms that had been promised in the Plan of San Luis Potosí.*

In Ciudad Juárez, on 21 May 1911, the following individuals are gathered in the Border Customs Building: Francisco S. Carvajal, representative of the government of Porfirio Díaz; Dr. Francisco Vázquez Gómez, Francisco Madero, and José María Pino Suárez, representatives of the Revolution, to deal with the cessation of hostilities throughout the national territory, and to consider:

I. That General Porfirio Díaz has made manifest his decision to resign the presidency of the Republic before the end of the current month; II. That we have reliable reports that Ramón Corral will likewise resign the vice presidency within the same time span; III. That to administer the law, Mr. Francisco León de la Barra, Secretary of Foreign Relations in the government of General Díaz, will exercise Executive Power on an interim basis and will convoke general elections within the terms of the Constitution; IV. That the new government will study current opinions in every state within the constitutional order and will determine what indemnities will be paid for damages caused directly by the Revolution. The two parties represented by this conference, due to the foregoing considerations, have agreed to formalize the present agreement: From this day hostilities between the forces of General Díaz

---

5. Javier Garciadiego, *La Revolución Mexicana: Crónicas, documentos, planes y testimonios* (Mexico City: UNAM, 2008), 117–19. Translated by Tim Henderson.

and those of the Revolution will cease throughout the territory of the Republic; in each state the necessary steps will be taken to reestablish and guarantee peace and public order.

Transitory: We shall proceed with the reconstruction or repair of the telegraphs and railroads that are currently down. This is signed in duplicate. Francisco S. Carvajal, Francisco Vázquez Gómez, Francisco Madero, José María Pino Suárez.

Document 13. Porfirio Díaz's Letter of Resignation[6]

The fall of Ciudad Juárez to the rebels finally persuaded Porfirio Díaz that his position was untenable, and he resigned as president of Mexico on May 25, 1911, with the brief letter that follows. Díaz went into exile shortly after his resignation, dying in Paris on July 2, 1915, at the age of eighty-four.

To the Secretaries of the Honorable Chamber of Deputies:

The Mexican people—those people who have so generously showered me with honors, who proclaimed me their leader during the War of Intervention, who patriotically supported me in all of the works I have undertaken to advance the industry and commerce of the Republic—those same people, Honorable Deputies, have risen up in armed millenarian bands, declaring my presence in the exercise of Supreme Executive Power to be the cause of their insurrection.

I don't know a single deed imputable to me that could have motivated this social phenomenon; but I will allow, without conceding, that I may unwittingly be culpable, and that possibility makes me the least appropriate person to rationalize and judge my own culpability.

Therefore, respecting, as I have always respected, the will of the people, and in accord with article 82 of the Federal Constitution, before the Supreme Representation of the Nation, I resign, without reservation, the office of Constitutional President of the Republic with which the people honored me; and I do this still more willingly when to retain that office would necessarily lead to the continued shedding of Mexican blood, destroying the Nation's credit, squandering its riches, depleting its resources, and exposing its politics to international conflicts.

I hope, Honorable Deputies, that once the passions that accompany all revolutions are calmed, a more conscientious and truthful study will be made in the national consciousness, a correct judgment that allows me to die, carrying in the

---

6. Porfirio Díaz's resignation letter, *Milenio*, accessed January 18, 2022, https://www.milenio.com/cultura/natalicio-porfirio-diaz-decia-carta-renuncia. Translated by Tim Henderson.

depths of my soul a fair correspondence of the esteem that throughout my life I have devoted and will forever devote to my countrymen. With all respect.

Mexico, May 25, 1911.

Porfirio Díaz

Document 14. Intimate Madero[7]

While many saw much to admire in Francisco I. Madero personally, his presidency has largely been judged a failure. Although his devotion to democracy seems to have been genuine, he was overly idealistic to the point of naïvete. He soon disappointed those of his supporters who yearned for sweeping social reforms, for he did not disband Díaz's army and many of the elites of the old regime continued to wield influence. At the same time he had few admirers among those elites, who viewed him as weak and vacillating, unwilling or unable to contain the disruptive forces of revolution. Even some of his closest allies came to see him as unequal to the nearly impossible task he had undertaken by assuming the presidency of Mexico at a moment of profound upheaval. Among these was Roque Estrada (1883–1966), a journalist and lawyer who was an early supporter of Madero. He was jailed along with Madero in 1909 and later became Madero's private secretary, though he was among many who took Madero to task for his eagerness to compromise with elements of the old regime. Estrada later supported Venustiano Carranza, ran for president in 1920, and served as a judge and later president of the Supreme Court of Justice from 1941 to 1952. In 1912, he published an account of the early revolution that included some pointed observations on the background and character of the president.

I often thought that the Madero family, one of the wealthiest in the Republic, cannot be revolutionary. The principal industries and businesses in our country are in the hands of "cientificismo," that is, in the hands of those we are fighting against as agents of our economic, social and political condition; agricultural, industrial and financial competition played to the interests of that same wealthy family, for all are governed by economic laws and common tendencies. Whatever might benefit or harm cientificismo would have to also benefit or harm the interests of the Candidate's family. Even supposing that those interests moved in a different orbit (hypothetically), economic laws would produce common effects; and since revolutions—true revolutions—are not just political but are fundamentally economic, their as-yet-latent impact would be bound to harm the family's interests.

---

7. Roque Estrada, *La Revolución y Francisco I. Madero* (Guadalajara: Talleres de la Imprenta Americana, 1912), 262, 300–302. Translated by Tim Henderson.

My thoughts arrived at a more-or-less realizable outcome: Mr. Madero in Power. The natural influence of his family legitimately shaped his own interests, as well as the natural economic relation of those interests and those of the científicos—ties of friendship and society, etc., etc. Would this not inspire or modify his conduct as President of the Republic? Undoubtedly it would. That inspiration or modification would be unconscious in most cases, while in others it would be quite conscious, for we tend to convince ourselves in favor of what pleases and benefits us. And in this case, it is nearly certain that revolutionary interests would be defrauded.

These considerations led me logically to conclude that revolutions can only fulfill their true promise if they are led by men who belong to, or have emerged from, the social class that needs those revolutions. . . .

Madero performs acts of great philanthropy. It is said that he treats his servants with great kindness and that he attends to their physical and intellectual needs; the first by giving gifts, the second by establishing rural schools that he sustains with his own funds. These qualities are common throughout the Madero family.

Francisco I. Madero, in his zeal to be useful to the poor and to help them in various ways, privately studied medicine, inclining toward Homeopathy; and he provided his services to the needy entirely free of charge.

Frugal, strictly vegetarian, modest at the dining table, without any hint of ostentation. He never takes a drop of alcohol, not even beer.

At its base, his character contains frequent and enormous contradictions. If he seems generally willing to consider the advice or opinions of others, with a bit of observation one sees that opinions contrary to his own displease him, and that he has a profound aversion toward people who frequently contradict him; by the same token, he is inclined to feel great affection for those who support him invariably. This reveals a powerful factor in his knowledge of men: he believes the first group to be useless and stupid; if they are clearly intelligent and he is unable to refute their views, he deems those views misguided or even dangerous; at the same time, he finds the second group to be useful and intelligent. He is practically obsessed with the belief that he can know men immediately; with a conversation, for example.

At first, it struck me as strange that Madero thought people intelligent who were notorious for their limited intellectual faculties. As I observed this so frequently, I became preoccupied with finding the explanation; I believe that explanation is found in the preceding paragraph. In effect those people, owing to their limited intellect and the exaggerated respect they have for their "superiors," accept his judgments and projects without question and generally in good faith; and if they sometimes think differently, then they doubt their own ideas and suppose that it is their superiors who possess the truth. [I am not here considering those people who maliciously attach themselves to the will of the superior.] As we have already explained, we are prone to believe things that please us and to reject things that displease us; and since the basis of our judgments is ourselves, we undoubtedly find those who think like us to be intelligent and successful. It requires a heavy dose of brain power to distinguish *reason* from *sentiment*.

These contradictions are echoed in Madero's doctrines, and one often observes in him a mixture of prejudices and modern ideas that he has incompletely assimilated. His foundation is indeterminate, with no firm or solid tendency.

Madero is quite fond of smiles and hugs. But upon knowing him with some intimacy, one arrives at the conviction that not all those smiles and hugs are sincere; there is much in them that is artificial, and that artificiality is perceived by people who meet him for the first time.

It is not unusual to see acts of exaggerated altruism alongside of refined egotism in such a character.

I may be wrong in making these observations; they are the product of my limited wisdom. Tomorrow the historian will judge them serenely, and I hope that my observations help him in some way, even if it be to destroy them, for I understand that in the current circumstances it is very hard to be impartial.

Document 15. Report of Investigation of the Chinese Massacre[8]

War often frees people from the conventions of civilization and allows them to indulge their basest and least admirable instincts. The Mexican Revolution was no exception: casual cruelty and reckless bloodletting were commonplace during the entire period. The single most appalling episode of mob violence was the senseless massacre of hundreds of Chinese immigrants in the northern city of Torreón, Coahuila, in May of 1911. More than any other group—with the possible exception of Spaniards—the Chinese were the objects of irrational xenophobic hatred. Even the relatively enlightened Liberal Party (doc. 6) sought to ban immigration from China. It is perhaps worth noting that the Chinese fared no better in the United States, which had outlawed Chinese and other Asian immigration since 1882. An account of the massacre by G. C. Carothers, the American consular agent in the district, follows.

Torreón, Coahuila, Mexico, June 7, 1911

According to the best information that I can secure, 303 Chinamen and 5 Japanese were massacred on May 15, 1911, by the Maderista Revolutionary forces under Emilio Madero, Jesús Castro, Sixto Ugalde, Enrique Macias, and other leaders.

I did not know that the Chinese were being massacred until 12:00 o'clock on the 15th as I had not left my residence at which hour several Americans came

---

8. "Report of Investigation of Chinese Massacre," RG 59, Department of State Decimal File, 1910–1929, from 312.93/1 to 312.94/46, box 3832, National Archives, College Park, MD.

to my house and told me that all of the Chinamen in town had been massacred. All morning I had been endeavoring to get into communication with Mr. Emilio Madero but it was impossible until 3:30 P.M. at which hour he came to my house answering an urgent request from me and a number of refugees who were assembled at my residence. Mr. Madero told me that he was appalled at the massacre of the Chinese but that they themselves were to blame. That he had been informed by the leaders and soldiers of his forces that they had been fired on by the Chinese both on the outskirts and in the City, but that he had tried his best to stop the massacre and that at that moment, (about 4:00 P.M.) he thought that he had his men under control; that he had ordered all the Chinamen concentrated in the barracks where they could be properly protected. . . .

On June 4th I received instructions from Ambassador Wilson to tender my good offices to the Chinese Agent in assisting him in his investigation. . . .

On June 6th Foon Chuck arrived, and as he is a heavy investor in Torreón, I told him that I would like to have him accompany me on a trip through the Chinese Gardens in order that I might personally see the damage that had been done. . . .

At 3:00 P.M. we started out, arriving first at a garden near Doctor Lim's place, belonging to Lim Chang. Foon Chuck, acting as interpreter for me, questioned the men who are working at the gardens. They told me that on May 14th, about noon, 7 or 8 Maderistas arrived at their place, robbed them of everything they had and killed one. That on the morning of the 15th, at 2:00 A.M. a large bunch of Maderistas arrived and killed 7 more; that there had been 11 in all working at this place, only 3 having escaped, among them the one whom I interviewed.

We then crossed over to Doctor Lim's place where I also interviewed about eight Chinamen who were back at work. They told me that on Saturday, the 13th, between 8:00 and 9:00 A.M. a small bunch of Maderistas had arrived there and insisted upon their giving them money, which they denied having, upon which they were beaten over the backs with sabers but none killed. That on early Monday morning a large bunch of Maderistas arrived, demanding money. Upon being refused this, they killed three. They then gathered the rest of the Chinamen together and drove them to Torreón through the mud and water, forcing them to run, and every time a Chinaman slipped and fell to the ground, he was shot and trampled upon by the horses. Out of 20 odd that started towards town, 7 were killed. They told me that across the ditch Doctor Lim had another garden where 18 Chinamen worked and that they had all been killed.

We then went to a garden rented by Dan Kee and Wong Sam. There were 18 at this place and all were killed. We found the place in [the] charge of a Maderista guard. At this place, as well as all others, we found the houses absolutely ransacked, not a thing of any value whatever remaining. It looked as if the places had been searched for money.

We passed another garden belonging to Wong Quam which was again in working order where I was told that 6 had been killed on May 15th. We then crossed over to a large garden owned by Mah Due who had 20 laborers, out of which 19 had been killed and 1 wounded.

From there we went to Foon Chuck's garden, where he had 38 laborers, out of which 33 had been killed.

I interviewed the Superintendent, Ung Shung Yee, who told me that the Maderistas had arrived at the garden Saturday afternoon, the 13th. That they had spent the night and all of the 14th at this place, using it as a fort in firing upon the Federal soldiers who were entrenched about 600 yards between the gardens and the City of Torreón. That they had taken the ladders and crawled up behind a high wall from which place they shot. This is evidenced by the ladders still being in position and the imprints of the rifle barrels on the top of the wall. It is also evidenced by a number of bullet holes on the outside of the wall, showing that the Maderista fire had been returned by the Federals. Ung Shung Yee told me that the Chinamen had been forced to cook the meals for the Maderistas during part of two days; that they had been much abused by them but that none had been killed until the 15th when the Maderistas started to run them out like rabbits, shooting them down as they ran, without any provocation whatever. At this garden the machinery of the pumping installation was robbed of all parts that could be detached, all of the windows and doors of the houses carried away, and everything in the houses either destroyed or stolen.

Next we went to the Chinese Laundry where four had been killed, and the laundry practically demolished. Bombs had been thrown on the roof, the windows and doors either destroyed or stolen, the machinery broken to pieces and everything that could be carted away, stolen. I might mention here that a dance was given by the Maderistas on the second floor of this building, on the night of the 16th. From the laundry 22 Chinamen escaped into the adjoining house where they were hidden by the wife of Mr. J. Cadena. . . .

The Puerto de Shanghai building was next visited. All of the doors and windows of the building were destroyed. The Chinese Bank, which had been moved into this building a few months before, was demolished, safes blown open and contents taken, furniture destroyed, all papers and valuables stolen. Seventeen Chinamen were killed here. I am told that many on the second floor had been cut to pieces and the pieces thrown out through the windows. Hong Si Jack, Cashier of the Chinese Bank, a relative of Kan Tu Wei, President of the Chinese Reform Association, was among the killed. The store called "El Puerto de Shanghai" also occupied part of this building. It contained a stock of about $30,000 and was completely sacked.

We then visited the Wah Tick building, commonly known as the "Chinese Bank Building." On the second floor of this building the Chinese Reform Association has its headquarters, lodge room, library, with private banquet hall in basement.

Here there were 18 Chinamen, of which 10 were killed, the others escaping. The building was considerably damaged, especially to doors and plate glass windows. The Laguna Bank and the offices of Sr. Rafael Aldape Quiroz, a private banker, and a store owned by an Arab, also occupied the ground floor of this building. All these places were demolished by the mob and the Maderistas, thinking that they belonged to Chinamen. The Maderistas rode their horses into the building, shooting and slashing everything in sight. The mob finished the work by carrying off everything of value. The large safe belonging to the Reform Association had a hole about 6 inches in diameter blown into it through the back, surrounded by hundreds of holes, evidently from steel bullets or chisels.

The next place we visited was the Chinese Railroad Hotel and Restaurant which was completely sacked of all furniture, dining room and kitchen fixtures. None were killed here but nine employees were killed, who had escaped from the building. Nothing but the stove and a few tables was left. . . .

At every place I visited I questioned every Chinaman, through Mr. Chuck as interpreter, as to the question of their Chinamen firing on the Maderistas and met with indignant denials in every case. They asked me how would it be possible for them to have fired on the Maderistas when the Maderistas had been with them, forcing them to cook and serve them and used their places as forts during 36 hours before the massacre.

I also questioned them very closely as to General Lejero's having invited them to resist the attack on the City of Torreón and as to his having given them guns and ammunition, but have been unable so far to find one single person outside of the Maderista forces who will affirm that he saw a Chinaman fire a gun.

I have talked with a number of Maderista leaders who all tell the same story, that they were attacked by the Chinese from the garden in entering the City and that in their anger they killed all they could find until they received orders to stop, after which they protected and took the balance to the cuartels. . . .

ADDENDA

I have been told by persons who claim to have been present, that on the fifth of May, a leader of the Maderistas by the name of Jesús C. Flores, who assisted at the taking of Gomez Palacio, made a speech in the Plaza at Gomez Palacio, in which he told his hearers that it was necessary to run the Chinamen out of the country; that they did the work that the Mexican women ought to do; that they had monopolized the gardening industry, and that they were not good citizens; that they would get together the money that they made and send it out of the country, instead of spending it here as other foreigners did. Jesús C. Flores was killed during the attack on Torreón, May 18th.

Document 16. Zapata Meets Madero[9]

One of the most iconic scenes of the revolution occurred during the first meeting between peasant leader Emiliano Zapata and the victorious revolutionary leader Francisco I. Madero, which took place not long after the signing of the Treaty of Ciudad Juárez. Although the real falling out between the two men was still months away, the issues that divided them were obvious from the outset. Zapata insisted that stolen lands be returned to the villages, while Madero prioritized the disbanding of Zapata's irregular forces, giving only vague assurances that the "promises of the revolution" would be fulfilled. It would soon become clear that the chasm between these two demands was unbreachable.

On the 8th [of June], after lunch, Madero and the southern chief exchanged impressions of the situation and problems of Morelos. Madero began by congratulating General Zapata for his performance, and after learning about the revolutionary forces he had at his orders, he opined that, the Revolution having triumphed, it would be convenient to disband those forces, since they had no reason to remain under arms.

"I am informed, General," said Madero, "that there have been difficulties between yourself and General Figueroa that must be done away with. It's not helpful that among the good elements of the Revolution such differences should exist."

"Mr. Madero," Zapata replied energetically, "Figueroa is not a loyal revolutionary. At the beginning of May he sent his brother don Francisco to make compromises with the government, and he declared publicly that there would be peace in the south because they had already agreed to an offer made them by the dictator. If these arrangements came to nothing, it was only because the revolution triumphed before they expected it to. However, if you believe that General Figueroa is a good element of the Revolution, so long as he doesn't meddle in the affairs of Morelos, everything is fine, and I will refrain from intervening in the affairs of Guerrero. But frankly, I don't want to deal with someone who, upon the outbreak of the struggle, entered into suspicious dealings with the government and tried to set me up when we agreed to attack Jojutla. I also have in my possession the propositions that were made to get me to defect from the Revolution and join the government, which, I was assured, are the same as the ones made to Figueroa. My only answer was to return to Cuautla. Mr. Madero, did you authorize General Figueroa to send his brother to make those arrangements with the dictator?"

"No, General," Madero answered, "I believe that you prejudged or have been badly informed. General Figueroa is like you, a good element of the Revolution and these problems are unacceptable, for they only harm our cause. I want you to

---

9. Gildardo Magaña, *Emiliano Zapata y el agrarismo en México* (Mexico City: Instituto Nacional de Estudios Históricos, 2019), 1:214–18. Translated by Tim Henderson.

end this bad blood, for it will probably lead to the kinds of intrigues that, sadly, are many."

"As you order, Mr. Madero," said Zapata. "But time will reveal who General Figueroa is and what he does. What interests us, of course, is that the lands be returned to the villages and that the promises of the Revolution be fulfilled."

"All that will be done; but in due time and according to the law, because these are delicate matters that cannot be resolved lightly or with the stroke of a pen. They must be studied, processed and resolved by the state authorities. What matters most in the short term," the Chief of the Revolution once again insisted, "is that you proceed with the disbanding of your revolutionary forces, because the triumph has now been secured and there is no longer any reason for them to remain armed."

Zapata then told Madero that he was well disposed to complying with all his orders, that he would disband his forces as requested and that he was absolutely confident that Madero would make good on the promises made by the Revolution, above all respecting the return of the stolen lands; but he expressed some doubts that the Federal Army would loyally support him in power.

"It is our natural enemy," he said. "Or do you believe, Mr. Madero, that because the people overcame the tyrant, these men are going to change their manner of being? You've seen what's happening with the new governor, Mr. Carreón. He completely favors the hacendados, and if this is happening now that we are triumphant and with weapons in hand, what will happen if we submit to the will of our enemies?"

"No, General," Madero replied. "The time when we needed arms has passed. Now we must pursue the struggle on other grounds. If the current governor of Morelos does not guarantee the revolutionary interests of the state, then he will be replaced with someone who will do his duty. But we must be prudent and not proceed violently, something for which both our enemies and public opinion would reproach us. The Revolution must guarantee order and be respectful of property."

The southern leader stood up, and without leaving his carbine (from which he had not been separated even while eating), he approached Madero and pointed to the gold chain that hung from his vest, and said:

"Look, Mr. Madero. If I, taking advantage of the fact that I am armed, take your watch and keep it, and at some later time we meet again and we are both armed with equal strength, would you have the right to demand that I return it?"

"Why not, General? And I would even have the right to ask for an indemnity for the time that you had it improperly," the Chief of the Revolution answered.

"Well, that is exactly what has happened to us in the state of Morelos," replied Zapata. "A handful of hacendados have taken lands by force from the villages. My soldiers, the armed peasants and the rest of the people, demand that I tell you, with all due respect, that they want you to proceed with the restitution of their lands."

Madero repeated to Zapata that all of the promises would be fulfilled, that he must have faith that everything would be worked out satisfactorily; and also that he would choose, among the revolutionary elements from different regions of the country that were best organized, some contingents to make up a set number of irregular corps of the Army.

"Mr. Madero," said Zapata, "we want you to visit our state to see our needs and return the land to the villages as soon as possible."

"I will study the case of Morelos minutely so as to resolve things fairly. And as a reward for the services that you have rendered to the Revolution, I am going to see to it that you are able to acquire a nice ranch," said Madero to the southerner.

Without hiding his displeasure, Zapata took a step backward and struck the floor loudly with his carbine. Then, in a respectful but somewhat altered tone that was heard by everyone present, he said:

"Mr. Madero, I did not join the Revolution to become an hacendado. If I value anything, it is the confidence that the rancheros have in me, for they believe we are going to give them what we have offered, and if we abandon those people that made the Revolution, they would be justified in again taking up arms against those who forgot their promises."

Madero, smiling, got up from his chair and said:

"No, General Zapata, understand what I am trying to say; that I will comply with my promises and also that those who have given valuable services like you and many other leaders should be duly rewarded."

"The only thing we want, Mr. Madero, is that the lands that were stolen from us by the 'científico' hacendados be returned to us," confirmed the southerner.

Madero left the room. . . . After about 25 minutes he returned, and he promised Zapata that as soon as his work schedule permitted he would go to Morelos, accepting the invitation Zapata had made. Thus ended that interesting interview, after which Zapata returned to Cuernavaca.

Document 17. Manifesto to the Nation[10]

Bernardo Reyes (b. 1850) was perhaps the most distinguished military man of the Porfiriato. He served multiple terms as governor of the northern state of Nuevo León, and was briefly (1900–1902) secretary of war in President Diaz's cabinet. He represented forces that were critical of the influential científico faction, and he and his supporters

---

10. Isidro Fabela, ed., *Documentos históricos de la Revolución Mexicana: Revolución y régimen maderista* (Mexico City: Fondo de Cultura Económica, 1965), 1:285–94. Translated by Tim Henderson.

*were incensed when the elderly Díaz chose a member of that faction—Ramón Corral—to
be his vice president, an office to which Reyes aspired. Díaz sent Reyes on a diplomatic
mission to Europe—a fairly standard means of eliminating potential threats—and Reyes
was enough of a Díaz loyalist to meekly comply. He returned in 1911 as a Madero
supporter, but soon grew disillusioned with Madero and announced his candidacy for the
presidency. In September he was badly beaten by a mob of Madero supporters; he and
his supporters subsequently sought to postpone the election without success, after which
Reyes withdrew from the race and went to San Antonio, Texas, where he proclaimed his
rebellion in November. He crossed back into Mexico in early December, but his rebellion
collapsed even before it began. He was arrested and imprisoned in Mexico City.*

Divisional General Bernardo Reyes to his fellow citizens:

Saving the Fatherland from the unfortunate circumstances afflicting it requires
the efforts of all its children. To demonstrate the urgency of that work of National
salvation, I will fill in the necessary background.

In 1909 . . . the noble Mexican People, grateful to one of the Nation's heroic
defenders and outstanding governors for bringing them peace and prosperity,
decided, without opposition, to nominate him for a seventh time as the Nation's
First Magistrate, his term to run from 1910 to 1916. Unfortunately, General Díaz
went against National Opinion, which wanted me as Vice President of the Republic, imposing in that position Mr. Ramón Corral, a man without merit and a member of the pernicious *científico* oligarchy.

The imposition of that candidacy might have been tolerated in earlier times
when the President was still young, but in 1909 it provoked the fear that Mr. Corral
would go on to govern the Nation if President Díaz were to become incapacitated or
die within his constitutional term. The Mexican people rebelled. . . .

[Díaz's *científico* allies] used all means, even the most reprehensible, to bring
about their unpopular plan. The Judiciary, which in a healthy society protects the
persecuted and afflicted, in Mexico served as the instrument of that group. They
unleashed all of their anger against me and my followers, and we saw something
that was never seen in the earlier days of the Porfirian administration: Troops were
sent against me as I was peacefully governing the State of Nuevo León; my friends
were imprisoned on spurious charges; governors and functionaries were imposed
upon, forcing them to abandon the posts to which they had been popularly elected,
just because they cultivated good relations with me.

I believed that popular opinion was inflamed and headed toward armed Revolution against General Díaz, and that this would cause serious evils within the
Country and dangers from abroad. Given that popular opinion tacitly named me
as Chief of the coming Revolution, I excused myself from leading it. I judged that
my leaving the country would bring about a situation where, since the President's
decrepitude was advancing rapidly, power would soon pass to Corral, who was

completely lacking in prestige. I foresaw that, if the change were brought about in any other way, disastrous anarchic movements would result. My prognosis was confirmed by the events that we are now witnessing. And so, due to these considerations, and hard pressed by the circumstances of the moment, I left the country. . . .

My expectation of that vigorous resistance was an error, as was demonstrated by the incredible, unforeseeable events that unraveled with vertiginous speed after my departure.

Citizen Francisco I. Madero . . . fled from San Luis Potosí, where he had been imprisoned. He then formulated a revolutionary plan in which he gave life and passion to public opinion, which was already inclined to welcome him.

In that plan he called upon the people to demolish the Dictatorship, do away with the tyrannical oligarchy, establish liberty and effective suffrage, and ensure there would be no reelection.

The Government, which was considered powerful within our Country and throughout the civilized world, fell apart within six months of the plan's appearance. . . .

In April of 1911, while the Government was still in flux, I was called from Europe to place myself at the head of the Government's armed forces. Taking the country's situation into account, I explained that I would return only if the *científico* group was eliminated from the Administration and if I were permitted to compromise with the revolution, which to my mind was justified. . . .

By the time I arrived in Mexico, the government of General Díaz was no more, and in its place was a provisional government emanating from the treaties of Ciudad Juárez. I could see that national opinion, almost unanimously, wanted Francisco I. Madero as their candidate for President of the Republic in the elections that were soon to take place; and when my old supporters sought to nominate me to occupy the same post, I told them that the Nation was still roiled by recent catastrophes, and, for good of that Nation, we should avoid a new upheaval. It would be patriotic, therefore, for us to adhere to the popular will, which welcomed Madero's candidacy. To confirm my judgment and inform the entire Republic of my ideas about the situation, as well as to encourage my supporters to accept it, I sent out a manifesto on 12 June 1911, [though I soon changed my views and sent out a] second manifesto on 4 August of the same year. Below I will reproduce the relevant portion, for it will clarify the reasons why I later accepted the candidacy that I had earlier rejected.

". . . [I]n this brief period (less than two months), I have seen that my dreams of uniting myself and my contingents with those of the Chief of the Revolution have been in vain. Some of his ardent proselytes rejected me and my followers, hurling all manner of insults through the press; and those offensive manifestations of intransigence, which Madero nobly and energetically opposed, were followed by still other more serious events, for they came from the authorities imposed by the revolution. I have personally been surveilled by the police and Maderista troops. . . .

"As before, and yet again, I am required to accept my nomination for the Presidency of the Republic; and freed from commitments for reasons I've explained, and considering the new circumstances of the country, I am convinced that I must not vacillate in attending to those requirements when they have to do with putting myself at the service of the Fatherland; for that reason I emphatically declare that I accept the candidacy I am offered, and if the public vote elevates me to the presidency I shall satisfy the legitimate national aspirations for Peace, Liberty, and Justice." . . .

After publishing this manifesto, I believed that there would be a free election. . . .

Very soon the facts demonstrated that neither the results of the Revolution nor the promises of its Chief would be respected. The promises written on the banner that represented the overwhelming opinion of the people and around which was grouped the phalanges that struggled for the triumph of Liberty were not respected, nor was the solemn pact of Tehuacán.

No sooner did political parties begin to organize in opposition to Mr. Madero's candidacy than they encountered all manner of outrages: imprisonment, murder, and other violent and unjustified persecutions by the Maderista gang, delivered in demagogic outbursts, supported by imposed authorities, and backed by carbines in the hands of the revolutionary caudillo's personalist followers. . . .

In addition, the election's constitutional requirements were violated, so that true suffrage was impossible in those conditions.

From the foregoing, it can logically be deduced that the election of Francisco I. Madero and Lic. José María Pino Suárez as President and Vice President of the Republic is completely null and void, and against the bastard Government that resulted from this election, the people, who brought about the triumph of the revolution that brought with it the promise of liberty and effective suffrage, have the duty to rise up; their banner is stained with the blood of all who sacrificed themselves in the war or who were murdered in the electoral preparations; torn and tattered, that banner has been mockingly hurled in the face of the Mexican people by the man waved it only for his sordid ambitions.

The nation has been able to size up this man, whose only greatness lies in committing crimes and outrages against liberty, and who is liberal only in distributing the highest public posts among his family members and others of his cabal. He has distributed the nation's treasures to those favored few so they can cover who knows what expenses, bankrupting the Treasury. From what they have seen fit to confess, we know this amounts to tens of millions. The unfettered power, the insatiable hoarding of gold, the nepotism sustained by demagogy—this has been the sad ending of a revolution that promised so much, that was based on the defense of right that the sacred wind of liberty burned into the people's soul. That revolution has been distorted and mocked by the man who led it, and in the few months that he has exercised his pernicious influence in the country, he has dragged it into anarchy.

Soledad Encampment, Tamaulipas, November 16, 1911

Document 18. The Plan of Ayala[11]

Relations between Zapata and Madero deteriorated swiftly after their June 1911 meeting (doc. 16). In defiance of Madero's wishes, Zapata refused to disband his forces. Soon landowners and their allies were accusing the Zapatistas of atrocities and demanded military action; Interim President Francisco León de la Barra, who had served as foreign secretary in the Díaz government, was happy to oblige, sending troops under the command of the ruthless General Victoriano Huerta. By the time Madero was elected and assumed the presidency, Zapata was his bitter enemy. The Plan of Ayala was the Zapatista declaration of war against Madero, but it was also a blueprint for the kind of revolution envisioned by the Zapatistas. They came to regard the document as a sacred text, one that should be embraced by all of Mexico's factions.

Liberating Plan of the sons of the State of Morelos, affiliated with the Insurgent Army which defends the fulfillment of the Plan of San Luis, with the reforms that it believes necessary to increase the welfare of the Mexican Fatherland.

The undersigned, constituted into a Revolutionary Junta to sustain and carry out the promises made to the country by the Revolution of 20 November 1910, solemnly declare before the civilized world which sits in judgment on us, and before the Nation to which we belong and which we love, the propositions we have formulated to do away with the tyranny that oppresses us and to redeem the Fatherland from the dictatorships that are imposed upon us, which are outlined in the following plan:

1. Taking into consideration that the Mexican people, led by Francisco I. Madero, went out to shed their blood to reconquer liberties and vindicate their rights which had been trampled upon, and not so that one man could seize power, violating the sacred principles that he swore to defend with the slogan "Effective Suffrage and No Reelection," thereby insulting the faith, cause and liberties of the people; taking into consideration that the man to whom we refer is Francisco I. Madero, the same who initiated the aforementioned Revolution, who imposed his

---

11. Manuscript from November 25, 1911, Carso Center for the Study of Mexican History, Mexico City. Reprinted in Gustavo Casasola Zapata, ed., *Historia gráfica de la revolución mexicana, 1900–1970*, 3rd ed., vol. 2 (Mexico City: Editorial Trillas, 1992). Translated by Tim Henderson.

will and influence as a governmental norm upon the Provisional Government of the ex-president of the Republic, licenciado Francisco León de la Barra, causing with this deed much bloodshed and many misfortunes to the Fatherland in a cunning and ridiculous fashion, having no goals to satisfy apart from his own personal ambitions, his boundless instincts for tyranny, and his profound disrespect for the fulfillment of the preexisting laws emanating from the immortal Constitution of 1857, written with the revolutionary blood of Ayutla.

Taking into account that the so-called chief of the Liberating Revolution of Mexico, don Francisco I. Madero, due to his great weakness and lack of integrity, did not bring to a happy conclusion the Revolution that he began with the help of God and the people, since he left intact the majority of the governing powers and corrupt elements of oppression from the dictatorial Government of Porfirio Díaz, which are not and can never in any way be the representatives of the National sovereignty, and that, being terrible enemies of ourselves and of the principles that we defend, are causing the ills of the country and opening new wounds in the breast of the Fatherland, making it drink its own blood; taking also into account that the aforementioned don Francisco I. Madero, current president of the Republic, tried to avoid fulfilling the promises he made to the Nation in the Plan of San Luis Potosí . . . nullifying, persecuting, imprisoning, or killing the revolutionary elements who helped him to occupy the high post of president of the Republic, by means of false promises and numerous intrigues against the Nation.

Taking into consideration that the oft-mentioned Francisco I. Madero has tried to silence with the brute force of bayonets and to drown in blood the people who ask, solicit, or demand the fulfillment of the promises of the Revolution, calling them bandits and rebels, condemning them to a war of extermination, without conceding or granting any of the guarantees that reason, justice, and the law prescribe; taking equally into account that the president of the Republic, Francisco I. Madero, has made of Effective Suffrage a bloody mockery by imposing, against the will of the people, the licenciado José María Pino Suárez as Vice-President of the Republic, imposing also the governors of the States, designating such men as the so-called Ambrosio Figueroa, cruel tyrant of the people of Morelos; and entering into collaboration with the científico party, feudal hacendados and oppressive caciques, enemies of the Revolution he proclaimed, with the aim of forging new chains and continuing the mold of a new dictatorship more opprobrious and more terrible than that of Porfirio Díaz; so it has become patently clear that he has not respect for life or interests, as has happened in the State of Morelos and other states, bringing us to the most horrific anarchy registered in contemporary history. Due to these consideration, we declare Francisco I. Madero incapable of realizing the promises of the revolution of which he was instigator, because he has betrayed all of his principle, mocking the will of the people in his rise to power; he is incapable of governing because he has no respect for the rule of law and for the justice of the people, and is a traitor to the Fatherland, humiliating the Mexicans by blood and fire because they wish for freedom and an end to the pandering to científicos, hacendados and caciques who enslave us; today we continue the Revolution begun by [Madero], and will carry on until we defeat the dictatorial powers that exist.

2. Francisco I. Madero is disavowed as Chief of the Revolution and as President of the Republic for the reasons expressed above. We shall bring about the overthrow of this functionary.

3. We recognize as Chief of the Liberating Revolution General Pascual Orozco, second of the caudillo don Francisco I. Madero, and in case he does not accept this delicate post, we shall recognize as chief of the Revolution General Emiliano Zapata.

4. The Revolutionary Junta of the State of Morelos manifests to the Nation, under formal protest, that it adopts the Plan of San Luis Potosí as its own, with the additions that shall be expressed below, for the benefit of the oppressed peoples, and it will make itself the defender of the principles that they defend until victory or death.

5. The Revolutionary Junta of the State of Morelos will not admit transactions or agreements until it has brought about the defeat of the dictatorial elements of Porfirio Díaz and of Francisco I. Madero, for the Nation is tired of false men and traitors who make promises like liberators, and upon attaining power forget those promises and become tyrants.

6. As an additional part of our plan, we make it known: that the lands, forests and waters that have been usurped by the hacendados, científicos or caciques in the shadow of venal justice, will henceforth enter into the possession of the villages or of citizens who have titles corresponding to those properties, and who have been despoiled through the bad faith of our oppressors, and they shall maintain that possession with weapon in hand, and the usurpers who believe they have rights to those lands will be heard by the special tribunals that will be established upon the triumph of the Revolution.

7. In view of the fact that the immense majority of Mexican villages and citizens own no more land than that which they tread upon, and are unable in any way to better their social condition or dedicate themselves to industry or agriculture, because the lands, forests, and waters are monopolized in only a few hands; for this reason, we expropriate without previous indemnization one third of those monopolies from the powerful proprietors, to the end that the villages and citizens of Mexico should obtain ejidos, colonias, and fundos legales for the villages, or fields for sowing or laboring, and this shall correct the lack of prosperity and increase the well-being of the Mexicans.

8. The hacendados, científicos or caciques who directly or indirectly oppose the present Plan, shall have their properties nationalized and two thirds of those properties shall be given as indemnizations of war, pensions to widows

and orphans of the victims who are killed in the struggles surrounding the present Plan.

9. In order to execute the procedures respecting the aforementioned properties, the laws of disamortization and nationalization shall be applied, as convenient; for our norm and example shall be the laws put into effect by the immortal Juárez against ecclesiastical properties, which chastised the despots and conservatives who have always wanted to impose upon us the ignominious yoke of oppression and backwardness.

10. The insurgent military chiefs of the Republic who rose up in arms to the voice of don Francisco I. Madero in order to defend the Plan of San Luis Potosí, and who now forcefully oppose the present Plan, will be judged traitors to the cause that they defended and to the Fatherland, for presently many of them, in order to placate the tyrants, or for a fistful of coins, or owing to schemes or bribes, are shedding the blood of their brothers who demand the fulfillment of the promises that were made to the Nation by don Francisco I. Madero.

11. The expenses of war will be appropriated according to article XI of the Plan of San Luis Potosí, and all of the procedures employed in the Revolution that we undertake will be in accordance with the same instructions that are set out in the mentioned Plan.

12. Once the Revolution that we are making has triumphed, a junta of the principal revolutionary chiefs of the different States will name or designate an interim President of the Republic, who will convoke elections for the organization of federal powers.

13. The principal revolutionary chiefs of each State, in council, shall designate the governor of the State, and this high official will convoke the elections for the proper organization of public powers, with the aim of avoiding forced appointments that bring misfortune to the people, like the well-known appointment of Ambrosio Figueroa in the State of Morelos and others, who condemn us to the precipice of bloody conflicts sustained by the dictator Madero and the circle of científicos and hacendados who have suggested this to him.

14. If President Madero and the rest of the dictatorial elements of the current and old regime want to avoid the immense misfortunes that afflict the Fatherland, and if they possess true sentiments of love for it, they must immediately renounce the posts they occupy, and by so doing they shall in some way stanch the grievous wounds that have opened in the breast of the Fatherland, and if they do not do so, upon their heads shall fall the blood and anathema of our brothers.

15. Mexicans: consider the deviousness and bad faith of a man who is shedding blood in a scandalous manner, because he is incapable of governing; consider that his system of Government is tying up the Fatherland and trampling upon our institutions with the brute force of bayonets; so that the very weapons we took up to bring him to Power, we now turn against him for failing to keep his promises to

the Mexican people and for having betrayed the Revolution he began; we are not personalists, we are partisans of principles and not of men!

Mexican people, support this Plan with weapons in your hands, and bring prosperity and welfare to the Fatherland.

Liberty, Justice, and Law. Ayala, State of Morelos, November 25, 1911

General in Chief, Emiliano Zapata; signatures

Document 19. Ambrosio Figueroa's Plea[12]

To Emiliano Zapata's great dismay, in July of 1911, his nemesis, Ambrosio Figueroa, was named governor of the state of Morelos. Figueroa was from a fairly affluent background, and although he had cooperated with Zapata in the early days of the Madero revolution, he was ideologically sympathetic to the hacendados. In the letter below, he exaggerates the atrocities committed by the Zapatistas and urges Madero to violently suppress them. Figueroa would later rebel against the dictatorship of Victoriano Huerta, during which struggle he was captured and executed.

Cuernavaca, 27 December 1911
Señor President of the Republic
Don Francisco I. Madero
Mexico.
Friend of my highest consideration and respect:

Materially obligated by the abnormal circumstances of this State, which are growing worse by the day, I am taking the liberty of distracting you in order to communicate the following facts of which you may be unaware.

Firstly, the Zapatistas are daily committing many grisly murders of defenseless victims, often on the flimsiest pretexts and other times with no pretext apart from the itch to spread panic every place they go. Lately there have been many murders of women, elderly people, and even of totally defenseless children, and I see no other remedy for such a grave evil than the immediate suspension of individual guarantees, as you offered to do in our last meeting.

The people of this State have been rising up almost en masse and proclaiming Zapatismo, without anyone containing them or being able to contain them. I have repeatedly urged the humble classes of the villages to bring their complaints against the landowners to the courts so that they may prove the dispossessions of which

---

12. Isidro Fabela, ed., *Documentos históricos de la Revolución Mexicana, Revolución y régimen maderista* (Mexico City: Fondo de Cultura Económica, 1970), 2:471–72. Translated by Tim Henderson.

they claim to be victims and receive full justice; that when any abuse or outrage is committed against them, they notify the competent authorities immediately and everything will be done to give them satisfaction. But none of this gets practical results. The spirit of rapine, idleness and extermination that has always been notable among these poor villages has now awakened with such unbridled zeal, it is like a torrent that overflows; it will be hard to contain if we don't shed the blood of the murderers and bandits.

You, Mr. President, please do me the favor of contemplating this and agreeing on the means to end the many crimes and outrages that have so badly alarmed and dismayed the peaceful inhabitants of this State; I beg you to send me sufficient forces to guard the villages and haciendas and to carry out the campaign against the Zapatistas, to prevent them from continuing to expand. . . .

I beg you to forgive the length of this letter and accept as always these protestations of friendship, subordination and respect from your friend,

Ambrosio Figueroa

Document 20. There Shall Be No Distribution of Lands[13]

Madero's fundamental conservatism in agrarian matters is amply demonstrated in this letter to Fausto Moguel, the director of the newspaper El Imparcial. His reverence for the law led him to essentially sanction land thefts that had been carried out behind a façade of legality during the Porfiriato. Positions of this sort lend great credibility to the claim that Madero was willfully blind to the radical tenor of the times.

Chapultepec, 27 June 1912

Esteemed Sir:

Since I was invested by my fellow citizens with the honorable position of President of the Republic I have not taken the trouble to refute mistaken reports circulating in the press, which frequently refer to offers that I have made and failed to follow through on. But some newspapers, especially the one that you so effectively edit, have so insistently repeated "that among the promises of the Revolution was the distribution of land to the proletariat and the offer to divide the *latifundios* remaining in the hands of a small number of privileged individuals, which harms the poorer classes" (this in an editorial published yesterday). I want to rectify this matter once and for all.

I beg you to carefully review the "Plan of San Luis Potosí" and all the speeches that I gave before and after the Revolution, as well as the program of government

---

13. Fabela, *Documentos históricos de la Revolución Mexicana* (1965), 3:481–83. Translated by Tim Henderson.

that I published after the Conventions of 1910 and 1911. If in any of these I expressed such ideas, then you will have the right to say that I have failed to fulfill my promises.

I have always advocated the creation of small landholdings; but that is not to say that we are going to despoil any landowner of his property; indeed, the agrarian policy of the government and its proposals to create small landholdings are well known.

In the same speech that you comment on, considering only one phrase, I explain the government's ideas. But it is one thing to create small property by means of constant effort, and another to break up the great landholdings, which I have never considered doing, nor have I offered to do in any of my speeches or proclamations. It is completely absurd to think that the government should acquire all of the great landholdings to distribute them for free among small landowners, which is how the distribution of lands is generally conceived. The government purely and simply does not have the money to carry out such an operation, at least not without taking out a loan so colossal that the only result will be the bankruptcy of the country.

I beg you, then, to correct your views, not just this once but from now on.

The only promise that till now has not been fulfilled in its fullest extent is the one regarding the restitution of lands to those who have been stripped of them in an arbitrary fashion and the prosecution of all officials who, during the past administration, fraudulently handled public funds; for from the time that the Plan of San Luis was modified, by virtue of the Treaties of Ciudad Juárez—so advantageous to the nation—the new government has had to adjust all its acts to the Law and recognize as valid the decisions of the earlier courts and the legitimacy of all acts of the past administration.

For this reason, it is difficult to restore lands to those who have been unjustly despoiled of them, for it would entail declaring subject to review all cases where the dispossessed have been upheld by legal rulings.

Despite this, the government has for some time been studying a project to comply with its promise as far as possible, restoring ejidos to the villages that have been despoiled of them and acquiring some large properties for division, for in this manner we may achieve the same end indirectly.

Along with this letter I will transcribe to you Article 3 of the Plan of San Luis, which is the only one that seems to have been misinterpreted, and you will be able to read it attentively to see that it contains no promises of the distribution of lands.

I hope, given your journalistic integrity, that this clarification will put an end, once and for all, to the unfair charge that I offered to distribute lands and have not complied with my promise. I remain very attentively and in friendship,

Francisco I. Madero

Document 21. Plan Orozquista[14]

By early 1912, the most serious threat facing the Madero regime was not the Zapatistas, but another rebellion that arose in the northern state of Chihuahua. A thirty-year-old ex-muleteer named Pascual Orozco—who, together with Pancho Villa, had secured Madero's victory by taking Ciudad Juárez—now turned against the government he had helped bring to power. The reasons for his rebellion are obscure: he probably resented Madero for failing to reward him adequately for his services; and he, like Zapata, may have been incensed by the slow pace of popular reforms. While surely his rebellion claimed to be popular, nationalist, and reformist, he had few qualms about accepting financial support from the immensely wealthy Terrazas-Creel family, whose domination of Chihuahua and hostility to social reforms had helped trigger the revolution. His plan recommends some fairly standard reform measures but seems mostly preoccupied with painting Madero as a puppet of the United States, a charge that was manifestly untrue. Orozco's plan, excerpted below, is also sometimes called the Plan de la Empacadora (Plan of the Packing House). Orozco would later back the dictatorial government of General Victoriano Huerta. He fled to Texas when Huerta was overthrown, where he was killed by police in 1915.

1. The initiator of the revolution, Francisco I. Madero, distorted and violated the Plan of San Luis Potosí.

2. Francisco I. Madero made the revolution with money from American millionaires and with the indirect and clandestine support of the Government of the United States. This is demonstrated by Madero's own declarations.

3. Francisco I. Madero's ranks included American filibusters, as well as filibusters of other nationalities, who killed Mexicans. . . .

5. Francisco I. Madero falsified the popular vote and brought the pressure of armed force in the elections that elevated him and José María Pino Suárez to the Presidency and Vice Presidency of the Republic.

6. Francisco I. Madero imposed interim governors by force of arms, . . . violating the sovereignty of the States.

7. Two days after usurping power, Francisco I. Madero contracted for and received fourteen million dollars from Wall Street on the pretext of expanding the services of the National rail lines, an expansion that was not needed. The real purpose of those funds was to pay a debt contracted for the Revolution to the house of Waters Pierce Oil Co., of the United States, through conduct of the two power holders in Mexico, whom Madero named beforehand, counselors of the National Lines.

---

14. Garciadiego, *La Revolución Mexicana*, 151–57. Translated by Tim Henderson.

8. Francisco I. Madero has brought harm and humiliation to the Nation by placing its fate into the hands of the American Government, by means of unworthy indulgences and promises that affect its nationality and integrity.

9. For the aforementioned crimes and offenses we declare Francisco I. Madero and his accomplices to be traitors to the Fatherland and find them in violation of the law.

10. Having used fraud and armed force in the elections of October 1911, we declare null the elections for President and Vice President and disavow Francisco I. Madero as President and José María Pino Suárez as Vice President and as President of the Senate. . . .

34. To improve and invigorate the working class, the following measures till be taken:

I. The tiendas de raya, which use vouchers, scrip and accounting gimmicks, will be suppressed.

II. Workers' wages will be paid entirely in cash.

III. The hours of work will be reduced to ten hours maximum for those who earn a daily wage and twelve for those who do piecework.

IV. Children younger than 10 will not be permitted to work in factories, and children ages 10 to 16 will only work six hours per day.

V. Wages will be increased to harmonize the interests of capital and labor, in a way that will not cause economic conflict that will obstruct the industrial progress of the country.

VI. We demand that the factory owners house their workers in hygienic conditions, that they provide them with health care and improve their condition.

35. Given that the agrarian problem in the Republic demands an urgent and considered solution, the Revolution guarantees that we will resolve it upon the following general principles:

I. Recognition of the properties of those who have had peaceful possession of them for more than twenty years.

II. Validation and perfecting of all legal titles.

III. Return of stolen lands.

IV. Distribution of all unused and nationalized lands throughout the Republic.

V. Expropriation on grounds of public utility, with prior appraisal, of the large landowners who do not habitually cultivate their properties; and the land thus expropriated will be distributed to foment intensive agriculture.

VI. In order not to harm the treasury or use reserve funds, much less increasing the foreign debt by contracting loans overseas, the Government will issue special agrarian bonds to pay for the expropriated lands, and it will pay the holders of those bonds 4 per cent annual interest until the loan has been paid off. This will be done every 10 years with the proceeds from the payment for the distributed lands; it will comprise a special fund destined for said amortization. . . .

The present Revolutionary Plan duly fulfills national needs and aspirations. We are confident that the people will heed our call.

General Headquarters, Chihuahua, March 25, 1912

Document 22. Félix Díaz Addresses the People of Veracruz[15]

Félix Díaz (1868–1945), nephew of don Porfirio, played a major role in the revolution. The rebellion that he declares in the following proclamation is characteristically vague regarding its precise goals, beyond reclaiming the honor of the Mexican army. Díaz's rebellion received scant support and quickly fizzled. Its leader was arrested and taken to Mexico City, where he was sentenced to death for treason. President Madero commuted that sentence to life imprisonment.

To the people of Veracruz:

In the proclamations that are currently circulating here and throughout the Republic, I fully detail the goals I pursue in attempting to overthrow the current governmental regime that is taking the Nation, by giant steps, to complete ruin and absolute disrepute.

For now, it is sufficient to say that I have two principal aims: First, to establish the peace we are all so anxious for, because I am convinced that it is and must be the supreme national aspiration; that this horrible bloodletting, the fight of brother against brother, which the current regime encourages with its indescribable abuses, must cease. Second, to elevate the noble Navy and the glorious National Army to the place of prestige and decorum to which those of us who have the honor of belonging to those bodies aspire; that we should never again endure the indelible outrage of seeing bandits hanging from the gallows sporting the insignia of the highest ranks.

Peace to the Nation, honor to the Army and Navy: for those ideals I will fight with weapons in hand and with justice as my guide. I do not come to destroy, I come only to repair the immense damage done to the Republic by those men who, with their utopian promises, cruelly deceived the people who followed them blindly into the revolution of 1910.

---

15. Fabela, *Documentos Históricos de la Revolución Mexicana* (1965), 4:160–61. Translated by Tim Henderson.

People of Veracruz:

In this beautiful land, cradle of the Reform Laws, three times heroic city, where my life's companion was born, I have launched my movement, and, fully confident in your supreme loyalty and valor, I will achieve the ends we all hope for.

In the few hours that have passed, we have been able to remain mutually satisfied, since I have been and continue receiving shows of adherence and affection from you. I have the satisfaction of knowing that I have not trampled anyone's rights, that I have respected and will ensure that all legal dispositions that regulate social life are respected, and above all, I have the immense pride of being able to say that the occupation of the first port of the Republic has not cost a single drop of blood.

Lend me your aid; I appeal to the goodwill of all the true patriots and, united, we will try with our conduct to get ourselves and others to see that our aspirations are just, and that the means of attaining them will always be persuasion and justice. Our triumph will be one more source of glory for this city where our movement began.

Receive with my gratitude the highest show of love of my heart.

Veracruz, October 16, 1912.

Document 23. The Government Is Not Respected or Feared[16]

During Francisco Madero's presidency, the Senate was controlled by holdovers from the Díaz administration; the Chamber of Deputies—the lower house of Congress—was controlled by Díaz supporters until the congressional elections of mid-1912. At that time, a core of progressives began styling themselves the "Bloque Renovador" (Renovating Bloc), comprising the loyal opposition in the Chamber. They grew increasingly critical of the Madero government. One of the Bloque's more prominent members, Luis Cabrera, delivered an influential speech in December of 1912 in which he lambasted the Madero government for its neglect of thoroughgoing agrarian reform. In the manifesto below, renovators take Madero to task for his lack of forcefulness in suppressing counterrevolutionaries, charging that by failing to "govern with the revolution" his administration was inviting its own destruction. Their pleas turned out to be prophetic, for only three weeks after this critique there began the coup that would put an end to Madero's presidency.

---

16. *"Memorial del Bloque Liberal Renovador al presidente Madero sobre la situación prevaleciente,"* January 23, 1913, Memoria Política de México, accessed January 19, 2022, http://www.memoriapoliticademexico.org/Textos/6Revolucion/1913-M-BLR.html. Translated by Tim Henderson.

January 23, 1913

Honorable President of the Republic:

The redeeming Revolution of 1910, essentially civilian and popular, defeated the Dictatorship. And you, [Mr. President], were anointed by the people's votes, with frenzied demonstrations of love, in democratic functions that had been neglected for three and a half decades. The resurgence of democracy and the vindication of political rights were triumphs that will immortalize your name as an eminent Republican.

The Plan of San Luis Potosí was the political banner of the Revolution. It embodied your thoughts, your program of Government, your political and social ideals.

The Plan of San Luis embodied the national spirit. The revolutionaries were those who whispered of political change, who despised the Dictatorship, who longed for the rule of Law, the advent of democracy, the redemption of the people through work and culture. The ideas of Revolution thrived in the press, in the cathedrals, in the courts, in social gatherings, in the sanctuaries of conscience. The Revolution triumphed on the field of battle because it flourished, like a mighty catapult, in public opinion.

But the Revolution became the Government. It won Power, but the Revolution has not governed with the Revolution.

And this, in the opinion of the Renovating Bloc, was the first error of the Government of the Revolution.

And this first error has diminished the power of the Government and the prestige of the revolutionary cause.

The Revolution is headed for ruin, dragging down the Government that emanated from it, simply because it has not governed with the revolutionaries. Only with revolutionaries in Power can the revolutionary cause move forward. The dealings and compromises with individuals of the defeated political regime are the real cause of the instability of the Government emanating from the Revolution. This is clear and elemental: How can people perform the high political or administrative functions of the Government of the Revolution, insisting on the triumph of the revolutionary cause, when they were not, are not, and can never be identified with that cause, when they did not feel it, think it, love it, if indeed they *cannot* love it? . . . The activities of these infidels have prospered in many states of the Republic, boiling and fermenting into hatred of the Legal Government, like a toxic yeast that sooner or later will move the country backward, undoing the redemptive work of the Revolution. . . . The keys to the Church have been placed in the hands of Luther. . . .

The counterrevolution was natural and logical. But it is also natural and logical that it could have been snuffed out by a stronger, more popular Government than the country has had. And yet, the opposite has happened. Why? First . . . because the Revolution has not governed with the revolutionaries. And second, because the Government has committed another error: that of thinking . . . that the counterrevolution can only be defeated by force of arms. And so we have this civil war that may well end with the collapse of the strongest Government the Republic has ever known. The Government has forgotten, despite being itself the best proof of the thesis, that revolutionaries only triumph when they have the strong and unshakable support of public opinion.

The counterrevolution is on its way to winning over public opinion. And what has the Government of the Revolution done to keep its prestige intact, to maintain the support of public opinion, as it did in better days? Nothing. Absolutely nothing. This Government seems to commit suicide, little by little, because it is determined to devote itself unceasingly to the foul labor that the natural and sworn enemies of the Revolution have undertaken to discredit it. The Government, believing it is respecting the Law, has allowed the Law to be violated in an attack on its very existence. The counterrevolution has become ever more dangerous and widespread, doubtless not because the counterrevolutionary nuclei are stronger and the bands of bandits more numerous, but because they are winning minds by means of propaganda of the press that day by day violates the Law with impunity, working ever harder to discredit the Government, and because everyone now thinks the Government is weak. [The Government] is insulted, calumniated, defamed, and disparaged, all with impunity. The press has been infiltrating its poisonous virus into the popular consciousness, and this will lead to a day when people will oppose the Government violently and unyieldingly, in the same way that earlier they stood up against tyranny. . . . The Government that is not respected or feared, is surely destined to disappear. . . . If the scandalous press were legally suppressed, the source that strews the seeds of counterrevolution throughout the Republic would be blinded. The Government would be respected and feared, it could calm spirits and the pacification of the country would accelerate greatly. Far more threatening than the Zapatistas who burn fields and murder women are the Zapatistas of the pen who shape national opinion. And much more worthy of consideration are the former, who wield the burning torches, than the latter, who tarnish the noblest attributes of thought.

We must, then, conclude that the counterrevolution seems to be fomented by the Government itself, fomented by the lenience of the Ministry of Justice toward the scandalous press. . . . If the Ministry of Justice had used the law to put a stop to the excesses of the press in the Federal District, there would today be only a serious press and a restrained opposition press, one that is more helpful than prejudicial. The State Governments would have imitated the Central Government, and this chorus of insults arising from our national soil, the moral force of the counterrevolution and the forge that strews sparks and fires spirits, would not exist. But it is clear that all, or nearly all, of the functionaries of the Judicial Branch are enemies of the current Government; they are indulgent toward the Government's enemies, allowing them to ridicule it to the point of ignominy, even while they are firm or criminally indifferent toward its supporters. In sum, the Ministry of Justice is the worst enemy of the current Government, and it must urgently, without delay or contemplation either change the personnel of that Ministry as well as that of the Judicial Branch or change the procedures that have been followed until today. . . .

We protest to you, Mr. President, our most profound consideration and our most absolute loyalty.

Mexico, D.F., 23 January 1913

Document 24. Two Corridos[17]

In the largely illiterate society of Mexico during the 1910s, folk songs known as "corridos" often carried news of battles and political events; they also recounted the age-old woes of soldiers forcibly separated from their sweethearts and other loved ones. Below are two of the most famous of the revolutionary corridos.

La Adelita

At the top of a steep mountain range
A regiment was encamped,
And a brave girl followed them,
Who was madly in love with the sergeant.

Adelita was popular among the troops,
The woman that the sergeant idolized.
She was so brave and pretty
That even the colonel revered her.

And the man who loved her so much
Was heard to say. . . .

If Adelita were to leave with another
I would follow her by land and by sea
If by sea, in a warship
If by land, in a military train.

If Adelita wanted to be my wife,
And if Adelita were my woman,

---

17. "La Adelita" and "La Valentina," El Corrido Mexicano, https://corridomexicano.com/letras/la-adelita.html; https://corridomexicano.com/letras/la-valentina.html. Translated by Tim Henderson.

I would buy her a silk dress
To take her to the barracks dance.

And after the cruel battle ended
And the troops returned to their encampment,
The sound of a woman sobbing
And prayers were heard in the camp.

And hearing her the sergeant feared
He might lose his beloved forever.
He hid his sorrow beneath a shroud
As he sang thusly to his love. . . .

He said that he was dying. . . .

And if by chance I die in the war
And they go to bury my corpse,
Adelita, I beg you before God,
Do not cry for me.

La Valentina

Valentina, Valentina,
I want to tell you something.
A passion controls me
It is what made me come here.

They are going around saying
That evil will follow me;
It matters not if it's the devil,
I too know how to die.

Just because I drink tequila,
And tomorrow I drink sherry,
Just because you see me drunk,
Tomorrow you will see me no more.

Valentina, Valentina,
I lay down at your feet.
If they're going to kill me tomorrow,
Let them kill me right now.

III. The Huerta Interregnum, 1913–1914

In February 1913, the Madero government was brought to an end when the leaders of a pair of failed rebellions—federal army general Bernardo Reyes and Félix Díaz, nephew of Porfirio—broke out of prison and launched a violent coup that raged for ten days in the streets of Mexico City. The man Madero entrusted with his defense—General Victoriano Huerta—betrayed Madero at the urging of American ambassador Henry Lane Wilson, who invited him and Félix Díaz to celebrate an agreement at the American Embassy (docs. 25–26). Huerta maneuvered to send Díaz packing and assumed dictatorial powers. Almost immediately his government was besieged by rebellions, the most forceful and best organized being led by wealthy northerner Venustiano Carranza (doc. 27).

Huerta faced a still more formidable foe in newly elected U.S. president Woodrow Wilson, who was appalled at the brutal manner with which Huerta had seized power and the antidemocratic manner in which he wielded that power (docs. 28–29). He eagerly sought a means of bringing about regime change, and he was furnished with a pretext in April 1914 when a minor episode in the port of Tampico was elevated to the stature of an international crisis that was followed by an armed takeover by U.S. Marines of the all-important port city of Veracruz. The intervention was denounced by nearly all factions, though it clearly brought major benefits to Huerta's enemies (doc. 30). Like the rebellions against Madero, those against Huerta were united only by their shared loathing of the dictatorship; some, like the Zapatistas, took a long view and announced themselves prepared to oppose any government that did not adopt their program as its own (doc. 31).

By the summer of 1914 the military tide had turned decisively against Huerta (docs. 32–33), and Huerta was compelled to resign in July. Unfortunately for Mexico, Huerta's exit did not end the civil war, which became still more violent and more factionalized.

Document 25. The Tragic Ten Days[1]

Beginning on February 9, 1913, the already-beleaguered government of Francisco I. Madero came under a sustained and determined assault from within the capital city. Two of Madero's leading antagonists—Generals Bernardo Reyes and Félix Díaz—were both in prison in Mexico City, having led earlier failed rebellions, and both were sprung from prison by zealous cadets from the military academy. Reyes was killed while attacking the National Palace on the first day of the revolt, and leadership devolved to Díaz. It was no secret that the American ambassador to Mexico, Henry Lane Wilson, loathed Madero. He and several of his fellow diplomats became heavily involved in the coup, with Wilson greenlighting the defection of Madero's top general, Victoriano Huerta, and later hosting Díaz and Huerta in the American Embassy where they would agree to share power. Wilson was later harshly criticized for his intervention and his failure to persuade Huerta to spare the lives of Madero and his vice president, José María Pino Suárez. Although Wilson vehemently denied having a role in the executions, he was clearly not unduly distressed by the news. The executions were widely condemned, including by the incoming U.S. president Woodrow Wilson (who was no relation to the ambassador). President Wilson dismissed Ambassador Wilson in July 1913.

Below are letters and telegrams exchanged between Ambassador Wilson and U.S. secretary of state Philander Knox, beginning with Wilson's harsh assessment of the Madero government on the eve of the coup. Also included is a brief statement by Madero responding to the diplomats' request that he resign his presidency.

Wilson to Knox, February 4, 1913

Confronted by the intolerable conditions which exist throughout the country, the administration of President Madero remains impotent to remedy or offer any solution for the rapidly accumulating dangers. The Cabinet is divided into warring factions of radically conflicting views, all petty intrigues and liliputian politics which have little to do with the salvation of the country or the restoration of national prestige at home or abroad. The kind of government that must necessarily be evolved out of a situation like this could not be otherwise than that which exists, viz, one that is impotent in the face of domestic ills and disorders and truculent, insolent,

---

1. U.S. Department of State, *Papers Relating to the Foreign Relations of the United States, with the Address of the President to Congress, December 2, 1913*, docs. 786, 790, 793, 794, 799, 805, 808, 815, 834, 836, 837, 839, 841, 844, 854, and 877 (Washington, D.C.: U.S. Government Printing Office, 1920). Hereafter cited as *FRUS*, followed by year and document number. Madero statement in Isidro Fabela, ed., *Documentos histórico de la Revolución Mexicana: Revolución y Régimen Maderista* (Mexico City: Fondo de Cultura Económica, 1965), 5:85. Translated by Tim Henderson.

and insincere in its international relations. A Government which came into power with an altruistic program, and with party pledges of a free press, free elections, free education, and the division and distribution of great estates finds itself, after a period of a little more than a year, in a position of not having accomplished any of its high-sounding measures for the relief of the Mexican population but responsible for the sacrifice of thousands of human lives, the destruction of vast material interests, aggravation in the condition of the poorer classes, for unspeakable barbarities, and for desolation and ruin of over a third of the area of the Republic. Liberty of the press does not exist either in fact or pretense. In the matter of free elections, which constituted so important a feature of the revolutionary program, the attitude of this Government has been a travesty and a disappointment even to those who did not accept the revolution with enthusiasm. Hardly had the new Government been seated in power until it began, by intrigues in some cases and by the exercise of force in others, to interfere in State elections, deposing some governors and imposing others. . . .

The President's speech, delivered to the diplomatic corps on New Year's Day, can leave very little doubt in the mind of anyone as to this administration's conception of its obligations to foreigners who have come hither with their energy and capital and have given to this country whatever of progress it has achieved and whatever of prestige it enjoys throughout the world. . . .

Wilson to Knox, February 9, 1913—2 p.m.

Revolt against Government has started; Felix Díaz and Reyes and other prisoners have been released. Reyes killed this morning while attacking National Palace, which is still in control of Madero, who is now holding Cabinet meeting there. Severe fighting in Cathedral Square in front of the National Palace. Two hundred reported killed and wounded. Díaz is said to have 3,000 troops. Schuyler has just returned from automobile trip through city and reports large but perfectly orderly crowds in main streets and heavy patrols, of mounted police. People crying "Viva Díaz" and "Death to Madero." Hard attack being made on arsenal and barracks near Embassy.

Wilson to Knox, February 10, 1913—noon.

The President and Cabinet have abandoned the palace; whereabouts unknown. General Huerta, whose loyalty is questioned, is in charge of the palace. Practically all of the local State authorities, police, and rurales, have revolted to Díaz, who is intrenching himself strongly.

No protection can be obtained for resident foreigners and the diplomatic establishments. In conjunction with my diplomatic colleagues, who heartily approve such action, I am organizing a foreign guard for the protection of foreign lives and property, which I hope to have in good working order before night, as we anticipate an invasion of Zapatistas from the south. Department should take immediate steps to dispatch of war vessels of sufficient size to produce an impression and with marines to render aid where necessary. And on the border equivalent steps should be taken.

Wilson to Knox, Mexico, February 11, 1913—10 a.m.

Public opinion, both native and foreign, as far as I can estimate, seems to be overwhelmingly in favor of Díaz. . . .

Wilson to Knox, February 11, 1913—2 p.m.

I have been notified informally by Díaz that if he is successful in the battle today, he will expect that the United States will immediately recognize his belligerency.

Wilson to Knox, February 11, 1913—6 p.m.

Serious and possibly prolonged fighting between the Federal and revolutionary forces is now taking place in the heart of this city, violating the rules of civilized combat and entailing untold loss of life and destruction of noncombatant property and depriving of any guaranties of protection the 25,000 resident foreigners. I am convinced that the Government of the United States, in the interest of humanity and in the discharge of its political obligations, should send firm, drastic instructions, perhaps of a menacing character, to be transmitted personally to the Government of President Madero and to the leaders of the revolutionary movement.

If I were in possession of instructions of this character or clothed with general powers in the name of the President, I might possibly be able to induce a cessation of hostilities and the initiation of negotiations having for their object definite pacific arrangements.

Knox to Wilson, February 12, 1913—5 p.m.

Your telegram February 11, 6 p.m. The conjecture that drastic instructions might enable the Embassy to induce a cessation of hostilities leading to negotiations for peace does not convince the President of the advisability of any such instructions at the present time. If the Embassy's representations under such instructions should be disregarded the enforcement of such representations, with the accompanying message to Congress looking to authority for measures of actual war, might precipitate intervention, which should not be considered except as a last resort and if found justified after deliberate consideration of the whole Mexican question, including the situation of foreigners throughout the Republic. Action at present looking to intervention might, moreover, precipitate many of the evils of actual intervention and might, indeed, subject American interests in the City of Mexico to increased dangers under the cloak of the present turmoil. Drastic representations, furthermore, might radically affect the issue of military supremacy at the capital, which is one for the determination of which it is not now expedient for this Government to become responsible, and is, moreover, one which, once definitely settled, may well create a better situation than has existed for some time. As to the situation of foreigners in the capital, bad as it is, nothing seems thus far called for beyond the precautionary dispositions already made as to ships and so forth. . . . The Department is gratified to note that there are no indications that Americans or other foreigners as such have thus far been subjected to more than the ordinary perils incident to such an unfortunate condition.

Wilson to Knox, February 14, 1913—2 p.m.

Mr. Lascurain[2] this morning expressed to me unofficially his conviction that something must be done to terminate the present dreadful situation. He intimated to me in confidence that he thought the President ought to resign. I told him that public opinion, both Mexican and foreign, was holding the Federal Government responsible for these conditions and urged him to take some immediate action leading to a discussion between the contending elements. I suggested the desirability of calling together the Senate and arranging an armistice during its deliberations. He is profoundly impressed with what he believes to be the threatening attitude of our Government.

Wilson to Knox, February 15, 1913—7 p.m.

In order to supplement the work done with Mr. Lascurain in our interview Friday morning [Feb. 14], I requested the British, German, and Spanish Ministers to come to the Embassy last night to consider situation and resolve upon some action. Conference lasted from 1 o'clock in the morning until nearly 3. The opinion of the assembled colleagues was unanimous and clear that we should at once, even without instructions, request President Madero to resign in order to save further bloodshed and possible international complications, the idea being that the Executive Power should be turned over to Congress. The Spanish Minister was designated to bear to the President our joint views, it being understood that his representations, while frank, were to be in the way of advice and supposedly unofficial. This morning he went to the palace and entered slightly in advance of 30 Senators, who had come on a similar mission. He went over the points which had been discussed the night before and stated the conclusion which had been reached, saying that it was our unanimous opinion that the President should resign. The President replied that he did not recognize the right of diplomats to interfere in a domestic question; that he

---

2. Pedro Lascuráin (1856–1952) was secretary of foreign affairs in the Madero government. He worked to persuade Madero to step down. After the Huerta coup, as constitutionally next in line to the presidency, he assumed presidential duties for about forty-five minutes before surrendering power to Victoriano Huerta. His presidency is considered the shortest in history.

was the Constitutional President of Mexico and his resignation would involve the country in chaos; that he would never resign, but if necessary would die in defense of his rights as the legally elected President. . . .

Mr. Lascuráin had worked very hard to bring this movement about, and the attitude of the President moved him so profoundly that he broke down and wept. . . .

Madero's Statement, February 15, 1913

To the Governors and Political Bosses of the Territories of the Republic:

This morning a foreign Diplomat, representing some of his colleagues, approached me to say that the solution that they saw to the conflict was my resignation. I answered them that I did not recognize any right to intervene in the affairs of the country; that I knew better than they what suits the Mexican nation and that I would die in my post.

For this and other reasons, I have come to consider imminent an intervention by the United States, which is what motivated my telegram to President Taft, but in those moments I had just celebrated a conference with the American Ambassador that was quite satisfactory, in that he has assured me that nothing will be tried in this sense, which I communicate to you with satisfaction.

Until now, for fear of a foreign conflagration, I have done everything possible to arrange an armistice or some satisfactory solution, but in view of the unpatriotic attitude of Félix Díaz and Mondragón, who haven't even been willing to observe a daily three hour truce so that non-combatants can satisfy their needs, we are carrying out operations with all vigor and we expect results very soon, for the enemy is growing smaller in a narrower circle; they are extremely demoralized and many are deserting, while our forces are in excellent spirits and growing daily more numerous.

Francisco I. Madero

Wilson to Knox, February 18, 1913—5 p.m.

General Huerta has just sent me an official note announcing that he has arrested the President and his Cabinet, and asking that President Taft and the resident Diplomatic Corps be informed thereof. The Diplomatic Corps was assembled at the moment General Huerta's note was received, and after consultation I made acknowledgment, coupled with the request that he unite with all Mexican elements for the maintenance of order. In my own name I stated that I confidently relied on his ability and good intentions to carry his expressions of patriotism to good effect, and expressed the hope that he would place the army at the disposal of the Mexican Congress. I also said I would convey the statements in his note to President Taft and to General Díaz, as requested in his note.

Wilson to Knox, February 18, 1913—midnight.

Apprehensive of what might ensue after the downfall of President Madero, I invited General Huerta and General Díaz to come to the Embassy to consider the preservation of order in the city. I discovered after their arrival that many other things had to be discussed first; but, after enormous difficulties, I got them to agree to work in common on an understanding that Huerta should be the Provisional President of the Republic and that Díaz should name the Cabinet, and that thereafter he should have the support of Huerta for the permanent Presidency. They thereupon left the Embassy to put into effect common order, which they had agreed upon for the public peace. I expect no further trouble in the city, and I congratulate the Department upon the happy outcome of events, which have been directly or indirectly the result of its instructions.

General Huerta to President Taft, February 18, 1913.

I have the honor to inform you that I have overthrown this Government. The forces are with me, and from now on peace and prosperity will reign.

Wilson to Knox, February 19, 1913—5 p.m.

. . . I have been assuming considerable responsibility in proceeding without instructions in many important matters, but no harm has been done, and I believe great benefits have been achieved for our country, and especially for our countrymen in Mexico. Our position here is stronger than it has ever been. . . .

Wilson to Knox, February 20, 1913—6 p.m.

The installation of the Provisional Government . . . took place amid great popular demonstrations of approval. A wicked despotism has fallen, but what the future contains can not now be safely predicted. . . . At the request of the wife of the ex-President I visited General Huerta today, in company with the German Minister, and unofficially requested that the utmost precaution be taken to prevent the taking of his life or the life of the Vice President, except by due process of law. General Huerta replied that he would have sent the President and Vice President out of the country last night but feared to assume the responsibility, in view of the possibility of an attack on the train. He said that every precaution was being taken to guard the life of these two persons and that they would probably be tried, but upon what charges he did not state. Madero, the Vice President and some generals are still confined in the National Palace, and I understand Madero is being severely treated. This feature of the situation I think should be brought to the attention of the President; I suggest that instructions be sent for me to deal unofficially with General Díaz in the matter of reprisals as an intermediary with General Huerta. I urgently recommend the retention of all American warships in Mexican waters until further advices [*sic*]. . . .

Knox to Wilson, February 20, 1913—11 p.m.

While it is the general duty of this Government to conserve for use on behalf of its own citizens and its national interests the influence it possesses, nevertheless General Huerta's consulting you as to the treatment of Madero tends to give you a certain responsibility in the matter. It moreover goes without saying that cruel treatment of the ex-President would injure, in the eyes of the world, the reputation of Mexican civilization, and this Government earnestly hopes to hear of no such treatment, and hopes to hear that he has been dealt with in a manner consistent with peace and with humanity.

Wilson to Knox, February 23, 1913—1 p.m.

Last night Mr. de la Barra told me that the Government, intending to transfer the President and Vice President to the penitentiary where it would be possible to make them more comfortable and where they would be in security until the public passions have subsided, removed them from the Palace at about 11.30 and en route to the penitentiary the party was attacked, according to the Government's published reports this morning, and in the struggle which followed both the President and Vice President were killed. President Huerta in a published letter explains the occurrence in this way and also states that all the circumstances will be made the subject of a rigid judicial investigation.

Wilson to Knox, February 26, 1913—4 p.m.

The Government of Madero during its entire existence was anti-American; neither appeals nor veiled threats affected it in its incomprehensible attitude; during the last three, and perhaps six, months of its existence it presented the aspect of a despotism infinitely worse than that which existed under General Díaz. Though the new Government resulted from an armed revolution and at certain critical stages events occurred for which the responsibility has not yet been definitely fixed, and which must be deplored by the civilized opinion of the world, it nevertheless assumed office according to the usual constitutional precedents, and therefore is, in my opinion, clothed with the form of a representative Provisional Government. The new administration is evidently approved and accepted by Mexican public opinion and especially by the more respectable part thereof; it is equally approved and accepted by the foreign elements in Mexico; the Cabinet is united, active, and moderate in its policy, acting in full concert with the President, with prevailing public opinion, and with the army. Anti-American sentiment has almost entirely disappeared and the new Government is showing decided pro-American proclivities. The prospects for settlement of all of our existing complaints against Mexico in a prompt and just way are excellent. If this Government can not be maintained, chaos must inevitably result and the demands and necessity for intervention could hardly be resisted.

Moved by these considerations, which I believe to be also entertained by my colleagues, I am endeavoring in all possible ways, and frequently on my own responsibility, to aid this Government to establish itself firmly and to procure the submission and adhesion of all elements in the Republic. It is assumed that in the course which I have adopted I have the approval of the Department of State and the President, and an expression to that effect will enable me to proceed with great vigor and more confidence in a delicate question, work which I believe to be not only in the interest of our Government but also in the interest of the peace of this continent.

Document 26. The Pact of the Embassy[3]

As we saw in the preceding set of documents, U.S. ambassador Henry Lane Wilson invited the victorious coup leaders, Félix Díaz and Madero's erstwhile defender, Victoriano Huerta, to the American Embassy, where they signed the following pact. The agreement is sometimes referred to as the "Pact of the Ciudadela" after the armory from which the coup was launched.

In the City of Mexico, at 9.30 p.m. of February 18, 1913, Generals Félix Díaz and Victoriano Huerta met together, the former being assisted by Attorneys Fidencio Hernández and Rodolfo Reyes and the latter by Lieutenant Colonel Joaquín Maas and Engineer Enrique Cepeda. General Huerta stated that, inasmuch as the situation of Mr. Madero's Government was unsustainable and in order to prevent further bloodshed and out of feelings of national fraternity, he had made prisoners of Mr. Madero, his Cabinet, and other persons; and that he desires to express his good wishes to General Díaz to the effect that the elements represented by him might fraternize and, all united, save the present distressful situation.

General Díaz stated that his movements have had no other object than to serve the national welfare, and that accordingly he is ready to make any sacrifice which might redound to the benefit of the country.

After discussions had taken place on the subject among all those present as mentioned above, the following was agreed on:

> First. From this time on the Executive Power which has held sway is deemed not to exist and is not recognized, the elements represented by Generals Díaz and Huerta pledging themselves to prevent by all means any attempt to restore said Power.

3. *FRUS*, 1913, doc. 839.

Second. Endeavor will be made as soon as possible to adjust the existing situation under the best possible legal conditions, and Generals Díaz and Huerta will make every effort to the end that the latter may within seventy-two hours assume the Provisional Presidency of the Republic. . . .

There shall be created a new Ministry, to be charged specially with solving the agrarian problem and matters connected therewith, being called the Ministry of Agriculture. . . .

Third. While the legal situation is being determined and settled, Generals Huerta and Díaz are placed in charge of all elements and authorities of every kind the exercise whereof may be necessary in order to afford guaranties.

Fourth. General Félix Díaz declines the offer to form part of the Provisional Cabinet, in case General Huerta assumes the Provisional Presidency, in order that he may remain at liberty to undertake his work along the lines of his promises to his party at the coming elections, which purpose he wishes to express clearly and which is fully understood by the signers.

Fifth. Official notice shall immediately be given to the foreign representatives, it being confined to stating to them that the Executive Power has ceased; that provision is being made for a legal substitute therefor; that meantime the full authority thereof is vested in Generals Díaz and Huerta; and that all proper guaranties will be afforded to their respective countrymen.

Sixth. All revolutionists shall at once be invited to cease their hostile movements, endeavor being made to reach the necessary settlements

General Victoriano Huerta
General Félix Díaz

Document 27. The Plan of Guadalupe[4]

Carranza issued his "Plan of Guadalupe" on March 26, 1913. In stark contrast to many of the plans issued by revolutionary factions of the day, Carranza's "plan" was narrowly political, without so much as a passing reference to the sorts of social ills that, for most Mexicans, the revolution was supposed to remedy. Perhaps Madero's example had made him wary of overpromising, though it seems social reform was not high on his agenda.

Whereas, General Victoriano Huerta—to whom Francisco I. Madero, Constitutional President of Mexico, entrusted the defense of the institutions and the legality of his Government—on uniting with the rebel enemies in arms opposing the same

---

4. *FRUS*, 1913, doc. 883.

Government, to restore the former dictatorship, committed the crime of treason to reach power, by arresting the President and Vice President, as well as the members of the Cabinet, forcing them under duress to resign their posts, as shown by messages addressed by the same General Huerta to governors of the States, advising them that he had the Chief Executive of the Republic and the Cabinet as his prisoners; and,

Whereas, the legislative and judicial powers have recognized and protected General Huerta and his illegal and anti-patriotic proceedings, contrary to constitutional laws and precepts; and,

Whereas, several governors of States of the Republic have recognized the illegitimate government imposed by that part of the army which consummated the treason, headed by the aforesaid General Huerta, notwithstanding that the sovereignty of those very states, whose governors should have been the first to repudiate Huerta, had been violated—

We, the undersigned, chiefs and officers commanding the Constitutional forces, have agreed upon, and will sustain with arms, the following plan:

1. General Victoriano Huerta is hereby repudiated as President of the Republic.
2. The Legislative and Judicial Powers of the Federation are also hereby disowned.
3. The Governors of the States who still recognize the federal powers of the present administration shall be repudiated 30 days after the publication of this Plan.
4. For the purpose of organizing the army which is to see that our aims are carried out, we name Venustiano Carranza, now Governor of the State of Coahuila, as First Chief of the army, which is to be called Constitutionalist Army.
5. Upon the occupation of the City of Mexico by the Constitutionalist Army, the executive power shall be vested in Venustiano Carranza, its First Chief, or in the person who may substitute him in command.
6. The Provisional Trustee of the Executive Power of the Republic shall convene general elections as soon as peace is restored, and will surrender the power to the citizen who is elected.

The citizen who may act as First Chief of the Constitutionalist Army in the States whose governments may have recognized that of Huerta shall take charge of the provisional government and shall convene local elections, after the citizens elected to discharge the high powers of the federation have entered into the performance of their duties, as provided in the foregoing bases.

Signed at the Hacienda de Guadalupe, March 26, 1913

Document 28. Our Purpose in Mexico[5]

William Jennings Bryan, the American secretary of state, sent the following letter to the chargé d'affaires in Mexico, Nelson O'Shaughnessy, on behalf of the Wilson administration, on November 24, 1913. Statements of this kind marked a sharp shift in U.S. foreign policy. The Taft administration had championed so-called dollar diplomacy, which aimed to promote and protect U.S. overseas investments. As we have seen, U.S. ambassador Henry Lane Wilson abetted Huerta's coup, which he expected to impose the kind of stability that American capital required. Woodrow Wilson and his secretary of state, by contrast, disavowed the pursuit of selfish economic interests; instead, they claimed only to wish to help the Mexicans govern themselves in an orderly fashion, which, they reasoned, must begin with the ousting of Huerta. Paternalistic and moralizing, the Wilson administration's ideology would soon lead it to massive violations of Mexico's sovereignty.

The purpose of the United States is solely and singly to secure peace and order in Central America by seeing to it that the processes of self-government there are not interrupted or set aside.

Usurpations like that of General Huerta menace the peace and development of America as nothing else could. They not only render the development of ordered self-government impossible; they also tend to set law entirely aside, to put the lives and fortunes of citizens and foreigners alike in constant jeopardy, to invalidate contracts and concessions in any way the usurper may devise for his own profit and to impair both the national credit and all the foundations of business, domestic or foreign.

It is the purpose of the United States therefore to discredit and defeat such usurpations whenever they occur. The present policy of the Government of the United States is to isolate General Huerta entirely; to cut him off from foreign sympathy and aid and from domestic credit, whether moral or material, and to force him out.

It hopes and believes that isolation will accomplish this end and shall await the results without irritation or impatience. If General Huerta does not retire by force of circumstances it will become the duty of the United States to use less peaceful means to put him out. It will give other Governments notice in advance of each affirmative or aggressive step it has in contemplation should it unhappily become necessary to move actively against the usurper; but no such step seems immediately necessary.

Its fixed resolve is that no such interruptions of civil order shall be tolerated in so far as it is concerned. Each conspicuous instance in which usurpations of this kind are prevented will render their recurrence less and in the end a state of affairs will be secured in Mexico and elsewhere upon this continent which will assure the peace

5. *FRUS*, 1913, doc. 651.

of America and the untrammeled development of its economic and social relations with the rest of the world.

Beyond this fixed purpose the Government of the United States will not go. It will not permit itself to seek any special or exclusive advantages in Mexico or elsewhere for its own citizens but will seek, here as elsewhere, to show itself the consistent champion of the open door. In the meantime it is making every effort that the circumstances permit to safeguard foreign lives and property in Mexico and is making the lives and fortunes of the subjects of other Governments as much its concern as the lives and fortunes of its own citizens.

Document 29. Request to Use Armed Force Against Huerta[6]

Wilson displayed strong antipathy toward Victoriano Huerta, based on his unconstitutional seizure of power. During the first year of Huerta's regime, he had allowed weapons to flow to the northern anti-Huerta forces led by Carranza, Villa, and Obregón. In April he claimed to be forced by circumstances to take a strong stand against the regime, but it was clear that from the outset of his administration he had been searching for a pretext to intervene militarily in Mexico to oust Huerta from power. He found his pretext in the events narrated in the following speech delivered to both houses of Congress on April 20, 1914.

It is my duty to call your attention to a situation which has arisen in our dealings with General Victoriano Huerta at Mexico City which calls for action, and to ask your advice and cooperation in acting upon it. On the 9th of April a paymaster of the U.S.S. Dolphin landed at the Iturbide Bridge landing at Tampico with a whaleboat and boat's crew to take off certain supplies needed by his ship, and while engaged in loading the boat was arrested by an officer and squad of men of the army of General Huerta. Neither the paymaster nor anyone of the boat's crew was armed. Two of the men were in the boat when the arrest took place and were obliged to leave it and submit to be taken into custody, notwithstanding the fact that the boat carried, both at her bow and at her stern, the flag of the United States. The officer who made the arrest was proceeding up one of the streets of the town with his prisoners when met by an officer of higher authority, who ordered him to return to the landing and await orders; and within an hour and a half from the time of the arrest orders were received from the commander of the Huertista forces at Tampico for the release of

---

6. Woodrow Wilson, "Message Regarding Tampico Incident" (speech, Washington, D.C., April 20, 1914), UVA Miller Center, https://millercenter.org/the-presidency/presidential-speeches/april-20-1914-message-regarding-tampico-incident.

the paymaster and his men. The release was followed by apologies from the commander and later by an expression of regret by General Huerta himself. General Huerta urged that martial law obtained at the time at Tampico; that orders had been issued that no one should be allowed to land at the Iturbide Bridge; and that our sailors had no right to land there. Our naval commanders at the port had not been notified of any such prohibition; and, even if they had been, the only justifiable course open to the local authorities would have been to request the paymaster and his crew to withdraw and to lodge a protest with the commanding officer of the fleet. Admiral Mayo regarded the arrest as so serious an affront that he was not satisfied with the apologies offered, but demanded that the flag of the United States be saluted with special ceremony by the military commander of the port.

The incident cannot be regarded as a trivial one, especially as two of the men arrested were taken from the boat itself—that is to say, from the territory of the United States—but had it stood by itself it might have been attributed to the ignorance or arrogance of a single officer. Unfortunately, it was not an isolated case. A series of incidents have recently occurred which cannot but create the impression that the representatives of General Huerta were willing to go out of their way to show disregard for the dignity and rights of this Government and felt perfectly safe in doing what they pleased, making free to show in many ways their irritation and contempt. A few days after the incident at Tampico an orderly from the U.S.S. Minnesota was arrested at Vera Cruz while ashore in uniform to obtain the ship's mail, and was for a time thrown into jail. An official dispatch from this Government to its Embassy at Mexico City was withheld by the authorities of the telegraphic service until peremptorily demanded by our chargé d'affaires in person. So far as I can learn, such wrongs and annoyances have been suffered to occur only against representatives of the United States. I have heard of no complaints from other Governments of similar treatment. Subsequent explanations and formal apologies did not and could not alter the popular impression, which it is possible it had been the object of the Huertista authorities to create, that the Government of the United States was being singled out, and might be singled out with impunity, for slights and affronts in retaliation for its refusal to recognize the pretensions of General Huerta to be regarded as the constitutional provisional President of the Republic of Mexico.

The manifest danger of such a situation was that such offenses might grow from bad to worse until something happened of so gross and intolerable a sort as to lead directly and inevitably to armed conflict. It was necessary that the apologies of General Huerta and his representatives should go much further, that they should be such as to attract the attention of the whole population to their significance, and such as to impress upon General Huerta himself the necessity of seeing to it that no further occasion for explanations and professed regrets should arise. I, therefore, felt it my duty to sustain Admiral Mayo in the whole of his demand and to insist that the flag of the United States should be saluted in such a way as to indicate a new spirit and attitude on the part of the Huertistas.

Such a salute General Huerta has refused, and I have come to ask your approval and support in the course I now purpose to pursue.

This Government can, I earnestly hope, in no circumstances be forced into war with the people of Mexico. Mexico is torn by civil strife. If we are to accept the tests of its own constitution, it has no government. General Huerta has set his power up in the City of Mexico, such as it is, without right and by methods for which there can be no justification. Only part of the country is under his control. If armed conflict should unhappily come as a result of his attitude of personal resentment toward this Government, we should be fighting only General Huerta and those who adhere to him and give him their support, and our object would be only to restore to the people of the distracted Republic the opportunity to set up again their own laws and their own government.

But I earnestly hope that war is not now in question. I believe that I speak for the American people when I say that we do not desire to control in any degree the affairs of our sister Republic. Our feeling for the people of Mexico is one of deep and genuine friendship, and everything that we have so far done or refrained from doing has proceeded from our desire to help them, not to hinder or embarrass them. We would not wish even to exercise the good offices of friendship without their welcome and consent. The people of Mexico are entitled to settle their own domestic affairs in their own way, and we sincerely desire to respect their right. The present situation need have none of the grave implications of interference if we deal with it promptly, firmly, and wisely.

No doubt I could do what is necessary in the circumstances to enforce respect for our Government without recourse to the Congress, and yet not exceed my constitutional powers as President; but I do not wish to act in a matter possibly of so grave consequence except in close conference and cooperation with both the Senate and House. I, therefore, come to ask your approval that I should use the armed forces of the United States in such ways and to such an extent as may be necessary to obtain from General Huerta and his adherents the fullest recognition of the rights and dignity of the United States, even amidst the distressing conditions now unhappily obtaining in Mexico.

There can in what we do be no thought of aggression or of selfish aggrandizement. We seek to maintain the dignity and authority of the United States only because we wish always to keep our great influence unimpaired for the uses of liberty, both in the United States and wherever else it may be employed for the benefit of mankind.

Document 30. The American Intervention[7]

On April 21, 1914, U.S. forces occupied the port city of Veracruz, an action that was immediately denounced throughout Mexico. One of the more acerbic perspectives on the intervention was that of Ricardo Flores Magón (1874–1922), who, along with his brothers Enrique and Jesús, is considered to be among the most important precursors of the Mexican Revolution. In 1900, they began publishing the dissident newspaper Regeneración, *which exposed Mexico's many ills and harshly denounced the regime of Porfirio Díaz. Ricardo attended the first convention of the Mexican Liberal Party (see doc. 6) in 1901, and he soon emerged as one of that party's most influential ideologues. In 1904, facing imminent arrest for his political activities, he fled to the United States, where he would spend the remaining eighteen years of his life—eight of them in prison for violating the U.S. neutrality laws. He was consistently critical of government in general, and also of the United States for exerting undue political and economic influence in Mexico. This essay was printed in* Regeneración *(which was then being published in Los Angeles, California) on June 13, 1914. Somewhat surprisingly, instead of denouncing the Huerta regime, he focuses his wrath on two of its leading opponents, whom he accused of being in league with the Wilson administration. Although Huerta's enemies unquestionably benefited from Wilson's maneuver, the charge that both Carranza and Villa were puppets of the United States would be difficult to sustain in the light of subsequent developments. Flores Magón was arrested for the last time in 1918, and he died two years later in Leavenworth Prison in Kansas.*

The enemies of the liberty of the Mexican people assured us from the start of the crisis between Mexico and the United States that in less than a week the U.S. forces would have taken over the city of Mexico.

About two months have now passed and the American forces stationed in Veracruz have not advanced more than three miles into the interior of the country, which proves what we have said many times: that the United States was not prepared for a war with Mexico; that the United States wished to gauge the mood of the Mexicans who, it believed, mostly sympathized with Carranza and Villa, and for that reason would favor the American invasion, given that the invasion was brought on by all of the political acts of those two bandits in their relations with Wilson.

Wilson, upon seeing that, despite his friendship with Carranza and Villa, the Mexican people did not welcome the invasion, pulled the agrarian question out of his hat, overnight becoming an advocate of the distribution of land to the proletarians, thinking that in this way he could make the invasion acceptable to the Mexican

---

7. Ricardo Flores Magón, "La Intervención Americana," June 13, 1914, Memoria Política de México, https://www.memoriapoliticademexico.org/Textos/6Revolucion/1914LIA.html. Translated by Tim Henderson.

people and thus not face too much opposition. Fortunately, we Mexicans still have no confidence in the institution called government, whether headed by Mexicans or foreigners. From the bitter experience of four hundred years, the Mexicans—at least a good part of them if not all—have come to understand that government is tyranny in whatever form it takes, and so we cannot expect anything good from any government, be it our own or foreign. We have a duty to fight it to the death.

That Carranza and Villa are nothing but miserable servants of American capitalism has been demonstrated by *Regeneración* with such abundant facts that there can be no doubt. We have seen both of these ambitious men extend a hand to Wilson so he would help them defeat Huerta; we have seen them behind closed doors with diplomatic agents of Wilson, compromising the future of the Mexican people by allying with the enemy; we have seen an immense contraband of weapons destined for the Carrancistas pass under the noses of American authorities; we have heard Carranza and Villa declare, without turning red with embarrassment, that the American invasion was not an act of hostility toward the Mexican people, but only toward Huerta, as if those people killed by American soldiers were not Mexicans; we have seen them receive from United States capitalists not only arms and ammunition but also combatants, as is demonstrated by the large number of American dead and wounded and imprisoned from that nation in the battles of Torreón and environs.

But as if all this were not enough, there is a very recent fact that proves that Carranza, Villa and Wilson are working together to tie the hands and feet of the Mexican people so that the capitalists of all nationalities, but principally yankee, can exploit them at will. The Cuban steamship *Antilla* was about to arrive at Tampico with a cargo of arms and ammunition for the Carrancistas on Monday, June 8. Huerta ordered the gunboats *Zaragoza* and *Bravo* to block their landing, and Wilson then ordered that, if the Mexicans ships obstructed the unloading of arms and ammunition for the Carrancistas, then the American ships should attack the Mexican ships.

Referring to the aid that Wilson gave to his servants Carranza and Villa, *The Los Angeles Times* published a telegram from Washington dated the 7th of this month that says, in its relevant part: There is in Washington a unanimous opinion about the intention of the government of the United States, and that intention is that this port—Tampico—serve to provide the Constitutionalists with their war supplies. It is known—the telegram continues—that this government (Wilson's) has been informed that Villa lacks ammunition to continue his campaign toward the city of Mexico and that he must be provided with it so he can achieve his objective.

Coming from the town of Niagara, the same American newspaper published a telegram of the same date that in part says: "If the gunboats of Huerta dare to intercept the ships that carry cargos of arms and ammunition for the Constitutionalists, it is said here that the American warships will intervene." Who can doubt now that Carranza and Villa are the lackeys of the American capitalists!

Narciso Guerrero, a Mexican, was shot down like a dog in the streets of Veracruz on the 7th of this month by a second lieutenant of the twenty-fifth infantry of the United States army, which was garrisoned in that port. The motive for Guerrero's murder was that he protested against an outrage that was to be committed against him. Naturally, the killer was not bothered and the Mexican has remained quite dead. That is the civilization that the soldiers of American capitalism bring us!

In two weeks the famous peace negotiations have made no progress. Banquets and parties have flourished, as if this were the reason that the poor people sweat. And whatever agreement these men make, it will not benefit the Mexican people, who carry on their struggle, expropriating and killing authorities. The future of the Mexican depends on this struggle, not on the shenanigans carried out in aristocratic hotels. Onward, rebels!

According to the telegrams published in the American press on the 11th of this month, Wilson's desire is to put Villa or Carranza at the head of a provisional government that results from a final agreement reached by the Peace Commissioners in the town of Niagara. Wilson says it is necessary that Villa enter the city of Mexico and assume command of the Ministry of War or become the Supreme Chief of all the forces of the Republic, for the more the Constitutionalists are helped, the better if will be for the United States.

Meanwhile, Emiliano Zapata, the honorable and firm defender of the disinherited, has just made public his disgust with the intervention and the Peace Conferences. Zapata says that he has no ties of any sort with Carranza and Villa, and after condemning the revolt of those rogues as criminal, for it has no objective other than to perpetuate the system of capitalist exploitation under the name of Constitutionalism, he exclaims as a true revolutionary: "They call me the bandit Zapata; Zapata the bandit will continue to be the face of all the powers of the world until the people obtain justice, until the peon becomes the master."

These words of brave Zapata are the worthy corroboration of his attitude of a true revolutionary. What a difference between the subservience of Villa and Carranza and the dignity of the noble southern fighter!

Regeneración, 13 June 1914

Document 31. Manifesto to the Nation[8]

It is easy to see from the following excerpt why Emiliano Zapata was the one revolutionary figure esteemed by the likes of Ricardo Flores Magón in the previous document. He puts forth a stirring, if unrealistic, vision of a Mexico where the poor are privileged, where greed and corruption are constrained by a new administrative system, and where elections genuinely vindicate the interests of the majority. Suspicious of all government and unyielding as to the righteousness of his cause—especially as embodied in the Plan of Ayala—Zapata and what he represented would prove a formidable obstacle to the consolidation of every revolutionary government, and he would become a potent symbol for future generations of Mexicans as justice for rural people continued to prove elusive.

The Mexican nation is extremely rich. But its wealth is virgin, that is, it has not yet been exploited, and it consists of Agriculture and Mining. But that wealth, that inexhaustible river of gold that belongs to more than fifteen million inhabitants, is concentrated in the hands of a few thousand capitalists, and of those the greater part are not Mexican. Owing to a refined and disastrous egoism, the hacendado, the landowner, and the miner exploit only a small portion of the land, the forests, and the lode, helping themselves to their abundant produce and keeping the largest part of their properties entirely unexploited, even though the entire Republic presents a picture of indescribable misery. What's more, the bourgeoisie—not content to own vast treasures of which no one may partake—guided by their insatiable avarice, steal from the worker and the peon the product of their labor; they despoil the Indian of his small property and, still not satisfied, they insult and beat him, confident in the support of the courts, for Judges, the only hope for the weak, place themselves at the service of the scoundrels. And that economic disequilibrium, that social dislocation, that flagrant violation of natural laws and human attributes, is sustained and proclaimed by the Government, which in turn sustains and proclaims the execrable army, sacrificing its own dignity in the bargain.

The capitalist, the soldier, and the government have remained tranquil, unmolested either in their privileges or in their properties, while enslaved and illiterate people, with no patrimony and no future, condemned to work without rest and to die of hunger and exhaustion, make all the sacrifices. These miserable people spend all their energy producing incalculable wealth, and yet they cannot expect to receive even the most indispensable provisions to meet their most basic needs. Similarly, the economic organization is an administrative system of mass murder, a collective national suicide, an insult and a humiliation for honorable and conscientious men.

---

8. Emiliano Zapata, "Manifesto to the Nation," October 20, 1913, Memoria Política de México, https://www.memoriapoliticademexico.org/Textos/6Revolucion/1913-EZ-Manif.html. Translated by Tim Henderson.

This situation could not be prolonged, and so the Revolution broke out, engendered, like any collective movement, by necessity. This was the origin of the Plan of Ayala.

Before he became President of the Republic, don Francisco I. Madero signed the Treaties of Ciudad Juárez, which envisioned a possible rehabilitation of the weak before the strong and hoped for a resolution of pending problems and the abolition of privilege and monopoly. We could not foresee that this man would build his government upon the same vicious system, and use the same corrupt elements, that the caudillo of Tuxtepec[9] used to extort the Nation for more than 25 years. That was an absurdity, an aberration; but nevertheless, there was hope, for Madero basked in the good faith that came from having conquered the dictator. Disaster and deception were not long in coming. The revolutionaries became convinced it would be impossible to salvage their work or uphold their conquests within that morbid and rotten organization, which reached its crisis before being definitively overthrown: Francisco I. Madero fell, and Victoriano Huerta rose to Power.

We hold that a country cannot be governed using such an administrative system, for its policies are entirely contrary to the interests of the majority. Therefore, it cannot champion the principles for which we struggle. The Revolution of the South and Center must, as economic conditions improve, first reform institutions. Otherwise, it will be unable to carry out its promises.

This is why we will not recognize any government that does not acknowledge and, more importantly, guarantee the triumph of our cause.

There may be as many elections as one likes; there will be other men like Huerta, who sit in the Presidential Chair, brought there by armed force or electoral farse. The Mexican people may be assured that we will not rent out our banner or yield for one instant in our fight, until, victorious, we can guarantee the advent of an era of peace with a basis in Justice and economic freedom.

If, as has been predicted, those human savages in their silly uniforms, that rampaging mob with hands and minds stained with blood, manage in defiance of the law to carry out the repugnant masquerade they call elections, we shall energetically protest before all the people of the land to keep them from making bloody joke of the Constitution of '57.

Be advised, then, that we do not seek to defeat the current government in order to take over public posts and sack the national treasury, as has been done by the imposters who have heretofore been elevated to the top magistracies. Know once and for all that we are not fighting against Huerta alone, but against all the governors and the conservative enemies of the reformist army, and above all remember always that we do not seek honors, that we do not covet rewards, that we simply seek

---

9. That is, Porfirio Díaz.

to realize the solemn promise that we have made, of giving bread to the disinherited and a free, tranquil and civilized country to future generations. . . .

Reform, Liberty, Justice and Law.

Revolutionary Encampment in Morelos, 20 October of 1913.

General in Chief of the Liberating Army of the South and Center,

Emiliano Zapata

Document 32. How to End the Revolution[10]

The following letter was sent on March 3, 1914, to General Aureliano Blanquet, a key participant in the coup that brought Victoriano Huerta to power. Blanquet first served as Huerta's secretary of war and later (from June 1913) as vice president. The letter's author was Dolores Jiménez y Muro (1848–1925), a uniquely compelling, yet largely forgotten, figure of the revolutionary era. She displayed talent as a poet in her youth, but after the death of her parents she determined that radical politics was her true passion. She was arrested in 1904 for publishing articles critical of the Porfirio Díaz regime. While imprisoned she began publishing a journal that continued to criticize the regime while advocating on behalf of women. She was an early supporter Francisco Madero, but soon became disillusioned with the lack of reform and switched her allegiance to Emiliano Zapata. She was again imprisoned during the interim presidency of Francisco León de la Barra and was freed after mounting a hunger strike. She spent eleven months in prison during the dictatorship of Victoriano Huerta, during which time she composed the letter excerpted below, suggesting how peace might be attained. After her release she again joined Zapata and remained a part of his movement until Zapata's death in 1919. During the early 1920s she worked in the Cultural Missions Program of the secretary of education, which endeavored to bring schooling to rural Mexico.

Penitentiary of Mexico, March 3, 1914

General Aureliano Blanquet.

General: Mrs. Gutiérrez de Mendoza, my friend and companion in prison, says she has assured you that I am willing to help the government in its work of pacification. What she said is true: my wishes and aspirations are well known. . . .

Mrs. Gutiérrez de Mendoza also told me that I should explain to you my propositions in writing and with complete frankness. . . . In accordance with your

---

10. Gildardo Magaña, *Emiliano Zapata y el agrarismo en México* (Mexico City: Instituto Nacional de Estudios Históricos de las Revoluciones en México, 2019), 3:516–24. https://inehrm.gob.mx/work/recursos/zapata/libros/Emiliano%20Zapata%20agrarismo%20TOMO%20III.pdf. Translated by Tim Henderson.

invitation, then, I will begin by saying that I have no personal pretentions. I have been unjustly confined in this prison for six months and several days, after having spent 50 days in Belém (Prison). I await the sentence of my judges—whatever it may be—reserving the right to appeal it, and the proceedings of which I have been victim, before the public, if, as has been the case up to now, I do not get justice. Therefore, if the government accepts my services, I will see my trial to its end; and whenever I must leave the prison to carry out some commission with which you have entrusted me, I will return of my own free will and continue to live under the authority of my judges, for that is what propriety demands of me as an adherent of the cause to which I have been and am faithful: the cause of the People and of Justice. As for my general demands, there are two: One is that you carefully read what I am going to write about the current revolution, whose causes I have known since before it broke out, and whose progress I have followed step by step, often in its most intimate environment; and the second is that the government accept the peaceful methods that I will take the liberty of explaining. . . .

One of the great errors that impedes the reestablishment of peace is the tendency to consider the present revolution as the impulse of a handful of ambitious men trying to gain public office, and of a growing number of bandits whose only goal is robbery. I will not deny that there are ambitious men and bandits, although not in the quantities spoken of in the press: it is a very rare man who lacks ambition and, in general, such men are worthless; and the bandits, who are everywhere, will attach themselves to any banner so long as it helps them to carry out their misdeeds more successfully. But neither Vázquez Gómez nor Carranza fight just to become president, although neither would object to being president; nor do people sacrifice themselves just because certain people rule over our destinies; nor is the objective of the present struggle simply to steal from others, no matter how many people do that very thing. The revolutionary movement is simply the armed expression of the aspirations and purposes of an immense collective that forms the majority, and nearly the totality, of the Mexican Nation—people who dream that the revolution will settle the claims due them and establish laws that guarantee equity between capital and labor and rights for all. Thus, you have seen, General, that despite the undeniable energy of General Huerta and his collaborators; despite the great elements of the Nation that he holds in his hands; despite the many police he has at his disposal, who daily discover plots and conspiracies, and fill the jails of the Republic with political prisoners; despite the obliteration of the villages, and despite every kind of repressive measure he has been employing since February 18, 1913, with the goal of ending the revolution, the revolution keeps growing. What explains this? It is because the idea of justice and reform agitates every mind, inflames every heart, puts weapons in every hand, and predisposes everyone to self-sacrifice. Rigorous measures, instead of frightening people, bring calm to those who know no fear; it exasperates them and inspires them to seek vengeance. It seems that you have created new combatants from the blood of those who have died, and from the tears of those who mourn them. Pay attention, General.

As proof of what I have just expressed, I am going to briefly review the facts. I can attest to their veracity because many times I was a witness, and other times the author.

After both of my parents died, I abandoned the life to which I was accustomed and joined a philanthropic society. I would visit the hovels of the miserable people, bringing them a little bread and some consolation; and since everything I did was done with love, they saw me as a friend, and on many occasions they would share with me their sad confidences, a heartbreaking chain of misery, humiliation and injustice, which can be synthesized in these words: usurpation, despoliation, abuse. Their labor was not fairly compensated; they had to pay very dearly for their miserable homes, so that the owners could gain profits of 4, 5, and up to 6 per cent, even while the houses built for the wealthy would yield a 2 per cent profit at most. And if this were not enough, the landlords would demand a humiliating servility.

After seeing the miseries of the city, which grew out of the low wages paid to workers, I went to the countryside, where I saw still greater exploitation of man by man. Here, in addition to the low wages paid, we must add the dispossession of the lands of villages as well as of individuals. And there, among those illiterate people, as they told me of their misfortunes, I heard a cry of rebellion and protest, just like I had heard in the city. No one, except possibly their own conscience, had ever told them that they were men and not things; that they were children of God and not the property of those who despoiled and oppressed them. From that time I understood that the current revolution would not be long in coming, because ideas were sprouting everywhere.

A little after that I went to Mexico City, where I saw thousands of citizens joining the political clubs that would give rise to the revolution.

During the short struggle headed by Madero . . . something happened that I cannot allow to pass in silence.

After learning of the revolutionary movement that was to break out on November 20, 1910, several citizens came from various states, including leaders of fairly large groups of people, and they banded together, forming a Revolutionary Junta; they expedited a politico-social plan that recognized Madero as the supreme chief of the Revolution. Among those who threw themselves into the fight were Gabriel Hernández, who left here with three men, and the Miranda brothers, who headed up a group of their countrymen. Two days after entering San Agustín Taxco, where he recruited his first followers, Hernández had 86 men, and this number swelled from day to day until it reached nearly 4,000. The same thing happened with the Mirandas. And as for the others who stayed in the Federal District, organized but without reserve weapons, their numbers exceeded 12,000 when, at the start of May of 1911, they commissioned me to visit Madero. Soon they had passed 20,000, not counting the people who joined them on the 24th and 25th of the same month and, energetically and without appeal, demanded the resignation of the Dictator.

Very well, then: What inspired those men to gather and organize themselves so eagerly for the struggle? And why did they come from every class of people, if not for the ideas and aspirations I referred to earlier, ideas that inspired everyone, some to fight on the battlefields, some to provide support in other areas? The same thing is happening now, because this revolution is simply a continuation of that earlier one. In its first period its caudillo was Madero, because his words echoed the ideas and sentiments of the people who acclaimed him as an apostle, a redeemer; in the second period people took up arms against Madero, because he did not fulfill his promises and betrayed his own doctrines; and today the fight is against the government of General Huerta, because people see him as an obstacle to the establishment of their doctrine. That obstacle will be overcome and the revolution will end, because, I repeat, it is not personalistic. It is being fought because the people of Mexico feel the irresistible need to take steps along the road of their political and social evolution and to persevere in their efforts. . . .

This is not to say that there is no remedy for the evil that afflicts us; that there is no way to stop this civil war that threatens us with extermination. There *is* a way to achieve this. If I have dared to exhaust your attention by making this superficial and very brief review of the nature and causes of the current revolution; if I have spoken with a frankness that might bring me harm in my condition as a political prisoner: I have done so because I believe that the remedy exists, and that it is in the government's hands. Allow me to explain.

The people, for whom the laws and authorities have been instituted, have the right to form, abolish, or reform the former, and to elect or depose the latter, when there is reason for it; and since the government is for the people, it has the power to facilitate the exercise of these rights, without spilling blood or harming anyone.

Thus, we know that the Mexican people have resolved to reform their institutions. General Huerta, without having to resign as president of the Republic, can end the conflict by convoking the armed revolutionaries in a convention, not to hold elections, but rather to discuss the best way of presenting the people's aspirations and just demands, so that the Congress of the Union can comply with those demands and elevate them to the status of law.

If General Huerta resolves to take this step, freeing the political prisoners who agree with the disposition described above, and granting guarantees to all, peace will become a reality, and he will be celebrated by his contemporaries and in the annals of history. As for me, I am willing, if this comes to pass, to put my intelligence and every effort at the service of the government, and I will consider myself very fortunate to have contributed, although in a very small way, to obtaining the priceless benefit of peace.

I take pleasure on this occasion, General, to offer my respects. —Dolores Jiménez y Muro.

Document 33. The Taking of Zacatecas[11]

While the major revolutionary leaders were nominally allied in the fight against Huerta, discord among them was strong and growing. By the summer of 1914, victory was in sight. The final federal stronghold before the grand prize of Mexico City was the north-central city of Zacatecas. Pancho Villa was poised to take that city, but Carranza, not wanting to cede the glory to his rival, did his best to obstruct Villa in that endeavor, at one point trying to weaken him by ordering Villa to send 7,000 men from his Division of the North to serve under another general, and later demanding his resignation. Villa felt he had already made many concessions to the "first chief," and concluded that further cooperation with him was futile. Villa set his sights on conquering Zacatecas. The Battle of Zacatecas took place on June 23, 1914. It was the bloodiest battle of the war against Huerta, costing some 6,000 federal and 1,000 Constitutionalist lives, along with an unknown—but surely large—number of noncombatants.

The Battle of Zacatecas had far-reaching consequences. It spelled the end of the Huerta dictatorship; it helped to cement the legend of Pancho Villa; and it provoked an unbreachable split between the two most prominent leaders of the revolution in the north of Mexico, helping to precipitate the most violent phase of Mexico's brutal civil war.

It was the 23rd of June
I was among those present,
Zacatecas was taken
By the insurgent troops.

They'd already been attacking
For several days
When Pancho Villa arrived
To see what was going on.

Villa gave his orders
To everyone in formation
To start the battle
With a cannon shot.

Long live my General Francisco Villa!

Upon that cannon blast,
As had been agreed,

---

11. "The Taking of Zacatecas," http://www.laits.utexas.edu/jaime/jrn/tomzac1.html (website of Dr. Jaime Nicolopulos). Translated by Tim Henderson.

Brutal combat began
From the right side to the left.

It fell to Villa, Urbina and Natera
To attack La Bufa,
Because it was there
That their great banner must be seen.

The streets of Zacatecas
Were strewn with corpses,
As were the hills
Due to the grenade blasts.

From Guadalupe, El Grillo Hill,
Hill of La Bufa, on all sides,
Long live my General Villa!

Ah, beautiful Zacatecas!
Look how they have left you!
The culprit was the old man Huerta
Along with his wealthy friends.

Now Huerta is drunk
And his legs will get shakier
When he learns that Pancho Villa
Has taken Zacatecas.

And with that I will take my leave,
With the flower of violet,
Zacatecas has been taken
By the Division of the North.

IV. The War of the Factions, 1914–1915

The tensions that would soon erupt in the most violent phase of the civil war began before Huerta was defeated, and the dictator's absence did nothing to reduce those tensions. The Zapatistas insisted that Mexico's only hope for salvation lay in the subordination of all factions to their own Plan of Ayala, something that was unlikely indeed (docs. 34–35). The leading contender for national power was the faction led by Venustiano Carranza, which boasted the largest treasury, was best organized, and gained the allegiance of the revolution's most talented general in Álvaro Obregón. Obregón had his own doubts about Carranza and briefly flirted with an alliance with Pancho Villa, but that idea was scotched when Villa, in one of his famous fits of rage, nearly had Obregón executed (doc. 36). Villa made manifest his uncompromising hatred for Carranza and proposed an alliance with Zapata (doc. 37). A "Sovereign Revolutionary Convention" was held in October and November of 1914 in the city of Aguascalientes, which was dominated by the Villistas, even though the Convention adopted Zapata's Plan of Ayala. The Carrancistas (or "Constitutionalists," as they styled themselves) did not participate. Even so, the convention witnessed moments of considerable turbulence (doc. 38).

The Constitutionalists occupied Mexico City before making a strategic withdrawal to Veracruz, and fierce fighting began between the Constitutionalist and Conventionist factions. Mexico suffered almost unimaginable horrors during these times (doc. 39). The Constitutionalists, largely thanks to the military brilliance of their top field commander, Álvaro Obregón, decisively defeated Villa by mid-1915 (doc. 41); they were also able to employ a combination of propagandistic and military methods to weaken the Zapatistas to the point where they presented little real threat. Meanwhile, Woodrow Wilson grew increasingly impatient with the chaos prevailing in the south and by June had determined that the time had come for the United States to once again take sides (doc. 42).

Document 34. Zapata Writes to Woodrow Wilson[1]

Victoriano Huerta resigned the presidency and fled Mexico on July 15, 1914, and by the middle of August the last of his forces had surrendered. At that point, the Constitutionalist Army led by self-styled "First Chief" Venustiano Carranza made a triumphal entry into Mexico City. Unfortunately, the coalition that had ousted Huerta was hardly united. Factional leaders Pancho Villa and Emiliano Zapata had not endorsed Carranza's "Plan of Guadalupe," and the two men shared a deep-seated skepticism of the first chief's intentions. The coalition would soon dissolve into violent factionalism, and as the following reading makes clear, tensions were already rising upon the Carrancistas' initial occupation of the city.

As Ricardo Flores Magón had pointed out (doc. 30), one of the measures Woodrow Wilson had adopted in hopes of countering the manifest unpopularity of his Veracruz invasion was to profess support for agrarian reform, which seems to have encouraged Emiliano Zapata to seek his favor. In the following letter, sent from Zapata's general headquarters at Yautepec, Morelos, and dated August 23, 1914, Zapata gives his account of the origins of the revolution and expresses his antipathy for Carranza. The letter is also indicative of Zapata's growing intransigence on the matter of his Plan of Ayala, the national adoption of which, he suggests, is the only possible route to peace.

Esteemed Sir:

I have seen the declarations you have made in the press concerning the agrarian revolution that has been developing in this Republic for the past four years, and I am pleasantly surprised to learn that, despite the distance, you have precisely understood the causes and ends of that revolution, which has spread especially in the southern region of Mexico—a region that has endured land theft and extortion by the great landowners.

The conviction that you sympathize with the movement of agrarian emancipation inspires me to explain the facts and antecedents that the press of the City of Mexico, which is dedicated to serving the interests of the rich and powerful, has always persisted in misrepresenting with infamous calumnies, so that the rest of America and the entire world could never realize the deep significance of that great proletarian movement.

I will start by pointing out the causes of the revolution I lead.

Mexico is still in a full feudal epoch, or at least it was when the Revolution of 1910 broke out.

---

1. Isidro Fabela, ed., *Documentos históricos de la Revolución Mexicana: Emiliano Zapata y el Plan de Ayala y su política agraria* (Mexico City: Fondo de Cultura Económica, 1970), 21:96–100. Translated by Tim Henderson.

A few hundred large landowners have monopolized the usable land in the Republic. From year to year they have increased their domains; to do this, they have dispossessed villages of their ejidos or communal fields, and small landowners of their modest holdings. There are cities in the State of Morelos, such as Cuautla, that lack even the land needed to throw out the trash, and of course they lack the land that would be needed to increase the population. And it is the hacendados who—going from dispossession to dispossession, today with one pretext and tomorrow with another—have absorbed all the properties that legitimately and from time immemorial have belonged to the indigenous villages. These [hacendados] steal their crops and with them their means of sustaining themselves and their families.

To carry out such extortion, the hacendados have availed themselves of legislation, written under their influence, that allows them to take over huge extensions of land on the pretext that those lands are idle and not protected by legally correct titles.

In this way—with the complicity of the courts and often using even worse methods, such as sending the small landowners they aim to despoil to prison or the army—the hacendados have made themselves the only landowners in the country. The Indians, no longer owning land, have been forced to work on the haciendas for miserable wages even while they must endure mistreatment by the hacendados and their overseers and foremen, many of whom, being Spaniards or the sons of Spaniards, believe they have the right to act as if they were back in the days of Hernán Cortés. That is, as if they were the conquistadors and masters, and the peons simply slaves, subject to the brutal law of conquest.

The position of the hacendado with respect to the peons is exactly the same as that of the feudal lord, land baron or aristocrat of the Middle Ages with respect to their serfs or vassals. The Mexican hacendado uses his peon as he sees fit; sends him to prison if he likes; forbids him to leave the hacienda on the pretext that he owes debts that he will never be able to pay; and thanks to his control of the judges, whom the hacendado has corrupted with his money, and the prefects and political bosses, who are always his allies, the great landowner is, in reality, the absolute lord over lives and haciendas in his vast dominions.

This intolerable situation caused the Revolution of 1910, which set out principally and directly to destroy the monopoly of land in the hands of a few. But unfortunately, Francisco I. Madero belonged to a rich and powerful family, owners of large extents of land in the north of the Republic, and so naturally Madero did not delay in reaching an understanding with his fellow hacendados, and he passed legislation (legislation made by the rich, to favor the rich) as a pretext to not fulfill the promises he had made to destroy the overwhelming monopoly enjoyed by the hacendados by expropriating their farms on grounds of public utility and with corresponding indemnities, if their possession was legitimate.

Madero betrayed his promises and the Revolution continued, principally in the areas where the abuses and despoliations of the hacendados were most acute; that is, in the States of Morelos, Guerrero, Michoacán, Puebla, Durango, Chihuahua, Zacatecas, etc.

Later came the barracks revolt of the Ciudadela, or rather, the effort of the old porfiristas and conservatives of all stripes to once again seize power, because they feared that Madero would one day feel obligated to fulfill his promises. At that point the peasant population became justly alarmed and the revolutionary effervescence spread, and after the assassination of Madero it became a challenge, a true test of the Revolution of 1910.

By then the Revolution encompassed the entire Republic and, having learned from their earlier experience, the peasants no longer waited for the triumph to begin the distribution of land and the expropriation of the large haciendas. This has happened in Morelos, Guerrero, Michoacán, Puebla, Tamaulipas, Nuevo León, Chihuahua, Sonora, Durango, Zacatecas, San Luis Potosí; and it was so successful that it may be said that the people have seized justice for themselves, since the legislation did not favor them and the current Constitution is always more a hindrance than a defense or a guarantee for the working people, above all for the rural workers.

These workers have understood that they must destroy the old modes of legislation. In the Plan of Ayala they can see the essence of their dreams and the expression of the principles that must serve as the basis for new legislation, and they have begun to put that Plan into practice as the supreme law demanded by justice. And so revolutionaries throughout the Republic have restored lands to the dispossessed villages, distributed the monstrous latifundios, and confiscated the farms of the people's eternal enemies: the feudal lords, the caciques, the accomplices of the Porfirian dictatorship, and the authors and accomplices of the coup of the Ciudadela.

I can assure you that there will be no peace in Mexico if the Plan of Ayala is not elevated to the rank of constitutional law or precept and complied with by all parties.

This not only relates to the social question, or the need to distribute land, but also to the political question, or the method of selecting the interim President who must convoke elections and begin to carry out social reforms.

The country is tired of impositions; it no longer tolerates the imposition of masters and chiefs; it wants to participate in choosing its leaders, and given that we are talking about the interim government that must emanate from the Revolution and provide guarantees, it is logical and just that it be the genuine representatives of the Revolution, that is, the leaders of the armed movement, who choose the interim President. This is set out in article twelve of the Plan of Ayala, in contrast to the desires of don Venustiano Carranza and his circle of ambitious politicos, who want to elevate Carranza to the Presidency by subterfuge, or, better said, by means of a coup of audacity and imposition.

Only a convention of revolutionary leaders from the entire country can success-fully elect the interim President, because it will take care to choose a man who, due to his antecedents and ideas, gives absolute assurances. Carranza, as the owner or shareholder of large properties in the border States, is a threat to rural people, since he will follow the same policies as Madero, with whom his ideas are perfectly aligned, the only difference being that Madero was weak, while Carranza is a man capable of exercising the most tremendous of dictatorships, which will provoke a formidable revolution, bloodier, perhaps, than the earlier ones.

From the foregoing you will see that the revolution of the south is a revolution of ideals and not of vengeance or reprisals. That Revolution has made a formal commitment, before the country and the civilized world, to provide full guaran-tees, both before and after the triumph, to the lives and legitimate interests of both nationals and foreigners. . . .

For my part, I can tell you that I understand and appreciate the noble and exalted policy that, within the limits of respect for each nation's sovereignty, you have undertaken in this beautiful but not always happy American continent. And so long as that policy respects the autonomy of the Mexican people to realize their ideals, you can be assured that I will be among your many sympathizers in this sister Republic, and certainly not the least loyal of your servants, who sends you special affection.

The General
Emiliano Zapata

Document 35. Carranza's Emissaries Visit Zapata[2]

In late August 1914, three emissaries from Carranza—Luis Cabrera, Antonio I. Villarreal, and Juan Sarabia—traveled to Cuernavaca, Morelos, to confer with Emiliano Zapata and his representatives. Their mission was to find out if the Constitutionalists and the Zapatistas would be able to find common ground and unify their movements. Clearly the Zapatistas had little interest in joining the Constitutionalist movement, for, as the following report indicates, they demanded nothing less than complete subordination of the Constitutionalists to the Zapatistas and their Plan of Ayala.

---

2. "Report by Antonio I. Villarreal and Luís Cabrera on Their Interview with Emiliano Zapata," September 4, 1914, Memoria Política de México, http://www.memoriapoliticade mexico.org/Textos/6Revolucion/1914-InfAIV-LC-EZ.html. Translated by Tim Henderson.

We arrived at Cuernavaca on the afternoon of Thursday, August 27. General Emiliano Zapata was absent from the city, but we were told he would arrive the following day.

Meanwhile, on that same night, we were invited by Colonel Manuel V. Palafox, General Zapata's Secretary, to "exchange ideas" about the matter that motivated our trip

In [a] preliminary interview, we began to realize the spirit that animated the group, now in favor, now against the agreement that we managed to reach between the Revolution of the North and that of the South, as well as the relative predominance of the opinions of Mr. Palafox and Mr. [Alfredo] Serratos over all the others. During our second conference we could almost convince ourselves that the opinions of these two persons were the most probable anticipation of the opinion of General Zapata, when the time came to treat the matter with him.

With respect to the interchange of ideas, we began with total frankness and liberty, making our way of thinking known, that is, your ideas and those of most revolutionaries; but after a little while we came to understand that that this would be an exchange of ideas only in the sense that we would listen to the ideas of others without refuting them.

We can summarize the opinions of the revolutionary group we talked with in the following way:

"Francisco I. Madero betrayed the Plan of San Luis, so the Revolution of Ayala must be considered the legitimate continuation of the Revolution of 1910.

"The Revolution of Guadalupe is nothing more than an incident in the National movement that should be considered contingent to that of the South." . . .

According to the dominant opinion in the group with whom we discussed the question, the Plan of Ayala is so profoundly embedded in the conscience of the Southern revolutionaries that any change to it would be hard to accept; its derogation or fusion with another Plan would be impossible and it would not be sufficient that the leader of the Constitutionalist Army guarantee the fulfillment of the agrarian principles it contains, but it would be necessary that he accept and subscribe to and elevate the Plan of Ayala to the category of a Constitutional principle, intact, with no modification whatsoever.

Some small additions to the Plan, suggested by us, encountered strong objections. In the course of the conference we discussed some points not included in the Plan of Ayala, and we found that our criticisms of the defects of the Plan of Ayala were quickly interpreted as attacks on the substance of the Plan and on the Revolution of the South.

Predominating among them is the idea that the current state of things in Morelos and other zones dominated by Zapatismo, the agrarian question is already resolved; that is, the usurpations have been vindicated, the lands distributed and lands of enemies confiscated, and the only thing lacking is to legalize what's been done. . . .

As to the attitude of the Southern revolutionaries toward the Constitutionalists, we can say that it is one of complete mistrust. We believe this is due to the lack of collegiality shown by the Constitutionalist troops, who entered the City of Mexico without first procuring an agreement with Zapata. The federalist outposts that confronted the Zapatistas were replaced by Constitutionalist troops, which the Zapatistas viewed as an act of open hostility. They are skeptical because the Chief of the Constitutionalist Army has never made a declaration of political and agrarian principles, and they see the fact that the Chief of the Constitutionalist Army assumed the Executive Power of the Nation without agreement from all of the Revolutionary Chiefs of the country as frankly undemocratic.

In these conditions, General Zapata arrived at mid-day on Saturday, August 29. . . .

At three in the afternoon of Saturday we were called by General Zapata to meet with him personally.

The conference was held properly, then, between General Zapata and Palafox and Serratos on one side, and Villarreal, Cabrera and Sarabia on the other.

In the course of the meeting the intransigent voice of the secretary, Mr. Palafox, was raised. General Zapata spoke little.

We explained our proposals, to wit: To contribute to the union of the Revolution of the South with that of the North, for, given that both pursued the same objective, it would not be necessary to continue a struggle that had no reason to exist between groups of identical tendencies.

We managed to limit our exposition to soliciting what they would tell us of the conditions that the Revolutionaries of the South believed indispensable to bring about peace.

The results we hereby enumerate:

The celebration of a personal interview between the First Chief of the Constitutionalist Army and General Zapata had to be discarded, of course, as it was considered impossible from various points of view due to the irreducible demand that such a conference could only be held at the Headquarters of the Revolution of the South, that is, in Cuernavaca.

We suggested that the conference could be held in Mexico City, or at least in some intermediate point between the two cities, neutral or neutralized between the extreme advanced troops of both armies. This proposition was rejected out of hand, with various arguments, among them the strongest being that only Cuernavaca deserved their confidence, and that the Revolution of the South, as the oldest, had the right of preeminence.

Having rejected the idea of a personal meeting between both Chiefs, we went on to deal with a conference among Delegates.

Secretary Palafox suggested the idea . . . that the precondition and sine qua non for any agreement had to be the submission of the First Chief and of the

Constitutionalist Generals to the Plan of Ayala, signing to that effect an act of adhesion that accepted the mentioned Plan in all its parts. General Zapata approved the idea, insisting that submission to the Plan of Ayala must be prior and unconditional.

We proposed that the fundamental principles of the Plan of Ayala simply be incorporated into an agreement or convention, to which they replied that the condition of submission to all of the precepts of the Plan, both agrarian and political, was sine qua non, and prior to any discussion about other points, and that only after we had persuaded the First Chief to sign the act of submission to the Plan of Ayala could we begin to discuss a conference of Delegates. . . .

The conditions, then, that General Zapata demands of the First Chief of the Constitutionalist Army for an agreement to avoid war between the Revolutionaries of the North and those of the South are the following:

First. Before everything the First Chief of the Constitutionalist Army and the general who support him must sign an act of submission to the Plan of Ayala, not just in its essence, but in all its parts.

Second. While future conferences may be held, an armistice must be agreed to based on the surrender of the plaza of Xochimilco to the Zapatista forces.

Third. The First Chief of the Constitutionalist Army must withdraw at once from the Executive Power of the Nation. Failing that, the First Chief of the Constitutionalist Army may continue in the Executive Power so long as he admits to his side a representative of General Zapata whose agreement must be obtained on all major decisions and who will make the nominations for political posts.

Fourth. Once the three previous requirements are fulfilled, the First Chief of the Constitutionalist Army can name his delegates, duly authorizing them to discuss and sign agreements. Said conferences will be held necessarily in the headquarters of the Revolution of Ayala, and they will have the objective of treating the procedures for carrying out the dispositions of the Plan of Ayala.

Such is the substance of the conditions of arrangements mentioned by Mr. Palafox and supported by General Zapata, to solve the imminent conflict between the Revolution of the North and that of the South.

Document 36. A Dangerous Encounter[3]

Álvaro Obregón, a former chickpea farmer from the northern state of Sonora, first distinguished himself as a gifted military tactician in President Francisco Madero's effort to quash the rebellion led by Pascual Orozco in 1912. He further demonstrated his considerable skills in the fight against Huerta, during which he subscribed to Venustiano

---

3. Álvaro Obregón, *Ocho mil kilómetros en campaña*, 202–4. Translated by Tim Henderson.

Carranza's Plan of Guadalupe. He had reservations about Carranza, however, and after Huerta's defeat entered negotiations aimed at forming an alliance with Pancho Villa. The effort broke down largely due to events in Sonora, where José María Maytorena, a Villa partisan, was governor. Obregón hoped to see Maytorena replaced with the more neutral Juan Cabral. Villa, suspecting treachery, sought to remove pro-Obregón general Benjamín Hill from Sonora. At this time Obregón paid a visit to Villa to deal with the Sonora issue and to try to persuade Villa to participate in an upcoming revolutionary convention called by Carranza. Coinciding with Obregón's arrival, Villa received word that a clash had taken place between Hill's and Maytorena's forces, and he assumed Hill had acted on Obregón's orders. Obregón was also, by his own admission, intent on weakening Villa by taking some of his best soldiers. Villa's suspicions led to what Villa biographer Friedrich Katz described as "one of the best known and most dramatic confrontations in the history of the Mexican revolution," which Obregón later recounted in his memoir, Ocho mil kilómetros en campaña (Eight Thousand Kilometers on Campaign), *first published in 1917.*

As I entered the room, Villa rose from his seat and, without concealing his anger, said to me:

"General Hill believes he can play with me . . . ; you are a traitor, and I'm going to have you shot right away."

He then called to his secretary, Mr. Aguirre Benavides, who was in the next room watching all this, and said to him:

"Telegraph General Hill. Tell him, in the name of Obregón, to leave immediately for Casas Grandes."

He then turned to me again, and asked:

"Shall we send that telegram?"

To which I answered:

"You can send it."

Immediately upon hearing my answer, Villa ordered one of his assistants:

"Get on the phone and request twenty men from the 'Dorados' corps,[4] under the command of Major Cañedo, to shoot this traitor."

Then I said to Villa:

"Ever since I put my life at the service of the Revolution, I have felt I would be fortunate to lose it." . . .

Regarding Major Cañedo, who was to command the firing squad, I must state that at one time he had belonged the Army Corps under my command, and on my orders he was discharged and expelled from Sonora for being unworthy to serve in our army.

---

4. The "Dorados" (Golden Ones) were Villa's elite escort.

Even as I responded to Villa's feint, and when perhaps there was some danger he would murder me as he had done to others, General and Doctor Felipe Dussart—an individual I had dismissed for being unworthy of serving in the Constitutionalist Army—entered from the next room and, making a sign to Villa, began to clap and jump around to demonstrate his joy at my impending execution, exclaiming:

"Bravo, bravo, my general! This is how you should operate."

Villa was incensed that this despicable man was celebrating my execution, and he unleashed his fury on him, saying:

"Get out of here, you fool, you puppet, or I'll throw you out!"

While this drama was going on between Villa and Dussart, I continued walking around the room. After Villa had thrown Dussart out, he returned to me, and the two of us continued circling around the room. The man's anger was causing him to lose control of his nerves, and his every move revealed his agitation. I had no recourse except to try to convince Villa that murdering me would do me good, and so every time he said, "I'm going to have you shot right now," I would answer:

"You will be doing me a favor, because death will give me a personality that I don't have, and the only one harmed in this case will be you."

The firing squad had already arrived. My officers were being held in the room that had been prepared as my bedroom, and they only lacked the final word from Villa. Villa continued walking beside me around the room, when suddenly he left, heading toward the interior of the house. In the next room, where Aguirre Benavides and General Madero had been earlier, Fierro and some other of Villa's henchmen had arrived, men who were renowned for their love of crime.

Time passed, and our situation did not change at all.

When everything was ready for our execution, Mr. Canova, the special agent of the United States government, arrived, surely intending to talk with Villa; but he had to leave without doing so, because they would not allow him through the door. The news of the order for our execution had spread throughout the city, and groups of curious onlookers gathered around Villa's house to witness it. After an hour, Villa dissolved the firing squad and removed the guard at the door.

At around 6:30 p.m., he entered the room and, taking a seat, invited me to sit by his side. I have never accepted an invitation so eagerly. Villa, with emotion that anyone would have thought genuine, said to me in a rueful tone:

"Francisco Villa is not a traitor; Francisco Villa does not kill defenseless men, much less you, dear companion, who are my guest. I am going to prove to you that Pancho Villa is a man, and if Carranza does not respect him, he will learn how to do his duty to the Fatherland." That emotion, so expertly faked, continued to build, until sorrow silenced his voice completely and a prolonged silence ensued, which was disturbed only when a servant suddenly entered the room and said:

"Dinner's ready."

Villa stood up and, wiping away his tears, said to me:

"Come to dinner, dear companion, this is all over now."

I confess that I did not share Villa's opinion that it was all over, because my terror had not yet begun to wane.

Immediately after dinner, the officers who had been commissioned that morning to prepare the dance, and who had been put at liberty, along with those who made up the reception committee, went to the salon of the Theatre of Heroes to start the party. Villa begged to be excused from attending the dance, saying he was indisposed, and I arrived at the theatre at nine in the evening. The party was very lively, and we danced until the early hours of the morning of the following day. Most of the attendees were aware of the events that had transpired during the afternoon, and they came up with a thousand conjectures upon seeing us at the dance without making any commentaries.

Document 37. Villa Urges Zapata to Join Him in Disavowing Carranza[5]

Francisco Villa sent the following letter to Emiliano Zapata on September 22, 1914. The two men and the movements they headed had little in common other than distrust and hatred for Carranza, but that was enough to produce a tenuous alliance as the revolution entered its most violent phase.

Much esteemed companion and fine friend:

The Division of the North, which I command, can no longer tolerate the unpatriotic conduct of Venustiano Carranza, which aims in every way to divide us, to sow ruin in the country and inspire distrust overseas. His views are basically personalistic, so for him the happiness of the country is a myth that is of little or no interest. All my Generals and I understand that it is absolutely imperative that, as soon as possible, we take our nation back from the brink that the so-called First Chief of the Constitutionalist Army is trying to drive it off of with his inconsistencies and caprices. Therefore, today we disavow him as the nation's leader, and we hasten to ensure that he surrenders power to the true representatives of the people. Since Venustiano Carranza is obstinate and has not the smallest atom of patriotism, he will try to fight before abandoning power. For that reason, I am preparing to march immediately to the capital of the Republic, and if he does not surrender I will attack him and give him the punishment he deserves.

---

5. Isidro Fabela, ed., *Documentos históricos de la Revolución Mexicana: Revolución y régimen constitucionalista* (Mexico City: Fondo de Cultura Económica, 1960), 1:353–54. Translated by Tim Henderson.

You, whose patriotic feelings and good intentions are well known—for you have shown them in the attitude you adopted in 1910 and in your constant struggles on behalf of the well-being of the Mexican people—will surely once again put your valuable services at the disposition of the people. I expect with good reason that you, inspired by the same sentiment as I, will also disavow Venustiano Carranza and will equip and quickly prepare your forces so that as soon as I approach the capital of the Republic, together with my forces, we will attack and impose officials who will concern themselves with the true ennoblement of our fatherland. The carrier of this letter, your envoy, whom I have had the pleasure of receiving and treating with the consideration he merits, will give you more details and explanations of the specifics, which I cannot give you in this letter since I have little time available. I must immediately and urgently prepare our march to the South so that our movement will succeed and the strike will be more assured.

Hoping to soon have the pleasure of shaking your hand, I am pleased to offer myself as your affectionate companion, friend and servant,

Francisco Villa

Document 38. An Insult to the Flag[6]

The Sovereign Revolutionary Convention—where the great warlords who had arisen during the revolution's earlier phases were supposed to hash out their differences—met in the city of Aguascalientes, some 300 miles northwest of Mexico City, between October 10 and November 9, 1914. The convention had little prospect for success, given that the most important leaders, Villa and Zapata, were united in their loathing of Carranza. Each of the major revolutionary factions sent delegates, with their numbers being determined by the numbers of troops they had deployed in the fight against Huerta. The Zapatista representatives did not arrive until October 26. One of the leaders of that delegation was Antonio Díaz Soto y Gama (1880–1967), who hailed from the north-central state of San Luis Potosí and who had a resume in radical politics dating back to the early 1900s. He joined the Zapatistas after the overthrow of Huerta and became a staunch advocate of agrarianism and indigenous rights. His appearance at the Aguascalientes convention on October 27 quickly became the stuff of legend. The delegates to the convention had ceremoniously signed their names to a Mexican flag that had been provided by Constitutionalist delegate Álvaro Obregón. That flag was draped on the stage where Soto y Gama spoke. Soto y Gama refused the sign the flag, and, making matters worse, early in his speech he grabbed the flag and denounced it as a symbol of the reaction. This opinion caused an uproar that nearly got him killed.

---

6. *Crónicas y debates de las sesiones de la Soberana Convención Revolucionaria* (Mexico City: Biblioteca del Instituto Nacional de Estudios Históricos de la Revolución Mexicana, 1964), 1:509–14. Translated by Tim Henderson.

Lic. Soto y Gama (enters the tribunal and is applauded): Delegates, public in the galleries:

Never in my life have I wavered as I do upon taking to this podium, for this is the podium of the country, the podium of the Mexican Nation, which, having acted heroically, has put all of its blood, all of its love, all of its great soul at the service of the greatest cause there can be, which is the cause of the oppressed, of the disinherited, of the greatest number, those who in this poor country are eternally forgotten. It is not right that a Nation, a great Nation that the world sees and admires, should fall victim to the last and greatest disappointment, the saddest deception: namely, that the men who lead this Revolution, those who go into battle, should be divided in this Assembly, that they should rupture before the enemy that hides in the confessionals, in the Jockey Club, in their palaces, trying to stifle us and to destroy, once and for all, the great revolutionary work that has cost so much blood and effort.

We of the South come, more than anything, to work for union, which we hold above all other principles. Someone in this Assembly said, with an astounding lack of awareness, "Upon entering this Assembly we put aside all plans, we put aside the Plan of Ayala just as the Plan of Guadalupe." I asked myself if I had come to a reactionary assembly or an assembly of the few, or rather to one that is not a Military Convention, as Carranza's servile press has infamously labeled it, but a Great Revolutionary Convention that has inherited the principles of 1910; and thus the Revolution that was remade in the southern mountains by the genius of Zapata and all his men, and solemnly approved, tacitly by this Assembly that, I assure you, will in time adhere, not to the Plan of Ayala's attack on don Francisco I. Madero, before whose brave memory I bow, but to the great principles of the Plan of Ayala, which is to say: War on the oppressors! Onward to victory and glory! [Applause] . . .

Above all is the opinion that, when one came to this Assembly, it was not as a constitutionalist or a Villista or a Zapatista; it was as a Mexican [applause and bravos]. . . .

We come here honorably. I believe that my word of honor is worth more than a signature on this flag, this flag that in the final analysis is nothing more [he grabs the flag] than the triumph of the clerical reaction led by Iturbide. [Shouts of "No! No!"] I, gentlemen, will never sign this flag. We have made a great revolution that expressly opposes the lies of history, and we must expose the lie of history that is in this flag; what we call our independence was not independence for the Indian, it was independence for the creole race, for the descendants of the conquest, to carry on infamously mocking . . . [Shouts of "Why do you keep touching the flag?"] the oppressed, the Indians. . . . [Shouts, hisses, a motion for order]

Eulalio Gutiérrez: More respect for the flag! You are a traitor! . . .

[Excited voices: "Shameless! Leave the rostrum! Order!" Hisses, etc., etc. A great disorder. A voice: "We, those of us gathered here, have signed and vow to fulfill the words imprinted there!" Shouts of "Order!" Hisses, shouts: "Calm, gentlemen!"]

Secretary González: The Chair demands respect. There will be no shortage of those who wish to respond to Mr. Soto y Gama, the defenders of brave Allende,[7] who do not go into battle and come to speak of liberty and to insult the flag.

Eduardo Hay: May I have the floor, Mr. President?

[Various voices: "I ask for the floor! Order! Silence! Calm! Make the speaker sit down! Down with traitors! Out!"]

Hay: Let us have silence so we can answer. [More voices: "Down with the speaker! Down with the traitors!"]

Hay: Gentlemen, as patriots, I beg you to come to order.

Samuel Santos: [taking the flag and carrying it to the other end of the platform]: For our honor, let us withdraw the flag, and do us the favor of allowing all orators to speak. I respond with this flag. [Applause and hisses; Voices: "Order, Gentlemen! Order!"]

Hay: We have a way of answering, gentlemen. Meanwhile, let us be patriotic, let us keep order, let us permit the speaker the speak. Afterward we can talk among ourselves.

[The disorder continues]

Mateo Almanza: For the sake of reason, gentlemen. . . .

[Great disorder continues]

Almanza: Calm, a little calm, so we can hear the arguments of Mr. Soto y Gama. Those arguments are answered with other more forceful ones, without insults.

Soto y Gama: I never thought. . . .

The President: One moment, gentlemen. I expect civility in the Assembly that allows the orator to continue his argumentation. Later it will be answered. But we cannot have here a spectacle that deprives anyone of the right to speak so long as anyone in the Assembly wishes to hear him. The representatives of the South, who come here to express what they think and feel, are allowed to do so. Let us listen, and afterward the podium will be open to any who wish to respond.

Francisco Serrano: To clarify: The outrage to our flag cannot be destroyed with arguments.

David Berlanga: I think we can table a discussion. I prefer that the speaker take a seat and we finish with everything. [Voices: "No! No!"]

Antonio Ríos Zertuche: I ask for a clarification. We must hear all of the errors that the gentleman wishes to say.

The President: The best test of civility that we can give at the moment is to allow the orator to say whatever he pleases.

Soto y Gama: Gentlemen, it is truly unfortunate that this Assembly misunderstood me. I began speaking and continue to speak in the name of Mexico, in

---

7. Ignacio Allende (1769–1811) was second in command to Miguel Hidalgo, who launched Mexico's revolution for independence in 1810.

the name of the Fatherland. What I oppose is that the sacred name of Mexico be used simply as a mask for political machinations. We of the South have seen clearly that the signatures on that flag signify the desire to reach, in advance and through deception, a compromise that perhaps is contrary to the national interests, and to all the delegates met here. [Voices: "No! No!]

What I wish to point out is that the Fatherland is not the same thing as the symbol, just as God is not the same as the person who believes in Him, is not the same as statues or pieces of wood placed on altars, or a piece of cloth that is used as a symbol or representation. I come to speak precisely, to make clear the difference between symbols and reality. I come to make clear that here we are all Mexicans and patriots. None are more patriotic than those of the South, who justifiably feel themselves mocked by the so-called Independence of 1821, which brought the triumph of the clerical reaction, the triumph of Iturbide,[8] who was very far from a representative of the popular will. And you, gentlemen, have not allowed me to finish my thoughts, you have not allowed me to do an analysis of our National History. And if I made a mistake in saying that this is the flag that represents the triumph of Iturbide, then you are calling us, the patriots of the South, traitors. Well then, gentlemen, it is frankly impossible to speak at this podium, and it may well be necessary to go once again to the mountains to complain that Iturbide, who flew this flag, was the one who betrayed Hidalgo[9], the one who reestablished the rule of the hacendados, the creoles and the descendants of the Spaniards in the name of that symbol. We must respect that symbol for what it is worth. Discussion is permitted, everything can be discussed, even God is discussed in full socialism, and I have not come to discuss the flag. I will do that another time. I am not able, because I respect the ideas of others. I didn't come to discuss the notion of the Fatherland. I came here simply to make something clear: That we need complete freedom. That was the theme of my speech, it was the theme that got me cut off. I absolutely respect patriotism; it is crucial that the sacred words be respected, I will be the first to respect them because as I said: We did not come to talk about our own ideas; we came to learn the ideas of the Mexican people.

The Mexican people respect that flag, and I respect it. But don't use it as a rag that can cover up political machinations of the ambitious, whom I want nothing to do with, and whom I have wanted to fight since the start of this Assembly, since the start of Mexico. . . .

---

8. Agustín de Iturbide (1783–1824) was a royalist general who fought against Mexico's independence from Spain, but who in 1821 switched sides and secured independence. He was later crowned Emperor Agustín I, but ran afoul of Congress and was forced to abdicate in 1823.

9. Miguel Hidalgo (1753–1811) was a Roman Catholic priest who initiated the first phase of the Mexico's revolution for independence in 1810. He proclaimed his revolution as a vindication of Mexico indigenous people.

Here we have discussed an idea and not a symbol. And, what's worse, we have discussed our country's history, which is not finished, and probably many of you gentlemen did not understand. Perhaps Mr. Gutiérrez doesn't know the History of his country, doesn't know that Iturbide did not free the indigenous race for which he had fought. And it is precisely for this reason, gentlemen, that I'm telling this Assembly to its face that its duty is to defend the oppressed race and not to forget that that race is not emancipated, nor to forget that the true revolution is not that of the white people gathered here. We are aficionados of the politics of the dilettantes of the Revolution; and the true men who have made the Revolution, for whom the Revolution was made, are as much slaves as they were before the Plan of Iguala. That is my thesis and my affirmation.

If that flag has since been sanctified by the glorious defeat of '47 and by the glorious triumphs against the French Intervention, then I respect it, I bow before the three colors. But I meant to refer to the historic flag and to the damage done by the use of that flag to hide certain intrigues which are very clear and which I want to expose. [Applause]. If you allow me to hold the floor in these circumstances, I will continue speaking. [Voices: "Yes, continue!"] . . .

In the meeting in Mexico, Luis Cabrera pulled off a political maneuver. He had already accepted the resignation of Carranza, who is the only obstacle to national pacification, the evil man who has prevented the Revolution from coming to an end by killing off the reactionaries. Then Luis Cabrera, with a sophistry characteristic of men of officialdom, of men of laws, suddenly surprised them, obliging them to give their vote of confidence to Carranza. And now they are all tied up, they were brought to the Convention, and here in the Convention they tried to tie them up again with the insult to the flag, which is a ploy to tie up every one into a group that is committing the great madness that will ruin the Mexican Fatherland: the madness of putting a man above the Revolution, making believe that Carranza personifies the Revolution, that without Carranza the Revolution does not exist; making believe that without Carranza all will be sacrificed, that without the Plan of Guadalupe the Fatherland is lost.

That is what I come here to protest. We are playing with the word fatherland. First, the fatherland was Díaz; later, the fatherland was Huerta; and now, the fatherland is Carranza. The editorials in *El Liberal* identify Carranza with the revolutionary idea, saying that without him there is no Revolution, for Carranza personifies all revolutionaries, he has established a personalist military dictatorship. He did not embrace the preconstitutional period of reprisals against the reaction, or above all the broad principle of agrarianism; instead of enforcing that agrarian principle to protect the people of the countryside, he gave his officers, many of whom are here, palaces and sinecures, he corrupted them with gold and cash so that those revolutionaries could come here to make their propaganda and their demands.

I believe, gentlemen, that this is not the Revolution. It is the perversion of the Revolution. And we of the South, however little we may be worth, come to speak in the name of the true Revolution. And you, though you may be the leaders, if you are not Indians . . . if you are not identified with the Indians, then you cannot speak for them. Their source in the South is Morelos and Guerrero, the nucleus where the first insurrection of 1812 prospered, the continuation of Hidalgo's movement, the nucleus where Morelos and Guerrero[10] sacrificed themselves and where the men of Zapata have sacrificed themselves. The men of the South come to express and interpret the ideas of the Revolution. All is being ruined, and the people of Morelos greatly fear for their fate, for their land, for their elevation to the rank, not of citizens, but of free men who want an independent life. The Revolution of the South declares expressly . . . that the Revolution will not end unless the men of the North, many of them of the white race and many of them incapable of feeling, refuse to understand the longings of the indigenous people, because they have not always worked here. The Plan of Ayala, for the people of Morelos, for all of the oppressed people, broadly signifies the start of their life of liberty, the consummation of all their longings, the true consecration of their flag—without masks and without lies of patriotism—a flag that is no longer that of Iguala, but the flag of Hidalgo, the flag of the emancipation, the flag of legality, the glorious flag of progress, the flag that spurs the other Mexico, the other Mexico that gives to the oppressed and impoverished what they have never been given. To leave behind the conquerors and their gold, and to raise up the working man, the laboring man, the Indian who is dying of hunger. . . .

For the Mexican people; for the people of the South, and for the honor of this flag, that we must wave with a firm hand, and not with the hand of a hypocrite; for that flag; for the national flag, from which if anything must arise it is this word: Plan of Ayala, emancipation, justice for the humble; for that flag, for the principles of the Plan of Ayala, the men of the South come to fight. [Applause]

---

10. José María Morelos (1765–1815) and Vicente Guerrero (1782–1831) were leaders in the Mexican War of Independence who were both of mixed race.

Document 39. Accursed City[11]

The Aguascalientes convention resulted in two major factions: one, led by Venustiano Carranza, styled themselves the Constitutionalists; the other—an alliance of Pancho Villa and Emiliano Zapata—became the Conventionists. As the convention unfolded, the Constitutionalists occupied Mexico City, though they would soon relocate to the port of Veracruz to take advantage of trade and customs duties. Mexico City, according to the following excerpt, presented a sorry spectacle indeed during this period.

Francisco Ramírez Plancarte lived in Mexico City during the years 1914 and 1915, and he wrote a harrowing and minutely detailed chronicle of the horrors that befell Mexico's capital as it was occupied by successive revolutionary factions and lived through plague, famine, and violence both martial and criminal. A short sample follows.

When the Carrancistas arrived at the National Palace and City Hall, along with all the military hardware came the soldier's old ladies, or *"soldaderas,"* with their children. The soldaderas were as hardened as their husbands to the perilous life of the campaigns, for they followed their husbands wherever they went, like "the thread follows the needle" or the tail follows the eagle. Not wishing to stay at a lodging house or some hovel in the slums, they instead settled in foul promiscuity in the great patios of both palaces, as well as in the portal of the City Hall. They slept in alleyways on stinking and bug-infested bedrolls that during the daytime they would hang from the many stakes they nailed to the walls. In these places they picked off lice, cooked, ate, and washed clothing on paving stones from the patios that they had pried up; and they strung ropes between the columns, as well as from the handrails of the exterior staircases and balconies of both palaces, from which they hung their blankets and rags as calmly as if they were in the farmyards of their home villages. For cooking they used *"paranguas,"* primitive stone ovens they fueled with scaffolding from the construction that had been halted by the fighting. These let loose clouds of smoke that quickly blackened the walls, columns, ceilings, and doors, making them appear as ugly and deplorable as the *"tesqüindadas"* of the Tarahumara Indians.[12]

Add to this the swarm of disheveled, dirty, ragged women with their eternally puckered frowns—women of a repugnant migratory type—and the hordes of

---

11. Francisco Ramírez Plancarte, *La ciudad de México durante la revolución constitucionalista* (Mexico City: Ediciones Botas, 1941), 364–67. Translated by Tim Henderson.

12. The Tarahumara (or Rarámuri) Indians of northern Mexico celebrate fiestas lasting several consecutive days, attended by both sexes under the influence of "tesgüino," a drink made of fermented corn containing 10% alcohol. In these fiestas they lose all notion of morality and enter into the most abject promiscuity, practicing adultery, incest and rape with indifference. (Plancarte's note)

Yaqui Indians, dirty boys with dark, sweat-stained faces, dressed practically in hides and continually chewing, with mouths open, pieces of tortilla or cakes of cane sugar—then you will understand the grotesque aspect of these buildings with their horrible encampments, which may as well have been those of nomadic tribes or semi-barbarous gypsies.

Although the City Hall's functions were purely administrative, public services were not just badly attended but completely nullified, especially the sanitary services. Many residents and caretakers piled up trash in the middle of the streets in front of their homes. No cars were sent to collect the trash as in normal times, allowing the formation of large dumps in which were found dead dogs and rats that poisoned the atmosphere with their miasma, making the neglected state of the city that much more dreadful. Sometimes these trash piles were set ablaze, and the fetid clouds of smoke caused incessant weeping.

As for lighting, many streetlights were shattered, having served as targets in the shooting exercises carried out by our "liberators" during their carousing; many others were made useless by the hurricane and were not replaced by the Electric Company. So it is easy to deduce that at night the city remained enveloped in semi-darkness, which was a boon to criminals who everywhere committed misdeeds. And in those days there was a complete lack of police services, for the patrols that constantly roamed the city were preoccupied with repelling surprise attacks by the Zapatistas, who on several occasions made audacious incursions not only in the city's outskirts but also in the city center.

Despite everything, the documents that had provided immunity to the businesses and warehouses had not been confiscated from their owners, but the scarcity of food had come to such a decisive and sorrowful extreme that no one was willing, as in earlier days, to threaten to denounce those merchants for hoarding. Instead they preferred to beg them, using tender and expressive words of persuasion and debasing themselves before grocers and wholesalers in pathetic scenes: women of humble condition would kneel down before them and, in phrases broken by tears, beg for the "special" favor of selling them something to ease the hunger that afflicted the poorer classes.

The uninhabited plains of the southern part of the city . . . were constantly crossed by many sick and miserable-looking people who, carrying baskets, searched those sad scrublands of ash-covered nettles and thistles for chard, *quintoniles*,[13] mushrooms, purslane, or any other fresh plant they could boil and eat. They busily rummaged through piles of garbage in the hope of finding some crumbs or perhaps a chicken or other bird in a state of decomposition.

Cats were the "scapegoats." Seasoned for barbecue, everyone ate them till there was not a cat left in the city. In some remote parts of the city people slaughtered

---

13. A Mexican wild green of the amaranth genus. (Editor's note)

dogs, burros, mules and scrawny nags whose meat they quickly sold; no one tried to verify to what animal the meat pertained or if it was healthy to eat, such was the hunger that devoured the population. The hospitals threw sick patients into gullies; the lunatic asylums and orphanages likewise disposed of the unfortunates who stayed there, for want of means to maintain them. Assaults took place in the light of day, and everywhere increased. Many young girls, near children; graceful adult women; women approaching their autumnal years; women in late middle age; and even hellish old women—all, cynically and without circumlocutions or scruples, offered their sexual favors in the hope of easing their hunger.

Seeing in the streets these miserable people begging for sustenance, ragged and discouraged, their sad and pained faces the jaundiced color of the ascetic, one would have reason to think that the Capital City had become an immense "Court of the Miracles," as the slums of Paris were called during the Middle Ages.

Corn ceased to be a vulgar and prosaic food worthy only of Indians, barnyard fowl and swine. In its many forms—tortillas, biscuits, *tamales, atole, corundas, champurrados, arepitas, quesadillas, pozole*, etc., etc.—it was transformed into rich and succulent morsels worthy of the gods of Olympus. But in order to make it agreeable to us, and to make amends for our earlier scorn for such mean things, we instinctively contrived to give corn a new name, one that was more charming and affectionate: we called it *"maicito,"* pronouncing the word with a sweet and mellifluous tone, then exhaling a deep, sorrowful, romantic sigh.

Document 40. The Law of January 6, 1915[14]

When it became abundantly clear that the convention was not going his way, Carranza ordered his emissaries to withdraw. He subsequently abandoned Mexico City for Veracruz, where he could import war supplies and collect customs revenues. For the first months of 1915 the Constitutionalists focused their military efforts on defeating the forces of Pancho Villa in the north, since Villa was the stronger of the Constitutionalists' foes. The Zapatistas used the period of relative neglect to carry out an ambitious local program of agrarian reform. Venustiano Carranza, himself a large landowner and scion of landowning family, had little enthusiasm for agrarian reform, but advocates of agrarian reform—most notably Luis Cabrera—were among his top advisors. Cabrera had given an influential speech in 1912 in which he lambasted the Madero government for neglecting agrarian reform, and he persuaded Carranza that indifference to the

---

14. Venustiano Carranza, "Ley que declara nulas todas las enajenaciones de tierras," January 6, 1915, Memoria Política de México, https://www.memoriapoliticademexico.org/Textos/6Revolucion/1915NET.html. Translated by Tim Henderson.

matter could bring catastrophe. The result was the Law of January 6, 1915, which was authored by Cabrera. The law nullified all illegal land seizures and outlined a byzantine process whereby villages that lacked land sufficient to their needs could petition for land grants from the surrounding haciendas. At least as far as Carranza was concerned, the law was probably less about social justice than pacifying rebellious peasant communities and countering the appeal of Zapatismo. Carranza also began to offer generous amnesties to Zapatistas who surrendered to the Constitutionalists. While agrarian reform during Carranza's time in power was negligible, the Law of January 6, 1915, proved to be a potent symbolic weapon.

Considering: That one of the most generalized causes of unrest and discontent in the rural villages of this country has been the despoliation of the communally owned lands that were given to the villages by the colonial Government as a means of ensuring the continued existence of the indigenous class. This was done on the pretext of complying with the Law of June 25, 1856, and other provisions that ordered that those lands be converted into private property and divided among the inhabitants of the villages to which they belonged; but those lands instead ended up in the possession of a handful of speculators; ...

That the despoiling of the lands was done not only by means of alienations carried out by the political authorities in open contravention of the aforementioned laws, but also through concessions, compositions, or sales arranged with the ministries of Development and Finance, or on the pretext of surveys and demarcations favoring those who denounced exceedances in league with the so-called surveying companies;

That, according to the existing litigation, the rights of the villages and communities have always been abused, for according to article 27 of the Federal Constitution [of 1857] those villages and communities lacked the capacity to acquire or possess real estate, and they also lacked a juridical personality with which to defend their rights. ...

That with the indigenous villages deprived of the lands, waters, and woodlands that the colonial Government granted them, and with rural property concentrated in few hands, the mass of the rural population has had no other recourse than to provide themselves with life's necessities by selling their labor at a miserable price to the powerful landowners, and this inevitably led to the state of misery, abjection and de facto slavery in which an enormous number of workers have lived and continue to live;

That in view of what has been said, the need to return to the villages the lands of which they have been dispossessed is palpable, an act of elemental justice and the only effective means of ensuring the peace and promoting the welfare and improvement of our poor classes. This cannot harm the interests of the people who currently own the properties in question, because those interests have no legal basis, having been established in express violation of the laws that only ordered the division of communal properties among the villages' inhabitants, not their alienation in favor of outsiders; nor can those rights be sanctioned or legitimized by length of possession, because the aforementioned laws did not establish the purchasing requirements with respect to those properties, and because the villages to which they belonged were unable to defend them for lack of legal personality;

That it is likely in some cases it will not be possible to make restitution, whether because the alienations of the lands belonging to the villages were done in accordance with the law; or because the villages have lost their titles or the ones they have are deficient; or because it is impossible to identify the lands or determine their precise size; or for whatever reason. But the reason for impeding restitution, no matter how fair or legitimate it may seem, does not free the villages from their difficult situation, nor does it justify the continuation of that woeful situation; therefore it is necessary to overcome this difficulty in a way that can be reconciled with everyone's interests;

That the means of means of fulfilling this necessity cannot be other than the authorization of the superior military authorities in each place to carry out the needed expropriations, giving sufficient lands to the villages that lack them, and thus realizing one of the great principles of the Revolution and establishing one of the first bases upon which we will reorganize the country.

That providing the means for the villages to regain the lands of which they were despoiled, or to acquire the lands they need for their welfare and development, does not mean reviving the ancient communities or creating similar ones; it only means giving land to the impoverished rural population that lacks it, so that they can fully develop their right to life and gain freedom from the economic servitude to which they have been reduced; it is to be noted that the lands will not belong to the villages in common, but must be divided in freehold, albeit with the limitations necessary to prevent greedy speculators, especially foreigners, from monopolizing that property, as almost invariably happened with the division of the village ejidos and *fundos legales* that was done legally at the start of the Revolution of Ayutla.[15]

---

15. The Revolution of Ayutla began in 1854 with the overthrow of the dictator Antonio López de Santa Anna. It was followed by a spate of liberal legislation ("La Reforma") that culminated in the Constitution of 1857. The liberal reformers sought to end the "corporate" ownership of land by the Roman Catholic Church and the Indian villages, which still held lands granted them during the colonial period.

For these reasons I have thought it well to issue the following decree:

Article 1: The following are hereby declared null:

I. All transfers of land, waters, and woodlands belonging to the population centers made by political bosses, State governors, or any other authority, in violation of the Law of 25 June 1856, as well as of other relevant laws and dispositions.

II. All of the concessions, compositions, or sales of lands, waters, and woodlands made by the Secretaries of Development, Finance, or any other federal authority, from the first of December of 1876 until the present day, with which the ejidos, lands, waters, woodlands, distributed lands, or any other kind of property belonging to the villages, *rancherías*, congregations, or communities have been illegally invaded and occupied.

III. All of the proceedings of surveys and demarcations carried out during the period of time referred to in the preceding clause, by companies, judges, and other authorities under which the ejidos, distributed lands, and any other type belonging to the population centers have been illegally invaded and occupied. . . .

Article 3: The villages that need lands, but which lack ejidos or are unable to gain restitution because they have no titles, cannot identify the lands, or have had the lands taken from them legally, will be able to obtain a grant of land sufficient to the needs of their population; the land immediately adjacent to the interested villages, which is required for this purpose, will be expropriated by the national Government.

Article 4: For the effects of that law and the rest of the agrarian laws that are expedited, in accordance with the political program of the Revolution, we hereby create:

I. A National Agrarian Commission of nine persons and that, headed by the Secretary of Development, will have the functions that this law and the successive ones indicate.

II. A local agrarian commission, composed of five persons, for each State or Territory of the Republic, and with the attributions that the laws determine;

III. The private executive committees that in each State are needed, those that will be composed of three persons each, with the attributions that are indicated.

Article 5: The private executive committees will depend in each State on the respective local agrarian commission, which in turn will be subordinate to the National Agrarian Commission.

Article 6: The petitions for restitution of lands belonging to the villages that have been invaded or occupied illegitimately, and that are referred to in article 1 of this law, will be presented in the States directly before the governors, and in the Territories and Federal District before the superior political authorities, but in the cases in which the lack of communications or the state of war impeded the action of the local governments, the petitions may also be presented before the military chiefs who are specially authorized for the effect by the head of the Executive Power; these petitions will be awarded based on their founding documents.

Also to be presented before the same authorities are the petitions concerning concessions of land to grant ejidos to the villages that lack them, or that do not have titles sufficient to justify their right to have their claims upheld.

Article 7: The respective authority, in view of the petitions presented, will hear the opinion of the local agrarian commission about the justice of the claims and about the convenience, necessity and extension of the concessions of lands for grants of ejidos, and will decide whether or not the solicited restitution or concession will proceed; in affirmative cases, it will pass the file to the corresponding private executive committee, so that they can identify the lands, demarcate and measure them, and proceed to provisionally grant them to the interested parties.

Article 8: The resolutions of the governors or military chiefs will have a provisional character, but they will be executed right away by the private executive Committee, and the file, with all its documents and other data that are deemed necessary, will be remitted later to the local agrarian commission, which, in turn, will elevate it with a report to the National Agrarian Commission.

Article 9: The National Agrarian Commission will dictate about the approval, rectification or modification of the elevated resolutions to its knowledge, and in view of the opinion rendered by the Executive Power of the Nation, will sanction the claims or grants effected, expediting the respective titles.

Article 10: The interested parties that believe themselves harmed by the resolution of the head of the Executive Power of the Nation will be able to appeal to the courts to decide their rights within the term of one year, counted from the date of said resolutions, since beyond this term no reclamation will be admitted.

In the cases in which protests are made against claims and the interested party received a judicial resolution declaring that the restitution granted to a village shall not proceed, the sentence will only give right to obtain from the Government of the Nation the corresponding indemnization.

In the same term of one year they can appeal to the owners of the expropriated lands, demanding the indemnizations that must be paid to them.

Article 11. A regulating law will determine the condition in which the lands must remain that are returned or adjudicated to the villages and the manner and occasion of dividing them among the inhabitants, who meanwhile will work them communally.

Article 12. The governors of the States, or in some cases, the military chiefs of each region authorized by the head of the Executive Power, will appoint the local agrarian commission and the private executive committees.

Transitory. This law will enter into effect from the date of its publication as long as the current civil war does not end. The military authorities will publish it and tout the present law in each of the plazas or places that are occupied.

Document 41. Villa's Defeat in Celaya[16]

The war against Pancho Villa culminated in a series of bloody battles fought in the Bajío region of the center-west, the first two of which were fought near the town of Celaya in the state of Guanajuato on April 6–7 and April 15–16. The Constitutionalists were outnumbered, but their leading general, Álvaro Obregón, was by far the better tactician. Villa, overconfident and reckless, squandered his advantages by mounting mass cavalry charges which came at an appalling cost in lives. While Obregón's forces lost 695 men at Celaya, Villa's lost more than 6,000. The Battle of Celaya was followed by battles at León—where Obregón lost an arm—and Aguascalientes, all of which were disastrous for the Villistas. By the end of summer 1915, Villa's forces had been virtually demolished and no longer posed a threat to Constitutionalist dominance.

The following is a corrido, or folk song, giving the Obregonista perspective.

I am going with my 30-30
And my noble heart
To fight for Carranza
At the Fifth Convention.

Francisco Villa turned
His whole division around.
And Chief Carranza says:
"Ay, Villa! What a traitor!"

Francisco Villa tells them,
With courage and with heart:
"Withdraw from Celaya
And surrender the city."

From Celaya comes the answer
With courage and with heart:
"I will not leave Celaya,"
Said Álvaro Obregón.

Francisco Villa tells them
With courage and fantasy:
"If you do not leave Celaya
My artillery will open fire."

---

16. "Derrota de Villa en Celaya," *The Mexican Revolution: Corridos about the Heroes and Events 1910–1920 and Beyond!*, Arhoolie Records, https://arhoolierecords.bandcamp.com/track/derrota-de-villa-en-celaya. Translated by Tim Henderson.

Villa had many people
Scattered about everywhere,
And the Natera brigade.
Was in San Luis Potosí.

Álvaro Obregón said:
"Now let us see:
Either you've just killed me
Or I will take over."

On the hacienda of Santa Ana
En route to the city of León,
Is where General Obregón
Was wounded in the arm.

A first captain from
the Murguía brigade said:
"Boys, long live Obregón!
I will die in his company!"

What horrible butchery!
Ay, what terrible hours!
How they mowed the Villistas down
With their machine guns!

Villa was in Salamanca
With all of his Dorados,
And Amaro was in Celaya
With all his toughest troops . . .

The poor Villistas said:
"We are no longer so feared,
For everywhere we go,
We look like armadillos."

Those poor people
Were already defeated.
By troops who took Celaya
Like taking a drink of brandy.

Obregon defeated Villa,
Who was the key figure,
And the Division of the North
Lost all its glory.

From the first day of August
To the first of April,
In Celaya Villa lost,
For he did not throw his life away.

Villa, very disconsolate,
Ordered a cease fire,
And said in desperation:
"With Obregón I cannot win."

Now, before I leave,
 I say farewell to my friends.
And this is where the corrido
Of Celaya ends.

Document 42. The United States Must Act[17]

The following statement was issued by U.S. president Woodrow Wilson on June 2, 1915, even as Álvaro Obregón was laying waste to Pancho Villa's Division of the North. Wilson is being rather disingenuous in declaring that the United States had taken an attitude of neutrality toward Mexico's civil war, given that his intervention against Victoriano Huerta had powerfully influenced that war's course. Shortly after this statement was issued—in October 1915—the United States granted de facto diplomatic recognition to Carranza.

For more than two years revolutionary conditions have existed in Mexico. The purpose of the revolution was to rid Mexico of men who ignored the constitution of the Republic and used their power in contempt of the rights of its people; and with these purposes the people of the United States instinctively and generously

---

17. U.S. Department of State, *Papers Relating to the Foreign Relations of the United States, with the Address of the President to Congress, December 7, 1915*, doc. 741 (Washington, D.C.: U.S. Government Printing Office, 1924).

sympathized. But the leaders of the revolution, in the very hour of their success, have disagreed and turned their arms against one another. All professing the same objects, they are nevertheless unable or unwilling to cooperate. A central authority at Mexico City is no sooner set up than it is undermined and its authority denied by those who were expected to support it. Mexico is apparently no nearer a solution of her tragical troubles than she was when the revolution was first kindled. And she has been swept by civil war as if by fire. Her crops are destroyed, her fields lie unseeded, her work cattle are confiscated for the use of the armed factions, her people flee to the mountains to escape being drawn into unavailing bloodshed, and no man seems to see or lead the way to peace and settled order. There is no proper protection either for her own citizens or for the citizens of other nations resident and at work within her territory. Mexico is starving and without a government.

In these circumstances the people and Government of the United States cannot stand indifferently by and do nothing to serve their neighbor. They want nothing for themselves in Mexico. Least of all do they desire to settle her affairs for her, or claim any right to do so. But neither do they wish to see utter ruin come upon her, and they deem it their duty as friends and neighbors to lend any aid they properly can to any instrumentality which promises to be effective in bringing about a settlement which will embody the real objects of the revolution—constitutional government and the rights of the people. Patriotic Mexicans are sick at heart and cry out for peace and for every self-sacrifice that may be necessary to procure it. Their people cry out for food and will presently hate as much as they fear every man, in their country or out of it, who stands between them and their daily bread.

It is time, therefore, that the Government of the United States should frankly state the policy which in these extraordinary circumstances it becomes its duty to adopt. It must presently do what it has not hitherto done or felt at liberty to do, lend its active moral support to some man or group of men, if such may be found, who can rally the suffering people of Mexico to their support in an effort to ignore, if they cannot unite, the warring factions of the country, return to the constitution of the Republic so long in abeyance, and set up a government at Mexico City which the great powers of the world can recognize and deal with, a government with whom the program of the revolution will be a business and not merely a platform. I, therefore, publicly and very solemnly, call upon the leaders of faction in Mexico to act, to act together, and to act promptly for the relief and redemption of their prostrate country.

I feel it to be my duty to tell them that, if they cannot accommodate their differences and unite for this great purpose within a very short time, this Government will be constrained to decide what means should he employed by the United States in order to help Mexico save herself and serve her people.

V. The Early Trials of the Revolutionary Regime, 1915–1916

Although the Constitutionalists had triumphed over their enemies, it took years for the central government to expand its authority. The documents in this section provide insight into the slow and experimental consolidation of the central government, as well as the many ongoing difficulties with its adversaries.

In 1915 and 1916, most reforms took place at the state rather than federal level, and sometimes against Carranza's own policy preferences (doc. 43). Some of his governors supported the rights of women and of workers, levied production taxes on mine owners, and experimented with measures against alcohol and the clergy. Elsewhere, the enemies of the revolution continued to operate at full strength, whether Porfirian insurgents such as General Félix Díaz or the Conventionists. In Yucatán, Governor Salvador Alvarado worried about the strength of the old oligarchy (doc. 44); in response, Yucatecans engaged in the most significant mobilization of women and the grass roots anywhere in 1910s Mexico (doc. 45). Under these conditions, revolutionary projects continued to compete with one another. For example, the Felicistas devised a plan that borrowed from the agrarian precepts of the Conventionists (docs. 46–47). Meanwhile, Carranza began pulling back on his earlier promises of social reform and cracked down on organized labor (doc. 48).

In this context, Pancho Villa's raid on Columbus, New Mexico, and the subsequent U.S. invasion in the so-called Punitive Expedition highlighted the continuing strength of rebel movements and focused the revolution on the goal of securing national sovereignty (docs. 49–51). It also established Villa's own nationalist credentials (doc. 52) and contributed to the ill-fated decision of imperial Germany to seek an alliance with Mexico (doc. 53), a decision that contributed to the U.S. entry into World War I on the side of the Allies.

Document 43. "The Dry Law," Sonora, 1915[1]

While Carranza's Constitutionalists consolidated their authority at the national level, many of the most important social reform efforts came at the state level. In many respects, the states became "laboratories of the revolution" during the Constitutionalist era. The following document is the first decree issued by the military governor of Sonora, future president Plutarco Elías Calles. A heavy drinker, Calles considered alcoholism a scourge impeding the economic and social development of the people of Sonora. His first decree showed his determination to act on his own rather than as an agent of Carranza, who opposed Calles's efforts to end alcohol use.

General Plutarco Elías Calles, governor and military commander of the state of Sonora, in the use of his extraordinary faculties awarded by the first chief of the Constitutionalist Executive, in charge of the Executive Power of the Republic

Considering,

—That one of the causes of the decadence of the peoples has been the use of intoxicating beverages, which, aside from producing physical annihilation and the moral perversion of the individual, is also one of the principal reasons for economic malaise.

—That the correlation between crime rates and the use of alcoholic beverages is well known. Since the Constitutionalist government has the obligation to moralize the citizens that have fallen under their sway, and to attempt their betterment, it could not fail to set upon legislating this important issue immediately.

For that reason, I have decided to issue the following decree:

1) The import, sale, and production of intoxicating beverages in Sonora is strictly prohibited.

2) Intoxicating beverages are those containing any amount of alcohol.

3) Until the judicial branch has been reestablished, the executive [branch of the state] will punish violators of Article 1 by five years of imprisonment, recording the action in a document that will include a declaration of the responsible parties and the evidence in favor and against. Accomplices and accessories will be punished by prison terms of three and two years, respectively.

4) Crimes of drunkenness will be punished by the penalties already listed in the Penal Code, using the same summary proceeding established in the first part of Article 3 until courts have been reestablished.

---

1. Plutarco Elías Calles, *Decretos, circulares y demás disposiciones dictadas por el C. Gobernador y Comandante Militar del Estado de Sonora, General Plutarco Elías Calles, durante el año de 1915* (Hermosillo: Imprenta de Gobierno, 1915), 15. Translated by Jürgen Buchenau.

Transitional. This law will become valid upon publication in each municipality by the military chiefs.

"Constitution and Reforms"
General Headquarters in Molina, Son., August 8, 1915
General P. Elías Calles

Document 44. The Situation in Revolutionary Yucatán[2]

While Calles was battling alcohol consumption, another governor from the North—Salvador Alvarado—asserted Constitutionalist rule over the southern state of Yucatán. Alvarado aimed to break the hold of the so-called Casta Divina *(Divine Caste) over Yucatán's large estates, many of which were devoted to the production of henequen, or sisal. He also undertook popular mobilization and advanced women's rights. The following excerpt contains Alvarado's views on the hacendados of Yucatán. He did not, in the end, break their power.*

Mérida, Yucatán, January 25, 1916
Venustiano Carranza.
My respected chief and friend:

I confirm my telegrams related to the agrarian question, reporting that in this State the agrarian problem is very grave and has a special character.

The Indians here (200,000) have been despoiled of their lands by the great hacendados. The methods used to do this are well known, and the vexations and injustices they have caused are so notorious that even the current proprietors recognize it and offer money and remote lands in compensation. The Indians of this place are very intelligent and much inclined to organize. They have not lost the love of the land, and many hundreds of them yearly give up good wages to sow a few fields of corn many leagues away.

When I arrived in this region, I let it be known to these people in proclamations, conferences and speeches that I represented all of the revolutionary ideals. As an honorable man, I believe in fulfilling all administrative and revolutionary promises, upholding, in thousands of concrete cases, the rights of the oppressed and afflicted, and I have not failed to return stolen lands. When I arrived, I created a commission to demarcate lands, a process that went slowly and was not yet regulated by the Law of January 6. I arranged with the landowners that, while their property was being

---

2. Isidro Fabela, ed., *Documentos históricos de la Revolución Mexicana: Revolución y régimen constitucionalista*, XVII; Volumen 5 del Tomo I (Mexico City: Editorial Jus, 1969), 17:21–23. Translated by Tim Henderson.

surveyed and the Law regulated, they would lend land to the people of the villages. This resulted in corn harvests so abundant that we now have a surplus. This, sir, was done on borrowed lands, and it should give you an idea of what our workers could do on lands they own outright. Recently the Law was regulated in a way that I believe responds to the circumstances of the locality and resolves the problem forever. If you . . . decide this law should be repealed or modified, I beg you to give me instructions on how to satisfy the imperious need to give the people what they expect from the Revolution and to solve the problem.

You have an immense burden and little free time, but I beg you to give attention to this matter because, in addition to solving a tense local situation, the study that you make of the question might orient your thinking and lay a general foundation for a definitive resolution of this vital matter.

The hacendados here hate Mexico and they persecute everything that is Mexican. They do this with their gold—the gold they took from the lands they stole, which they use to foment opposition. At their earliest opportunity they will request annexation to the United States, which, as they see it, will free them from the horrors of the Revolution. *Proof*: Last February a commission composed of the principal leaders of this group (eight in number) left here to request annexation to the United States. Avelino Montes gave them 480,000 dollars for this effort.

Now Avelino Montes and the great landowners have gathered five million dollars so that Eleuterio Ávila can come to Yucatán, and Félix Díaz can go to Chiapas and Oaxaca, with the support of the clergy and of the "International Harvester Co." They do not cease for one moment to fight against this Government, and they have begun a formidable campaign in the U.S. press of attacks against President Wilson because, according to them, he permits a Mexican monopoly (The Regulating Commission) to dictate prices in that market. They have also organized associations of agriculturalists to urge Senators to attack the question vigorously. Already the [U.S.] Senate has ordered an investigation to see if we are violating the Sherman Act and the other five laws against the "trusts"; we have defended ourselves and we have absolute confidence we will win, even if there is an invasion. But what makes us seethe with rage is that the witnesses against us in the U.S. Senate are Yucatecan hacendados. . . .

The general opinion is that the best way to revolutionize this State is to organize the Indians, helping them to understand what they owe to the Revolution and to the revolutionaries who come from other states, for as long as the great capitalists have one peso, they will use it to defend their interests, which are in open conflict with the interests of the nation.

Here I represent the Revolution and the Center. I represent for the Indian the only hope of salvation from the clutches of the cacique's tyranny. The Center is the protector of the Indian, the laborer; for this reason, giving the Indians lands links them to Mexico.

I beg you to listen to Mr. Rolland,[3] who will explain to you in detail everything related to the regulation of the Law and the administrative work of my Government. I am also sending you a collection of my dispositions, law and decrees. I will not give you a detailed report because that would be very long and tedious, while in each of the dispositions I have shown how I interpret the needs of this place and the spirit of the Revolution. If you believe that I am mistaken in any of this I will do as you suggest, but I beg that you allow me to try my reforms for some time and observe how they work, here, on the ground, in practice.

My constant hope has been to do in this very short time all the good possible for the State in general and for the humble classes in particular, establishing the strictest administrative morality and the most virtuous line of conduct for me and my collaborators and subordinates as we carry out our duties.

I know I am not free of enemies; I am not inclined to make friends with merchants and rogues, and I have taken privileges and sinecures away from the capitalists and the powerful. I have always remained steadfast before their pretentions and they have never influenced my decisions in any way, so naturally they do not love me, which I consider an honor for any revolutionary.

I will not tire you further, and I am pleased to take this opportunity to reiterate my support and personal affection as your most devoted friend,

Salvador Alvarado

Document 45. The Woman in the Future[4]

Hermila Galindo (1886–1954) was one of the most important feminists and intellectuals within the Constitutionalist coalition. She advocated for sex education in schools, the right to divorce, and women's suffrage, and she believed that the Catholic Church stood in the way of feminist efforts to reform Mexico. These ideas were considered radical at that time. In 1916, Galindo participated in the first feminist congress in Mexico, convened by Yucatán governor Salvador Alvarado. Galindo was also the first woman to run for federal office, garnering a majority of the votes, but she was kept from her seat by a ruling restricting the franchise to men. Her religious references in this speech contrasted with Alvarado's intensely anticlerical state government.

---

3. Modesto C. Rolland, a revolutionary propagandist and technocrat who played a significant role in the revolutionary and postrevolutionary regimes.

4. Hermila Galindo, "La Mujer en el Porvenir, Primer Congreso Feminista de Yucatán, enero de 1916," *Ideas feministas de Nuestra América* (blog), accessed November 20, 2021, https://ideasfem.wordpress.com/textos/f/f13/. Translated by Jürgen Buchenau.

I consecrate these meditations to the virtuous ruler of Yucatán, General Salvador Alvarado, who has revealed himself as a profound sociologist with his laws and administrative dispositions; to the thinker and humanist who unravels and studies deep-seated social problems in order to find a definitive solution to them; and to the admirable innovator who promotes Feminist Congresses in Yucatán, aware that the remedy for many of the grave evils that afflict humanity will depend on them. In case they are worthy of being taken into account, (as St. Gregory said) the truth must be told even if it is the source of scandal.

Respectfully, HERMILA GALINDO

The prophecy in the Gospel has been fulfilled. "The times have come." "Blessed are they that hunger and thirst after righteousness: for they shall have their fill."

Just as a miner digs the earth to its deepest depths to extract its coveted treasures from its entrails; and just as a diver descends to the depths of the ocean to clutch a shell . . . that may contain a precious and beautiful pearl, so the Constitutionalist revolution has begun . . . to turn its promises into facts, and to transform theory into action upon the triumph of its weapons.

To the worthy Yucatecan woman fell the glory of being summoned to the First Feminist Congress in Mérida, where the "brain" of the Republic is located. Here, the climate inflames the blood and kindles the intellectual fire, here one is, due to the proximity of the sea, in perennial communication with God and in close fraternal embrace with all nationalities, with all races, with all men. I repeat that it was Yucatán's turn in the glory of hoisting the emancipatory banner of women, under the effective protection of a highly cultured Governor . . . a revolutionary who has interpreted the program of social and political reforms generated by the armed movement so well. . . .

How can we not heed this call of civilization and confraternity of women? I take advantage of this . . . opportunity to demonstrate once again the fervent zeal with which I dedicate my energies to promoting the holy cause that I have embraced and the intoxicating joy of putting my modest intelligence at the service of my sex. . . .

While there was only one step from hunter to warrior, to get from the nomadic tribe to the family took a whole phase. But the force, the Atlas of all times, was . . . the eternal dominator of the ages. . . . Man, feeling himself king of creation, . . . enslaved his conscience and his will under the iron rule of the strongest. Thus, slavery emerged spontaneously, and entire generations were born without control over their own bodies. . . . One was born a slave or a free citizen, a plebeian or a patrician, a squire or a colonist. . . . Meanwhile, the woman, because of her physical weakness . . . , was born, grew and lived as a thing, as an object of luxury or pleasure, as real estate that could be transferred, sold, taken hostage, killed or wounded with impunity. Her father and her husband controlled her life and death.

The sweet and peaceful doctrine of the Nazarene did not manage to manumit her, but it did succeed in improving her condition by establishing the right of equality among Christians.

But, while Jesus established equality before God, men . . . continued to keep women in obscure degradation until the Roman laws began to dignify them, recognizing some rights and instituting the dowry as a first step on the road to their emancipation.

. . . Man, recognized . . . in a woman the cornerstone of the family, divining . . . an inexhaustible wellspring of tenderness and inhaling for the first time the holy perfume of the mother, destined to perpetuate the species and to be the guardian and faithful preserver of the greatness of creation. . . . A thrill had run through his nervous system, and for the first time in the course of centuries, he paid homage to woman. The miracle came by way of a kiss and a sigh in one of those moments in which the spirit communes with God! From that sublime minute, . . . she already had a destiny; man had found merit in her. She could henceforth be the guardian of his younger children. She . . . learned to read and write; she tasted the divine joys of art, she accumulated in herself the virtue of the wife and the instruction of the artistic hetaira[5]. . . ; she wore the white robe of the matron or vestal, and she could file for divorce when she felt hurt or outraged, as a consecration of her independence.

But as we have seen, their manumission depended on marriage. In those remote ages as in the present age, . . . marriage was the purpose of their existence. The problem for women was as complex and difficult to solve then as it is now, in spite of the diversity of laws and customs. . . .

Sad as it is to say, man is born an animal and woman a female! In the latter, the nervous, muscular and digestive systems, the elevated functions of her brain, the inexplicable outbursts of her instinct, the most sublime traits of her superhuman self-denial, . . . the beauty of her skin and the softness of her features: all these are nothing more than the . . . means to reach a single and high end: maternity.

Maternal love, indispensable for the preservation of the species, was held up to be far superior to all affections, passions, habits, and instincts: to overcome all obstacles and to rule as absolute sovereign over all acts of feminine life. This is the only way to rationally explain the well-known cases of . . . aristocratic virgins abandoning homeland, home, family, religion, society, . . . to fall into the arms of the one who managed to captivate her, no matter her social status. . . .

The sexual instinct reigns in such a way in women . . . that no hypocritical artifice is capable of destroying, modifying or restraining it. . . .

Since marriage is the only lawful and moral means of satisfying it fully, according to the demands of society and according to the written laws, we are faced with a daunting problem. We have seen all of the difficulties in increasing the number of

---

5. In ancient Greece, a prostitute who was considered to be highly cultured.

marriages. Thinkers, statesmen and legislators have the duty to find a solution to this problem, since it involves the most serious evil that can happen to a nation: the decrease of the population and the degeneration of the race.

Of course, there are overwhelming reasons for amendments to the civil and penal codes that would increase punishment in cases of seduction and abandonment of women. When a woman surrenders herself into the arms of her lover, captivated and carried away by the inescapable sexual instinct, the man appears before society as a pleasant skull, an emulator of Don Juan Tenorio. The impunity of his crime makes him cynical, and he refers to his deed with the bossy tone with which a revolutionary chief would tell the story of the capture of a *plaza*.[6] But the unfortunate woman who has done nothing more than yield to a demand of her instinct . . . finds herself relegated to social contempt, her future cut short and thrown into the abyss of despair, misery, madness or suicide. How many times does the newspaper give an account of an unhappy woman who killed her own child in order to hide her transgression? Crime statistics are full of cases of infanticide and induced abortion, without counting those that remain hidden, proving the heavy burden of public vindictiveness against the sad woman who has committed a crime! For such cases, the well-understood charity of our statesmen has founded orphanages and nurseries. That is to say, their hypocrisy has invented a contrived means to leave unpunished their attacks on morality and their crimes against the Fatherland!

How many men of elastic conscience sit at the finest tables surrounded by honors and friends, wearing magnificent jewels and dressed in the impeccable costume of the gentleman and have no other means of living or other source of income to sustain that luxury than the filthy and criminal exploitation of some women, of some wretched women who fell for love and then forced by circumstances to become beasts of vice!

How many foreigners come to this country to make a real industry out of Mexican women, taking advantage of their abnegation and ignorance!

How many authorities allow these filthy trades, a mockery of morality and civilization, but are inflexible with the weak woman who has committed a crime!

To deserve the title of a just revolution, for equity to reign supreme, for the good of the race rather than for the pleasure of society, the revolution must extirpate all leprosy, sweep away all obstacles, reform the codes, open its arms to women, provide them with well-paid work . . . to improve nutrition, repress vices, encourage immigration, and multiply educational centers. . . . It will not be able to bring the good news to the bosom of families that will end idolatrous prejudices and extirpate profound worries.

---

6. Stronghold.

This noble and lofty mission corresponds to the Mexican woman. She alone has enough power to . . . throw into the purifying fire of truth all that is false, conventional and hypocritical in our heroic race. . . .

May God and honest men have pity on woman by procuring a reasonable way of life for her, and the evolution of our race will come, filling the coming generations with astonishment!

And with this, if the 19th century did not fulfill Victor Hugo's prophecy of emancipating women, the 20th century and the Mexican homeland will have fulfilled it.

Document 46. Plan Felicista de Tierra Colorada[7]

The triumph of the Constitutionalists in 1915 did not end the fighting in Mexico. Resistance continued from both Villistas and Zapatistas, and don Porfirio's nephew Félix Díaz also continued to battle the new government. This Felicista "plan" outlines some of the political positions of a movement usually labeled as "reactionary" due to Díaz's past and family connections. However, while this plan affirms the liberal property rights ensconced in the 1857 constitution, it calls for land reform, which suggests that even reactionaries understood the need to provide land to the rural dispossessed.

Gathered on the base of Tierra Colorado, Veracruz on the day of February 23, 1916, the undersigned decided to initiate an armed movement within the Republic, in combination with what other groups working for the reestablishment of order already started in various points of the country. We fight for the reorganization of our authority and institutions under the legal standards as of October 10, 1913, the date on which General Huerta dispersed the Congress of the Union legally elected by the people. Protesting and fighting until the end, persistent in the sole purpose of the salvation of country, through the elimination of anarchy, the re-installation of public authorities, the restoration of our institutions, and the improvement of our working classes, we agree on the following:

First: We designate the Army, entrusted with the task referred to in the preceding paragraph, with the name "National Reorganizing Army."

Second: We name the Citizen Félix Díaz the General in Chief of that Army.

---

7. Román Iglesias González, ed., *Planes políticos, proclamas, manifiestos y otros documentos de la Independencia al México moderno, 1812–1940* (Mexico City: Universidad Nacional Autónoma de México, 1998), 761–64. Translated by Madison Green.

Third: During the campaign required for the strengthening of institutions and the restoration of peace, we award to the aforementioned chief extraordinary powers over the branches of War, Finance and Government.

Fourth: The National Reorganizing Army shall support and enforce all decrees issued by the General in Chief, using the powers this act confers to it.

Fifth: We declare that General Victoriano Huerta interrupted the constitutional order in disbanding the Congress of the Union on October 10, 1913 and became a usurper of public functions. Officials who have incurred responsibilities for actions in direct connection with this act will be subject to the decisions of the law and the courts in that regard.

Sixth: We do not recognize any of the acts and contracts executed by . . . Huerta since October 10, 1913, nor any of the decrees, laws and general enforcement provisions issued by the so-called Congress of the Union that substituted the Twenty-Sixth legislature. Private interests, created in good faith under such acts, contracts and laws, shall be respected if they do not contradict the public interest.

Seventh: We declare null and void . . . all acts and contracts of the leaders and groupings that have usurped . . . functions that the Law reserves to officials elected by the people, in whom the national sovereignty resides essentially and originally and from which all public power must derive in order to be legitimate. . . .

Eighth: Upon the restoration of order and before the competent courts, the indigenous peoples and communities who believe they have been dispossessed of property the use or ownership of which legally corresponds to them, may make a claim against the dispossession, even when the perpetrators are protected by enforceable judgments. . . .

Ninth: Considering that the aspiration to own land is a legitimate manifestation of the desire to progress through work, and that the subdivision of rural property and its best use will increase public wealth, and consequently, the well-being of all social classes, the reorganizing movement will particularly address the distribution of land, for which a commission will be created as soon as order has been restored to study each and every one of the proposed formulas to address such aspirations. We accept the following as a secure and stable basis for the solution to be adopted:

a. The ejidos and goods of common use of which the pueblos have been unduly deprived shall be returned to them . . . following the procedures established by the law for expropriations on the grounds of public benefit. . . .

b. All federal and uncultivated lands not used as private property shall principally remain destined for the formation of agricultural colonies whose lots shall preferably be distributed among the individuals who have rendered services in favor of order, serving in the rank and file of the National Reorganizing Army.

c.   Through legal procedures, the Government of the Union shall expropriate . . . those parts of the latifundios (division of land into large estates) or haciendas (estates, plantations or ranches) necessary to satisfy the demand for land requested by the working class in each region, in accordance with the special law that will regulate the matter.

Tenth: The legal farms and ejidos still preserved by the villages cannot be distributed without the consent of the same communities. . . .

Eleventh: We declare null and void all the seizures that have taken place or ensued in violation of the constitutional precept declaring the abolition of the penalty of confiscation. All persons who by any title acquire confiscated property, whether owned, leased, possessed or occupied as free users, or of any other order, are obliged to return the movable or immovable property to their rightful owners at the time they claim them, without prejudice to the fact that the proprietors remain subject to the responsibilities that they have incurred according to the law.

Twelfth: We declare null and void the adjudications of real or personal property at auction or by any other means, originated by nonpayment of contributions or taxes, monthly pensions, interest or capital given in a due term loan and which were secured by mortgage or pledge. . . .

Thirteenth: No private or public property can be occupied by any authority or person without the full consent of its owners. . . . The case of occupation of property required by war operations is an exemption for the rules previously established; but such occupation will always be transitory and without ignoring the character and rights of the proprietor in any case, among them, compensation for damages caused.

Fourteenth: No agricultural, commercial or industrial enterprise may be subject to intervention unless by order of a competent judge.

Fifteenth: The inhabitants of the Republic shall enjoy full religious freedom. Without distinction, religions and cults shall exercise freely as guaranteed by the Constitution of 1857 and the Reform Acts.

Sixteenth: . . . When establishing the provisional government in the capital of the republic, we will install the Supreme Court of Justice of the Nation and the courts . . . and call the people of Mexico to elections of the legislative branch, after the issuance of an amnesty law that . . . facilitates the union of all Mexicans and ends hatred and revenge. Elected by the people, the Congress of the Union will call for elections of the other Powers.

Seventeenth: The newly established government shall recognize all contracts and concessions given by previous legitimate governments to Mexican and foreign citizens or enterprises, provided that they are in agreement with the provisions of law.

Eighteenth: The government of the Union shall encourage the establishment of a system of free education and the improvement and dissemination of public education to the popular classes.

Nineteenth: The National Reorganizing Army adopts the motto of Peace and Justice, which combines the aspirations of the Mexican people, and declares its use obligatory at the bottom of any official document.

Twentieth: Before beginning their service, all employees and officials appointed or elected in accordance with the rules listed above shall promise to "protect and uphold" the foundations established in this memorandum and, within them, the Political Constitution of 1857, its addenda and reforms and the laws emanating from it.

Constituents: You already know the intentions that lead us to victory or sacrifice; the time has come to take up arms to reconquer the freedoms that have ruthlessly been taken away from us . . . ; to rebuild our ravaged homes; to ensure our children the right to live as civilized beings in their own land; to eradicate through work and peaceful exercise of our rights the embarrassments we suffer today; to expel forever the hate and yearning for revenge that have transformed the national Mexican family into a blood stained fratricidal conflict; and finally, to punish those who intend to deprive us of our homeland.

Join me in the fight, even if we have to sacrifice our lives, which are worthless if we lose them to save the life of the republic that is about to succumb, bleeding and dying.

Félix Díaz

Document 47. A Conventionist Manifesto[8]

Like the Felicista plan, the Manifesto to the Nation and Program of Revolutionary Political-Social Reforms Approved by the Sovereign Revolutionary Convention, Jojutla, Morelos, *rallied Mexicans in opposition to the Constitutionalist government. This plan embodies the aspirations of the defeated Conventionist coalition and, most importantly, those of the Zapatistas. As a result, it foregrounds the central agrarian aims of Zapata's Plan of Ayala of 1911 as well as municipal and state autonomy. But it goes beyond these aims in also embracing improvements for industrial workers as well as economic nationalism.*

Program of Political-Social Reforms, approved by the Sovereign Revolutionary Convention.

---

8. Javier Garcíadiego, ed., *La Revolución Mexicana: Crónicas, documentos, planes y testimonios* (Mexico City: Universidad Nacional Autónoma de México, 2008), 329–39. Translated by Jürgen Buchenau.

After extensive study and prolonged debates that vibrated with the noble passion of the revolutionary, . . . the Sovereign Revolutionary Convention presents . . . the attached Program of Social and Political Reforms.

It features as its highest and most beautiful principle the return of land to the dispossessed and the distribution of the haciendas and ejidos among those who want to make them produce with the effort of their own hands.

There is nothing greater or more transcendental for the Revolution than the agrarian question, the basis and supreme purpose of the liberation movement, which . . . has already been betrayed twice: first, by Maderismo, which quickly forgot its promises; and second, by the disastrous faction of Venustiano Carranza. After repeated boasts of radicalism, purity and steadfastness, [that faction] has degenerated into an absurd form of reaction in an opprobrious . . . pact with the large landowners.

AGRARIAN QUESTION

The Revolution proposes to carry out the following reforms:

Art. 1. Destroy *latifundismo* by creating smallholdings and providing each Mexican who requests it with the amount of land sufficient to meet his and his family's needs, within the premise that preference will be given to peasants.

Art. 2. Return to the villages the ejidos and water of which they have been deprived, and award them to villages that need them. . . .

Art. 3. Promote agriculture by establishing agricultural banks to provide funds to small farmers, and by investing sufficient capital into irrigation works, the planting of forests, [and the building of] roads and any other kind of agricultural improvement works, so that our soil may produce the riches that it is capable of creating.

Art. 4. Foment the establishment of regional schools of agriculture and agricultural experimental stations in order to teach and apply the best methods of cultivation.

Art. 5. Empower the Federal Government to expropriate real property on the basis of the value that the respective owners have currently declared to the Treasury. Once the agrarian reform has been completed, adopt that value . . . as a basis for expropriation. . . .

THE WORKER'S QUESTION

Art. 6. Prevent the destitution and future exhaustion of workers by means of appropriate social and economic reforms such as moralizing education, laws governing work accidents and retirement pensions, regulation of working hours, provisions that guarantee hygiene and safety on shop floors (taller), factories and mines, and in general, through legislation that makes the exploitation of the proletariat less cruel.

Art. 7. Recognize the legal personality of workers' unions and societies so that entrepreneurs, capitalists and employers will have to deal with strong and well-organized workers' unions rather than the individual defenseless worker.

Art. 8. Provide guarantees to the workers by recognizing the right to strike and boycott.

Art. 9. Abolish in all businesses in the Republic the *tiendas de raya*, the system of vouchers for the payment of wages.

SOCIAL REFORMS

Art. 10. Protect natural children and women who are victims of male seduction by means of laws that recognize them as well as their ample rights and sanction the investigation of paternity.

Art. 11. Promote the emancipation of women by means of a just law on divorce that will base the conjugal union on mutual esteem or love and not on petty social prejudice.

ADMINISTRATIVE REFORMS

Art. 12. To meet the enormous needs of secular education and instruction . . . carry out the following reforms:

I. With federal funds, establish elementary schools in all the places of the Republic beyond the current reach of the benefits of instruction. . . .

II. Demand that more time be devoted to physical culture, manual labor and practical instruction in primary schools.

III. Found normal schools in each State, or regional schools where they are needed.

IV. Raise the remuneration and benefits of teachers.

Art. 13. Emancipate the National University.

Art. 14. In higher education, give preference to the teaching of manual arts and industrial applications of science over the study and promotion of the so-called liberal professions. . . .

Art. 16. Establish special procedures to enable artisans, laborers and employees to quickly and efficiently collect payment for their work.

Art. 17. Prevent the creation of all kinds of monopolies, destroy those already in existence, and revise the laws and concessions that protect them. . . .

Art. 19. Reform mining and oil legislation according to the following principles:

Favor mining and oil explorations; . . . prevent the monopolization of vast areas, grant broad and effective rights to the discoverers of metalliferous deposits; grant the State a proportional share of the gross production . . . ; declare . . . concessions null and void in case of stoppage or possible reduction of work for more than a specified period of time, without just cause; and in cases of waste of said riches or infringement of the laws protecting the life and health of the workers and inhabitants of the district. . . .

Art. 21. Declare that the land required for the construction of oil pipelines, irrigation canals, and all kinds of communication destined to the service of agriculture and the oil and mining industries may be expropriated for public utility.

Art. 22. Require foreign companies that wish to do business in Mexico to comply with the following prerequisites:

I. To establish in the Republic boards of directors sufficiently qualified for distributing dividends, rendering reports to stockholders, and exhibiting all types of records and documents.

II. To comply with the principle, unobserved until today, of submitting to the jurisdiction of the Mexican courts, which will be the only ones empowered to resolve any litigation that may arise in connection with the interests herein and, for the same reason, any lawsuits that may be filed against the companies.

Art. 23. Revise customs taxes, stamp duties and other federal levies in order to establish better grounds for appraisal; abolish the present exemptions and privileges in favor of the large capitalists; and gradually reduce protective tariffs without harming the interests of the national industry.

Art. 24. Exempt the articles of prime necessity from all kinds of indirect taxes.

Art. 25. Exempt artisans, small merchants, and farms of a negligible value from all kinds of taxes. . . .

Art. 28. Establish a progressive tax on inheritance, legacies and donations. . . .

Art. 30. Levy high taxes on the sale of manufactured tobacco and alcoholic beverages and establish prohibitive taxes on these when their manufacture is made with articles of primary necessity.

POLITICAL REFORMS

Art. 32. Ensure the independence of the municipalities, providing them with ample freedom of action that will allow them to attend effectively to communal interests and protect them from the attacks and oppression of the federal and state governments.

Art. 33. Adopt parliamentary rule as the form of government of the Republic.

Art. 34. Abolish the Vice Presidency of the Republic and the *Jefaturas Políticas*.

Art. 35. Abolish the Senate, an aristocratic and conservative institution par excellence.

Art. 36. Reorganize the Judicial Power on new foundations in order to secure the independence, ability and responsibility of its officials . . .

Art. 37. . . . Reform the electoral laws of the Federation and of the States, in order to prevent the falsification of the vote of citizens who cannot read or write.

Art. 38. Punish the enemies of the revolutionary cause by means of the confiscation of their property and in accordance with legal procedures. . . .

Reform, Liberty, Justice and Law

Jojutla, Morelos, April 18, 1916

Document 48. Carranza Moves Against Workers[9]

In the summer of 1916, the workers of Mexico City's electrical company struck to protest their poor working conditions, aided by the Casa del Obrero Mundial (House of the World's Worker). This anarcho-syndicalist labor confederation had played a significant role in the Constitutionalist victory over the Villistas and Zapatistas. Their pact with Carranza made available thousands of additional fighters in the so-called red battalions. These contributions were quickly forgotten, however, as the Carranza government occupied the headquarters of the union. The following selections from Carranza's decree of August 1, 1916, demonstrate his resolve to prevent strikes against public utility companies and to wipe out organized labor despite its valuable service to the Constitutionalist cause.

A work stoppage . . . becomes illegal in the moment when it is used not only as pressure on the industrialist, but also to damage society either directly or indirectly. . . . The conduct of the labor union is in the present case so much more unpatriotic and so much more criminal; it is driven by the maneuvers of the enemies of the government. In light of this, we have to immediately decree the measures that the situation demands. The lack of water, light, and transportation is intolerable for the population of the Federal District, as all public services have been paralyzed. . . .

Article 1: We will punish by death

1) Those who incite or propagate the work stoppage in those factories or businesses destined to provide public services; those who preside over meetings in which [such stoppages] are proposed, discussed, or approved; those who defend, sustain, subscribe to, or approve of them; those who attend such meetings or do not abandon them as soon as they learn of its objective; and those who attempt to enforce those resolutions once declared.

2) Those who take advantage of the work stoppage to destroy or damage the effects of the . . . businesses to which the operators desiring the work stoppage belong. . . .

---

9. Rosendo Salazar and José G. Escobedo, *Las pugnas de gleba, 1907–1922* (Mexico City: Editorial Avante, 1923), 205–7. Translated by Jürgen Buchenau.

3) Those who by threats or force prevent other people from carrying out the services provided by the workers in the companies against which a work stoppage has been declared.

Document 49. A Widow Gives an Account of Pancho Villa's Raid[10]

On March 9, 1916, a detachment of 500 men led by Pancho Villa attacked the town of Columbus, New Mexico, three miles north of the international border, in retaliation for U.S. president Woodrow Wilson's diplomatic recognition of the Carranza administration. Villa's men burned part of the city and killed some eighteen people, including eight soldiers and ten civilians. The raid angered the U.S. government and led to the sending of a "Punitive Expedition" into Chihuahua to find Villa. This first-person account gives some insight into that fateful day.

Testimony taken at El Paso, Tex., December 22, 1919, by Maj. Dan M. Jackson, in pursuance of an order of the subcommittee of the Committee on Foreign Relations of the Senate: Mrs. SUSAN A. MOORE, being duly sworn, testified as follows: By Maj. DAN M. JACKSON:

Q. Will you state your name to the stenographer?

A. Susan A Moore.

Q. You are the widow of John J. Moore?

A. Yes, sir.

Q. Where is your residence, Mrs. Moore?

A. I don't know just what you mean by that.

Q. Where do you live now?

A. At the Paso del Norte Hotel.

Q. Did you formerly live in Columbus, N. Mex.?

A. Yes, sir.

Q. For what length of time?

A. Five years.

Q. Do you recollect when you moved there?

A. 13th of December, 1912.

---

10. Testimony of Susan Moore, *Investigation of Mexican Affairs. Preliminary report and hearings of the Committee on Foreign Relations, United States Senate, pursuant to S. res. 106, directing the Committee on Foreign Relations to investigate the matter of outrages on citizens of the United States in Mexico* (Washington, D.C.: U.S. Government Printing Office, 1920), 1:956–62.

Q. Did you and Mr. Moore have any children?

A. No, sir.

Q. When did Mr. Moore die?

A. 9th of March, 1916.

Q. Will you kindly relate the circumstances attending his death. . . .

A. . . . . About 4.30 . . . in the morning I was awakened by some shots, and I laid still and listened; then directly I heard a number of shots, and I thought: "That is a machine gun," and in a little while I heard some more shots from this machine gun. I did not hear any noise around the house, so I hurriedly awoke Mr. Moore. I said to him: "Look, Villa has come in, and he is burning the town." He looked out. We were on the sleeping porch facing town. He said: "You are right; we had better get dressed." We hurriedly dressed in the dark so as not to attract any attention by making a light; then we went to the front of the house and listened and looked; not seeing or hearing anything, we drew the blinds within 6 inches of the bottom of the window so we could see out without being seen; then we went to the back of the house, and Mr. Moore stood at the pantry window, screening his body, and just put his head over so he could see, and I got up in front of the window, and he said to me: "If I were you I would not stand directly in front of the window; you might be hit by a stray shot, or someone might see you." I then went to the kitchen and sat down opposite the little kitchen table and watched the burning of the town through the kitchen window. From time to time I would go in where he was, and on one of those occasions I saw a dark object coming down the road. We watched it come to the front, and we decided it was a man on horseback. He was coming just as fast as he could come and did not even look toward the house. We watched him until he was well by, and then went back, and in a little while there were two more Mexicans on horseback come down, and they rode past.

I don't know why, but I watched the crowds come by, and then there were five and seven and nine, and as we watched these all pass I said to Mr. Moore: "Maybe we had better go to the mesquite bushes and hide." I says: "Some of these fellows may take a notion to come in." He says: "No; I don't think so; we have always been good to them, have harmed none of them, and carried them on our books; we have nothing to fear." We went back then to the back of the house, looked up the road, and I saw a large number coming down. We went to the front of the house. I counted 17. These stopped right in front of the house; a number of them got off their horses. There was a group that stopped beside the well and was looking at the top of the water. I again said to Mr. Moore: "I wonder if any of them will come in." He said: "No; I just think they want some water." I then looked out of the north window at Mrs. Walker's gate at the beginning of our land. There was a man on a white horse with a cape coat. He looked down the road to these men and motioned to them and then motioned to Mrs. Walker's house, and a number of them, about 10 I suppose, went over and began rapping on the door and looked in the windows.

I glanced up toward town, and I saw that the road was thick with them, and they were breaking from town just like a sandstorm; I guess the entire army was coming that way. It seemed to me like a quarter of a mile on either side of the house the road was filled with men. This man on the white horse; I looked back at him; then he motioned again toward our house, and there were 40 or 50 all around the gate, opened the gate and began pouring into the yard. Mr. Moore said to me: "We had better get in the dining room; we will have better protection." I hurriedly stepped to the dining room and then heard these men come up on the porch. They tried the door, which was locked, and then one of the leaders, who had been leaning on the fence previously looking at the water and house, he took the butt end of his gun and smashed in the west bedroom window.

When I heard the crash, I stepped where I could see, and I saw him just in the act of entering. Mr. Moore then opened the door. This leader came around, came in, and was followed by a number of men, just as many as could come into the house, and he said something to Mr. Moore, which I did not hear, and Mr. Moore said no. Then this man looked across Mr. Moore's right shoulder at me and said something else, which I did not hear. Mr. Moore again said no. Then this leader raised his gun and shot, and others raised their sabers, and a few began shooting and stabbing him. He made one rush for his gun, which stood right at the corner of the door, and they blocked his way, prevented him from getting it, and closed right around him. Just then I heard a number of steps on the back porch. The kitchen and dining-room doors were not locked, and a second later the dining-room door opened and the same Mexican who had been in the store the day before purchasing a pair of 32 overalls came in, with his gun just about on a level with my heart, and he said to me, "Gold, money." I told him in Spanish there was no money here; the money was in the bank in Columbus. I told him to take anything that he wanted only to leave us. He then saw a ring on my finger—my wedding ring. I started to put up my hand—show him my hands. He came around in front of me, grabbed hold of my hand, and started to take off this ring. The house was filled with Mexicans then from all sides, and one of his men stepped up and grabbed me by the right wrist and another one by the left. This, I knew, was very tight. I had my doubts whether they could get it off. I had tried it the day before with a silk string; and thought they would cut my finger off, so I tried to help them get off my ring. As I did, he noticed two rings on my right-hand, so he started to take these off. They were quite tight; I started to help him.

I looked out to see how Mr. Moore was getting along. He was about halfway across the porch and he was surrounded by these men, and the left side of his face was all bloody; there was blood all over him. I knew he was either dying or just at the point of dying—staggering. They got the two rings off then, and they started in on the other hand, and I looked out again and I saw Mr. Moore on the front steps. I knew then that he was absolutely killed. One man was taking off his rings, another man had his watch in his hand, and they were taking his clothes. I thought at that time that to save myself I would either have to outwit them or startle them, and the thought came to me to scream, and just as the wedding ring was leaving the last joint of my finger I screamed twice, and at the same time I looked toward Mr. Moore to attract their attention away from me to him, and their hold loosened on my wrist just a little. I gave one big jerk and jerked away from them. I pushed the dining-room door open, and I was shot at in the kitchen. There is a big hole there now about that big around. I ran across the porch, and as I stepped down I looked out toward the garage, and there were a number of Mexicans around the garage, and when they saw me they shouted, "Senora, senora, mira," and began laughing. The camp was about a mile from home, and I started to see if I could run there. I ran just as fast as I could. When I got within, say, about 100 yards—the bullets were flying very fast all the time—and I felt a sensation in my right leg. I knew I had been struck. I went ahead. In about 50 yards from there I fell. I knew I must not lay still, because it would mean certain death. So I got up again and went a little ways farther, and my right leg buckled up on me and I fell again. I got up again and went as well as I could, rather slowly. I had to kind of hop on one leg and carried my wounded leg. The fence was about—we had 20 acres inclosed—the fence, I think, was about 100 yards from where I was then. I thought if I could only get over the fence I would be so much safer.

I got up to the fence, and then went to get on the other side. I thought that would be impossible, because it was a rabbit-proof fence, buried about a foot in the ground; on the top was three barbed wires; I did not see how I could climb it; I knew I did not have strength enough to dig in with just my hands, but I tried, and I got over the fence without even catching any of my clothes; I fell right down side of the fence; I laid still a little while; the shots were coming just as fast as they could come; I looked back and saw that the house was almost surrounded by Mexicans in great numbers, and there were, I guess, 50 or more guns pointed in my direction, all shooting. There was a cluster of mesquite bushes about 25 feet from me; I thought if I could get over there and crawl under the mesquite bush and cover myself up with the dark coat they might think I was dead and stop shooting; I was unable to get up at all, so I dragged myself on my left side over to these bushes and got in around them as well as I could, and I had on a white waist and a gray skirt, and covered myself up so nobody would see that I was a woman, and turned my face in the other direction. I reached down; I felt that my clothes were all saturated with blood; it kind of sickened me. I thought, "Well, my time has come." I closed my eyes, and prayed, and was unconscious for the first time in my life. Later I was aroused by the sound of horses' hoofs, and I looked up and I saw the United States Cavalry; the Thirteenth Cavalry come across the corner of the 20 acres. I looked down at the house; I saw there was no one down there at all.

Document 50. Carranza and the Punitive Expedition[11]

The following document provides Carranza's response to the Punitive Expedition. Although Carranza did not mind the U.S. Army giving chase to Villa, he worried about the implications of the expedition for Mexican sovereignty and especially the possibility of a wider war.

TRANSLATED FROM *La Opinión*:

The First Chief of the Revolution issues an appeal to the people to be prepared for any emergency that may arise. I have not yet received any reply from the American Government and, from the reports sent in to the First Chief by the military commanders along the boundary line, I know that forces of the United States are being mobilized to cross into Mexican territory for the purpose, according to President Wilson's declarations published in the American press, to pursue and try to capture Villa and then deliver him up to the Mexican authorities, protesting that the expedition is nothing but punitive in its character and that the sovereignty of Mexico will be respected.

The Constitutionalist Government has suitably instructed the Confidential Agent of Mexico at Washington immediately to make the pertinent representation, for it will not admit, under any circumstances and whatever may be the reasons advanced and the explanation offered by the Government of the United States about the act it proposes to carry out, that the territory of Mexico be invaded for an instant and the dignity of the Republic outraged.

I am sure I am voicing the national sentiment and that the Mexican people will worthily perform their duty, no matter what sacrifices they may have to undergo in the defense of their rights and sovereignty.

If we should unfortunately be plunged into a war which the Government of the United States can never justify, the responsibility for its disastrous consequences will not lie with us but with those who serve as tools for the purposes of treacherous Mexicans who have labored within and without the country to bring about this result but upon whom the inexorable justice of the people will fall.

As this news might arouse the minds of our fellow-countrymen, I specially recommend that you exercise the utmost prudence and endeavor to maintain order while extending every guaranty to the North American citizens residing in your State.

With affectionate greetings,

V. Carranza

---

11. U.S. Department of State, *Papers Relating to the Foreign Relations of the United States, with the Address of the President to Congress, December 5, 1916*, doc. 589 (Washington, D.C.: U.S. Government Printing Office, 1925). Hereafter cited as *FRUS*, with date and document number.

Document 51. Calling Out U.S. Hypocrisy in the Punitive Expedition[12]

Two months and dozens of diplomatic notes later, the Carranza administration had grown even more alarmed. Not only had U.S. forces proceeded more deeply into Mexican territory than anticipated, but the chase had also rebuilt Villa's popular following, once again making him into a dangerous adversary.

Mexico, May 22, 1916

MR. SECRETARY: I am instructed by the First Chief of the Constitutionalist Army in charge of the Executive Power of the Union, to transmit to your excellency the following note:

1. The Mexican Government has just been informed that a body of American troops . . . has entered Mexican territory, and is at present . . . some 60 miles to the south of the frontier. The passage of these troops, again carried out without the consent of the Mexican Government, gravely endangers the harmony and good relations which should exist between the Government of the United States and that of Mexico. This Government is forced to consider this act as one violating the sovereignty of Mexico, and . . . urgently requests that the Government at Washington give the matter its most careful consideration with a view to define, once for all, the policy which it should pursue as regards the Mexican nation. . . .

2. As a result of the raiding of Columbus, New Mexico, by a band headed by Francisco Villa . . . the Mexican Government, sincerely lamenting the occurrence, and with a view to effectively protect the boundary, expressed the desire that the Governments of the United States and Mexico should reach an agreement providing for the pursuit of the raiders. The Mexican Government . . . made a concrete request that permission be given Mexican troops to pursue raiders into American territory under the same reciprocal conditions governing the passage of American troops to Mexican soil, in case such raids as that on Columbus should be repeated at any other point along the border.

As a result of this proposition . . . the Government of the United States . . . formed the opinion that the friendly attitude shown by the Mexican Government was sufficient to consider itself authorized to cross the frontier, and effectively, without awaiting a formal agreement in the matter, ordered a large body of American troops to enter Mexican territory in pursuit of Villa and his band.

3. The American Government . . . gave emphatic assurances to that of Mexico of its good faith, stating that the only object in crossing the boundary was to pursue and capture or destroy the band of Villa which had raided Columbus; that this act was not to be taken as signifying an invasion of our territory, nor an intention to

---

12. *FRUS*, 1916, doc. 714.

violate the sovereignty of Mexico; and that as soon as the object of the expedition had been practically accomplished, the American troops would be withdrawn from Mexican territory.

4. The Mexican Government was not informed that American troops had crossed the frontier until the 17th of March, when the fact was brought unofficially to its attention, through private sources from El Paso, that some American troops were already on Mexican territory. This Government then sent a note to that of the United States stating that inasmuch as the terms and conditions of the agreement to be formally made between the two countries for the passage of troops had not been decided upon, the American Government could not consider itself authorized to carry out the expedition. . . .

20. The Mexican Government considers it necessary to take advantage of this opportunity to request of the American Government a more categorical definition of its true intentions toward Mexico. . . .

28. The American Government justly desires the protection of its frontier. If the frontier were duly protected against incursions from Mexico there would be now no reason for the existing difficulties. The American Government understands perfectly the difficulties which exist in the protection of a boundary which possesses no natural advantages for its defense, and, notwithstanding its enormous resources, the American Government itself has been unable to afford an efficient protection along the more than 2,000 kilometers which it has to cover. . . .

30. The American Government incessantly demands from the Mexican Government an effective protection of its frontier, and yet the greater part of the bands which take the name of rebels against this Government are cared for and armed, if they are not also organized, on the American side under the tolerance of the authorities of the State of Texas, and, it may even be said, that of the Federal authorities of the United States. The leniency of the American authorities respecting these bands is such that in a majority of the cases the conspirators, who are well known, when they have been discovered and taken to prison, obtain their liberty by insignificant promises which allows them to continue in their efforts.

The Mexican emigrants who conspire and organize incursions from the United States side have now more facilities for doing harm than formerly, for they knew that any new difficulty between Mexico and the United States will prolong the stay of the American troops. They endeavor therefore to increase the possibilities of conflict and friction. . . .

The Mexican Government does not wish war with the United States, and if this should occur it will be as a consequence of the deliberate cause by the United States. To-day these measures of precaution by the American Government show that there is a desire to be prepared for such an emergency, or, what amounts to the same thing, they manifest an attitude of hostility on the part of the United States toward Mexico.

C. AGUILAR

Document 52. The Corrido of Pancho Villa[13]

This final document on the Columbus raid and the Punitive Expedition is a popular Villista corrido that celebrates the valor of their leader and ridicules the inability of the U.S. troops to locate and punish Pancho Villa. Some of the history told in this corrido does not match the timeline of the expedition, but the passion and emotion of the song display the deep conviction of the Mexicans rallying to Villa's cause.

In our Mexico, on February 23
Carranza let Americans cross over
20,000 men and 200 airplanes
Looking for Villa all over the country

The expeditionary searches began
And the airplanes took off into the sky
Going into several different directions
Looking for Villa in order to kill him

Francisco Villa placed on all the roads
A gravestone saying "here he is already"
The valiant, the valiant Pancho Villa
That's why they could never find him

When the neighbors came to Chihuahua
In the environs of the village of Parral
Pancho Villa set an ambush for them
And not a single one escaped

Oh what were the Americans thinking
Who wanted to conquer our soil
Although they have a large amount of cannons
The Mexicans have what it takes

Oh what were the Americans thinking
That fighting was a dance of *carquís*?
With their faces covered with shame
They had to return to their country

---

13. "The Ballad of Pancho Villa," Letras, accessed December 13, 2021, https://www.letras.com/cadetes-de-linares/corrido-de-pancho-villa/. Translated by Jürgen Buchenau.

I was born in the Sierra of Chihuahua
I'm the most faithful soldier in the battalion
Long live Villa, long live his Dorados
And long live the Revolution

Document 53. The Zimmermann Telegram[14]

This short document contributed to the decision of the Wilson administration to declare war on Germany and Austria in World War I. Authored by the German foreign minister, it assumed that Mexico might join an alliance against the United States in order to reclaim the land that it had lost in the U.S.-Mexican War (1846–1848). The kaiser especially aimed to take advantage of the nationalist indignation caused by the Punitive Expedition then still in the field. Written in cypher and decoded by British intelligence only with great difficulty, the telegram demonstrates a great power that had fundamentally misunderstood the situation and realities in revolutionary Mexico. But it also shows the extent to which a foreign power believed it could count on the nationalism of the Carranza government. Although Carranza was pro-German, he never considered such an alliance.

We intend to begin on the 1st of February unrestricted submarine warfare. We shall endeavor in spite of this to keep the United States of America neutral. In the event of this not succeeding, we make Mexico a proposal of alliance on the following basis: make war together, make peace together, generous financial support and an understanding on our part that Mexico is to reconquer the lost territory in Texas, New Mexico, and Arizona. The settlement in detail is left to you. You will inform the President of the above most secretly as soon as the outbreak of war with the United States of America is certain and add the suggestion that he should, on his own initiative, invite Japan to immediate adherence and at the same time mediate between Japan and ourselves. Please call the President's attention to the fact that the ruthless employment of our submarines now offers the prospect of compelling England in a few months to make peace.

Signed, ZIMMERMANN

---

14. Original cypher and transcription available at the National Archives website, https://www.archives.gov/education/lessons/zimmermann.

VI. The Constitutional Revolution, 1917–1920

This period featured the gradual strengthening of the Constitutionalist government, which included not only constant campaigns against its enemies but also a new constitution. This constitution broke new ground as the first such document in the entire world seeking to guarantee social rights and national control over natural resources (doc. 54).

The constitution was not immediately implemented and remained hotly contested, both inside and outside Mexico. In particular, classical nineteenth-century liberals, the Catholic Church, and the U.S. government fought its novel provisions (docs. 55–56). Despite their participation in the armed revolution, such as in the case of the famed soldaderas (doc. 58), women remained excluded from citizenship, at least at the national level. Nonetheless, the constitution did provide an immediate blueprint for a nationalist posture vis-à-vis foreign intervention of the type that had plagued Mexico since the infamous Pact of the Embassy in 1913, and Carranza proudly proclaimed to the nation that the principles of "the revolution" should be applied to international relations as a whole (doc. 57).

While the constitution promised to deliver land to campesinos, public education to all, and rights to workers, the government suppressed rebels who had inspired its social rights in the first place, including the Zapatistas. In April 1919, General Pablo González set a trap for Zapata, who was gunned down inside the hacienda of Chinameca. Thus ended the life of the one revolutionary protagonist most dedicated to the cause of land reform; at the same time, the heinous deed created one of the revolution's primary martyrs (docs. 59–60).

Meanwhile, a powerful new force arose: Obregón's faction from the northwestern state of Sonora. Widely considered the premier military leader, Álvaro Obregón had resigned his position in the Carranza administration in May 1917 in order to plot a presidential campaign. Along the way, a rumored extramarital affair troubled at least some of his allies (doc. 61). By June 1919, Obregón had emerged as the frontrunner in the 1920 presidential election, confronting Carranza with a program that focused on conciliation, even sacrificing some of the nationalist principles that Carranza had espoused (doc. 62). When Carranza attempted to block Obregón by imposing a candidate of his own, the Sonorans revolted (doc. 63) and overthrew the government in early May 1920. Carranza was assassinated during his escape from Mexico City. Although many historians regard this event—the last successful coup d'état in Mexican history to date—as the end of the revolution, warfare would continue for another nine years, and the work of implementing revolutionary reforms had just begun.

Document 54. The Constitution of 1917[1]

In September 1916, Carranza called for a Constitutional Congress to be held in Querétaro in December. Within two months, an assembly of elected delegates approved a sweeping new constitution that combined the political liberalism of its 1857 predecessor with striking provisions to safeguard social rights—the first constitution in the world to do so. The constitution also imposed strict limits on the Catholic Church and awarded economic patrimony to the nation rather than private owners. Although never implemented in its entirety, the 1917 Constitution structured political discourse for the remainder of the century.

Article 3. Instruction is free; that given in public institutions of learning shall be secular. Primary instruction, whether higher or lower, given in private institutions shall likewise be secular. No religious corporation nor minister of any religious creed shall establish or direct schools of primary instruction. Private primary schools may be established only subject to official supervision. Primary instruction in public institutions shall be gratuitous. . . .

Article 5. No one shall be compelled to render personal services without due compensation and without his full consent, excepting labor imposed as a penalty by judicial decree, which shall conform to the provisions of clauses I and II of Article 123. . . .

Article 10. The inhabitants of the United Mexican States are entitled to have arms of any kind in their possession for their protection and legitimate defense, excepting such as are expressly prohibited by law and such as the nation may reserve for the exclusive use of the army, navy and national guard; but they shall not bear such arms within inhabited places, except subject to the police regulations thereof. . . .

Article 27. The ownership of lands and waters comprised within the limits of the national territory is vested originally in the Nation, which has had, and has, the right to transmit title thereof to private persons, thereby constituting private property. Private property shall not be expropriated except for reasons of public utility and by means of indemnification.

The Nation shall have at all times the right to impose on private property such limitations as the public interest may demand as well as the right to regulate the development of natural resources, which are susceptible of appropriation, in order

---

1. U.S. Department of State, *Papers Relating to the Foreign Relations of the United States, with the Address of the President to Congress, December 4*, 1917, doc. 1144. (Washington, D.C.: U.S. Government Printing Office, 1926). Hereafter cited as *FRUS*, with date and document number.

to conserve them and equitably to distribute the public wealth. For this purpose, necessary measures shall be taken to divide large landed estates; to develop small landed holdings; to establish new centers of rural population with such lands and waters as may be indispensable to them; to encourage agriculture and to prevent the destruction of natural resources, and to protect property from damage detrimental to society. . . . Wherefore, all grants of lands made up to the present time under the decree of January 6, 1915, are confirmed. Private property acquired for the said purposes shall be considered as taken for public utility.

In the Nation is vested direct ownership of all minerals or substances which in veins, layers, masses or beds constitute deposits whose nature is different from the components of the land, such as minerals from which metals and metalloids used for industrial purposes are extracted; beds of precious stones, rock salt and salt lakes formed directly by marine waters, products derived from the decomposition of rocks, when their exploitation requires underground work; phosphates which may be used for fertilizers; solid mineral fuels; petroleum and all hydrocarbons—solid, liquid or gaseous. . . .

Legal capacity to acquire ownership of lands and waters of the nation shall be governed by the following provisions:

I.   Only Mexicans by birth or naturalization and Mexican companies have the right to acquire ownership in lands, waters and their appurtenances, or to obtain concessions to develop mines, waters or mineral fuels. . . . The Nation may grant the same right to foreigners, provided they agree before the Department of Foreign Affairs to be considered Mexicans in respect to such property, and accordingly not to invoke the protection of their Governments in respect to the same, under penalty, in case of breach, of forfeiture to the Nation of property so acquired. Within a zone of 100 kilometers from the frontiers, and 50 kilometers from the sea coast, no foreigner shall under any conditions acquire direct ownership of lands and waters.

II.   The religious institutions known as churches, irrespective of creed, shall in no case have legal capacity to acquire, hold or administer real property or loans made on such real property; all such real property or loans as may be at present held by the said religious institutions, either on their own behalf or through third parties, shall vest in the Nation, and any one shall have the right to denounce property so held. . . .

VI.   Properties held in common by co-owners, hamlets situated on private property, pueblos, tribal congregations and other settlements which, as a matter of fact or law, conserve their communal character, shall have legal capacity to enjoy in common the waters, woods and lands belonging to them, or which may have been or shall be restored to them according to the law of January 6, 1915, until such time as the manner of making the division of the lands shall be determined by law. . . .

Article 32. Mexicans shall be preferred under equal circumstances to foreigners for all kinds of concessions and for all public employments, offices or commissions, when citizenship is not indispensable. No foreigner shall serve in the army nor in the police corps nor in any other department of public safety during times of peace.

Only Mexicans by birth may belong to the national navy, or fill any office or commission therein. . . .

Article 33. Aliens . . . shall be entitled to the guaranties granted by Chapter I, Title I, of the present Constitution; but the Executive shall have the exclusive right to expel from the Republic forthwith, and without judicial process, any foreigner whose presence he may deem inexpedient.

No foreigner shall meddle in any way whatsoever in the political affairs of the country. . . .

Article 123. The Congress and the State Legislatures shall make laws relative to labor with due regard for the needs of each region of the Republic, and in conformity with the following principles, and these principles and laws shall govern the labor of skilled and unskilled workmen, employees, domestic servants and artisans, and in general every contract of labor.

I.   Eight hours shall be the maximum limit of a day's work.

II.   The maximum limit of night work shall be seven hours. Unhealthy and dangerous occupations are forbidden to all women and to children under sixteen years of age. . . .

III.   The maximum limit of a day's work for children over twelve and under sixteen years of age shall be six hours. The work of children under twelve years of age shall not be made the subject of a contract.

IV.   Every workman shall enjoy at least one day's rest for every six days' work.

V.   Women shall not perform any physical work requiring considerable physical effort during the three months immediately preceding parturition; during the month following parturition they shall necessarily enjoy a period of rest and shall receive their salaries or wages in full and retain their employment and the rights they may have acquired under their contracts. During the period of lactation they shall enjoy two extraordinary daily periods of rest of one-half hour each, in order to nurse their children.

VI.   The minimum wage to be received by a workman shall be that considered sufficient, according to the conditions prevailing in the respective region of the country, to satisfy the normal needs of the life of the workman, his education and his lawful pleasures, considering him as the head of the family. In all agricultural, commercial, manufacturing or mining enterprises the workmen shall have the right to participate in the profits in the manner fixed in Clause IX of this article.

VII.   The same compensation shall be paid for the same work, without regard to sex or nationality.

VIII. The minimum wage shall be exempt from attachment, set-off or discount.

IX. The determination of the minimum wage . . . shall be made by special commissions to be appointed in each municipality and to be subordinated to the Central Board of Conciliation to be established in each state.

X. All wages shall be paid in legal currency and shall not be paid in merchandise, orders, counters or any other representative token. . . .

XII. In every agricultural, industrial, mining or other class of work employers are bound to furnish their workmen comfortable and sanitary dwelling-places, for which they may charge rents not exceeding one-half of one per cent per month of the assessed value of the properties. They shall likewise establish schools, dispensaries and other services necessary to the community. . . .

XIV. Employers shall be liable for labor accidents and occupational diseases arising from work; therefore, employers shall pay the proper indemnity, according to whether death or merely temporary or permanent disability has ensued, in accordance with the provisions of law. This liability shall remain in force even though the employer contract for the work through an agent.

XV. Employers shall be bound to observe in the installation of their establishments all the provisions of law regarding hygiene and sanitation and to adopt adequate measures to prevent accidents due to the use of machinery, tools and working materials, as well as to organize work in such a manner as to assure the greatest guaranties possible for the health and lives of workmen compatible with the nature of the work, under penalties which the law shall determine.

XVI. Workmen and employers shall have the right to unite for the defense of their respective interests, by forming syndicates, unions, etc.

XVII. The law shall recognize the right of workmen and employers to strike and to lockout.

XVIII. Strikes shall be lawful when by the employment of peaceful means they shall aim to bring about a balance between the various factors of production, and to harmonize the rights of capital and labor. . . .

XIX. Lockouts shall only be lawful when the excess of production shall render it necessary to shut down in order to maintain prices reasonably above the cost of production, subject to the approval of the Board of Conciliation and Arbitration.

XX. Differences or disputes between capital and labor shall be submitted for settlement to a board of conciliation and arbitration to consist of an equal number of representatives of the workmen and of the employers and of one representative of the Government. . . .

Document 55. Three Mexican Perspectives on the Constitution[2]

The 1917 Constitution elicited mixed reactions in Mexico. Some, like the Porfirian intellectual Andrés Molina Enríquez, appreciated the independence that the Constituyente had shown with regard to Carranza's mandates. Constituyente member Luis Manuel Rojas, a former member of the Chamber of Deputies under Francisco I. Madero, believed that the new document had gone too far but applauded Carranza's followers. Finally, Madero's foreign minister, Manuel Calero, considered the new constitution null and void because it had not been approved by a duly elected Congress.

Andrés Molina Enríquez

The project of the First Chief had been made expressly in order to demonstrate his own lack of resolve to fulfill the promises of the revolution made in the decree of December 12, 1914:[3] nothing about social reforms; nothing about important purposes; . . . Deputies were sent the printed project with the clear and precise insinuation to approve it as it was. . . .

Although the majority of the chosen ones were people without intellectual preparation, they instinctively and decisively allied with the radicals and against Carranza, his group, and his project, which—as he had said—was a product of his experience and patriotism. Therefore, the Congress split between revolutionaries and Carrancistas on the very first day, and the group surrounding Carranza did not amount to even 30 percent. The radical revolutionaries—the majority—coalesced around the figure of General Alvaro Obregón. . . .

. . . In Señor Carranza's mind . . . lay a deep-rooted idea that the discussion of a project to reform the Constitution of 1857 was the issue at hand. But things in Querétaro did not go according to the dictator's liking. Beginning with the first ordinary session, Carranza's leaders understood that they did not control the Convention, and for the discussion of article 3, they wanted none other than the First Chief, with his ostentatious presence, to force the vote in favor of the projected article. The astonishing defeat they suffered made them return to reality.

---

2. Miguel León Portilla, Ernesto de la Torre, Moisés González Navarro, and Stanley Ross, eds., *Historia Documental de México* (Mexico City: UNAM, 1964) 2:481–84. Translated by Jürgen Buchenau.

3. On December 12, 1914 (Guadalupe Day), Carranza issued additions to his Plan of Guadalupe promising to implement social reforms. These reforms included land reform and defending the rights of labor, among many others. The announcement preceded the Law of January 6, 1915, excerpted in Section IV.

Luis Manuel Rojas

I sincerely believe in the singular merit of the Political Constitution of the United Mexican States, after its notable transformation in Querétaro, without it being inferred that I consider it a perfect work. On the contrary, I plainly confess that it has some visible blemishes, due to exaggerations or defects in important issues.

It was very fortunate that the First Chief, Don Venustiano Carranza, had displayed the very good sense to have drafted a calmly and well thought out general project of reforms to the Constitution of 1857 beforehand, which he then submitted to the free discussion of the entire assembly. It is clear that this circumstance explains the whole secret or reason for the success achieved in the Constituent Assembly. By the prestige and great authority of Señor Carranza, the general foundation and main ideas contained in the primitive project could not but prevail, after the most passionate debates. On the other hand, without question, the errors correspond to the modifications introduced during the discussion—errors entirely explicable and excusable by way of the inexperience, fervor and enthusiasm of a good number of the deputies who came to the convention fresh from the heat of the recent struggle and eager to break with the past without consideration or scruples. They were eager to correct the inveterate vices of Mexican society and to favor the popular classes of the country.

Among the most characteristic topics of the new "fundamental law," . . . the so-called labor and agrarian questions stand out. . . . Surely the deputies to the Constituent Assembly of Querétaro made their mistakes in these matters with the best of intention, and perhaps these mistakes will accrue to the detriment of the same popular classes that they tried to favor. . . . Similarly, the freedom of instruction . . . and, in general, issues relating to the clergy and the Catholic Church, suffered the influence of the passionate concerns . . . manifested in the peoples of Latin civilization in their great moments of convulsions. . . .

Manuel Calero

Parading material and moral strength afforded by the protection of the U.S. government, Carranza is determined to give the country a new constitution. For this project, he has counted on the servility of a part of the revolutionary military element . . . and on the abomination of some corrupt and hungry politicians. . . .

We solemnly protest against this nameless fraud, as well as against this attack on the law and the public liberties in our country. Our attitude is sincere because it is patriotic. Exiled, like many others, because of the criminal stubbornness of Carranza, we are not . . . united in a political cause; . . . but we are all liberals, determined to prevent the glorious work of the historic Mexican Liberal Party from perishing. We agree on the following propositions:

That the constitution of 1857 is the code of Mexican institutions that cannot be subverted without subverting those same institutions;

That any reform or addition to the constitution must be made by the procedures that it establishes, that is to say, by means of the cooperation of the two Chambers of the Congress of the Union with the state Legislature;

That the meeting of a constituent congress such as the one assembled in Quere-taro is an illegal act; therefore, the work of said congress is null and void;

That a government organized by virtue of a spurious constitution will be a usurper government, and the decrees that it approves as well as the commitments that it contracts in the form of loans, international agreements, etc., will be null and void and not binding on the Mexican people; . . .

That, consequently, it is not only a right of the people, but an obligation for every citizen . . . to procure the reestablishment of the Constitution of 1857 and to com-bat any Mexican government that is not organized under the terms by virtue of [that] constitution.

Document 56. The U.S. Government and the Constitution[4]

The Woodrow Wilson administration wasted no time registering its opposition to the new constitution, particularly the provisions in Article 27 regulating foreign-owned property. Secretary of State Robert Lansing also reminded the Carranza administration of its obligations to pay its debts.

Secretary of State Robert Lansing to Ambassador Henry P. Fletcher

DEPARTMENT OF STATE, *Washington, June 6, 1917—5 p.m.*

. . . You are instructed to bring the following to the immediate attention of Gen-eral Carranza:

This Government is reluctant to believe that it is the intention of the Mexican Government to depart from the assurances given by the Minister for Foreign Affairs who stated to the American Ambassador at an interview on February 20 last, in substance, that the effect of the new Constitution would be in no way prejudicial to existing property rights, calling attention at the same time to an article of the new Constitution which provides that no laws may be made retroactive and again at an interview on February 26, that it was not the intention of the Mexican Government to confiscate American property. Inconsequence [*sic*] of these assurances, and in view of the international responsibilities assumed by the Mexican Government toward other Governments in seeking their recognition on the basis of equality of rights, the Government of the United States has noted with grave concern evidences

---

4. *FRUS*, 1917, docs. 1269 and 1270.

of an intention on the part of the Mexican Government to give certain provisions of the Constitution adopted by the Constituent Assembly in January last, retroactive application to the rights of foreign owners of property in Mexico, to the extent of destroying or impairing those rights. This amounts to confiscation, and to this the Government of the United States cannot consent because, as the Mexican Government has already been informed by the Government of the United States, it cannot acquiesce in the direct or indirect confiscation of American owned properties or discrimination against American citizens with reference to their legally acquired rights and interests in Mexico.

In this connection attention is directed to the petroleum export tax decree of April 13 and supplemental regulations which appear to contemplate the confiscation of American rights by retroactive legislation, impairing contractual obligations and, inasmuch as action thereunder is required prior to the 10th instant, they call for immediate consideration.

The Government of the United States invites an expression of the views of the Mexican Government on the principles underlying this subject involving national interests of grave importance which cannot be adequately represented by the private property owners concerned but require direct discussion between the two Governments. Pending the consideration of this matter, the Government of the United States earnestly desires that the enforcement against American interests of any confiscatory or discriminatory enactments be suspended.

Fletcher to Lansing

AMERICAN EMBASSY, *Mexico City, June 7, 1917—6 p.m.*

Inasmuch as the President is sick in bed and your telegraphic instruction No. 234 of June 6, 4 p.m. cannot be complied with immediately I respectfully request reconsideration of that portion of it relating to petroleum taxes. I fear that representations along these lines now will prove fruitless and possibly harmful and may result in a refusal to discuss these questions on the usual Mexican ground that it is an interference in a purely domestic matter, thus precipitating a situation which I think we should avoid at this time. The House of Deputies has just passed a resolution calling on the President to propose a petroleum law based on Article 27 of the new Constitution and it was charged in the debate that the foreign petroleum companies are endeavoring by bribe to delay this legislation.

This Government is in a difficult position . . . [with] its deficit of about seventy million pesos, not counting prerevolutionary debts, at the rate of 5 million pesos monthly without present prospect of securing a loan. Money must be raised and petroleum and mining taxation bearing largely upon foreigners seems popular perhaps because of Mexico's inability to secure foreign financial assistance.

Document 57. The Carranza Doctrine[5]

Devoted to the defense of Mexico's national sovereignty, Carranza's foreign policy stands out as the area in which the president most faithfully implemented the aspirations of the Constitution of 1917. While his earlier pronouncements regarding the Punitive Expedition and the authority of Mexico to make its own laws defended national interests bilaterally, with regard to the United States, in September 1918, Carranza decided to use the annual state-of-the-nation address to Congress to lay out the principles of the diplomacy of the Mexican Revolution more broadly. Just a few months before the end of World War I afforded an opportunity to restructure the world order, Carranza made a strong argument for the rights of developing nations vis-à-vis the designs of foreign investors and the Great Power governments that defended the interests of those investors.

The Principles of Mexico's International Policy

Mexico's international policy has been characterized by the firmness in the development of the principles that sustain it. The results we have obtained are satisfactory enough for the Executive . . . during the year I report. The desire for the same practices as those adopted by Mexico to be followed by all countries and laws, but in particular Latin America, whose specific phenomena are the same as ours, have given such principles a most significant doctrinal character. That is especially true if one considers the fact that they were formulated by the . . . First Chief of the Constitutionalist Army, in charge of the Executive Power of the Union, in the middle of the revolutionary struggle. They had the object of showing the whole world her purposes and the yearnings for universal peace and Latin American fellowship. The guiding ideas of the international policy are few, clear, and simple. They limit themselves to proclaiming:

—That all countries are equal and need to respect each other's institutions, laws, and sovereignty mutually and scrupulously.

—That no country should intervene in any form and for any reason in the internal affairs of others. All [nations] must submit strictly and without exceptions to the universal principle of non-intervention.

—No person may claim a better situation than that of the citizens of the country where he will establish himself, nor make his status as a foreigner into a title of protection and privilege.

—Nationals and foreigners must be equal before the sovereignty of the country in which they find themselves; and finally,

---

5. "Don Venustiano Carranza, al abrir el Congreso sus sesiones ordinarias, el 1° de septiembre de 1918," in Luis González y González, *Los presidentes de México ante la nación* (Mexico City: Cámara de Diputados, 1966), 3:250–51. Translated by Jürgen Buchenau.

—That so far as possible, laws need to be uniform and equal without making distinctions based on nationality, except with regard to the exercise of sovereignty.

This set of principles profoundly modifies the current concept of diplomacy. [Diplomacy] may not serve to protect the interests of individuals, nor to put at their service the force and the majesty of a nation. Neither should it serve to exercise pressure over the governments of weak countries in order to obtain the modifications of laws that are not convenient to subjects of powerful countries.

Diplomacy needs to safeguard the general interests of civilization as well as the establishment of universal fellowship. The guiding ideas of policy in international affairs are about to be modified because they have proven ineffective in preventing international wars and in putting an end to the global confrontation in short order. Mexico has tried to contribute to the reform of the old principles and has sustained on various occasions its readiness to render its good offices for any agreement. Today, she hopes that the end of the war will be the beginning of a new era for humanity. A great many causes of wars and conflicts between the peoples will disappear the day in which the interests of individuals will no longer be a driving force for international politics.

To sum up, equality, mutual respect for institutions and laws, and the firm resolve not to ever intervene in the internal affairs of other nations for any reason whatsoever have been the fundamental principles of the international policy that the Executive under my charge has pursued. At the same time, Mexico has endeavored to obtain a treatment equal to the one it is granting; that is, consideration as a sovereign nation just like all other countries; that her laws and institutions be respected; and that no one interfere with her internal affairs in any way.

Document 58. The Story of a Soldadera[6]

Born María Francisca Luna in 1900, Nellie Campobello took her name after her stepfather, Dr. Ernest S. Campbell, whom her mother married after her husband's death during the 1914 Battle of Ojinaga. Despite her young age, Campobello became a trusted advisor for Villa and remained one of his staunchest defenders after his defeat. At once fiction and autobiographical, her first novel, Cartucho, is the only book-length depiction of the revolution authored by a woman. The novel consists of multiple vignettes set in the state of Chihuahua, and specifically the city of Parral, where the author lived in the 1910s. It is difficult to date many of the vignettes (not all of them are based on the author's own experience), but most of them appear to have reflected the years following the

---

6. Nellie Campobello, *Cartucho and My Mother's Hands*, trans. Doris Meyer and Irene Matthews (Austin: University of Texas Press, 1988), 21–22.

VI. The Constitutional Revolution, 1917–1920

Constitutionalist victory in 1915, when violence and rebellion continued until the federal government signed a peace agreement with Villa in 1920. The following episode describes a soldadera in the Villista army.

Nacha Ceniceros

A large Villista encampment at station X near Chihuahua. All was quiet and Nacha was crying. She was in love with a young colonel from Durango by the name of Gallardo. Nacha was a *coronela* who carried a pistol and wore braids. She had been crying after an old woman gave her advice. She went to her tent where she was busily cleaning her pistol when, all of a sudden, it went off.

In the next tent was Gallardo, sitting at a table and talking to a woman. The bullet that escaped from Nacha's gun struck Gallardo in the head and he fell dead.

"Gallardito has been killed, General."

Shocked, Villa replied, "Execute the man who did it."

"It was a woman, General."

"Execute her."

"Nacha Ceniceros."

"Execute her."

She wept for her lover, put her arms over her head, with her black braids hanging down, and met the firing squad's volley.

She made a handsome figure, unforgettable for everyone who saw the execution. Today there is an anthill where they say she was buried.

This was the version that was told for many years in the North of Mexico. The truth came out some time later. Nacha Ceniceros was still alive. She had gone back to her home in Catarinas, undoubtedly disillusioned by the attitude of those few who tried to divide among themselves the triumphs of the majority.

Nacha Ceniceros tamed ponies and rode horses better than many men. She was what's called a country girl, but in the mountain style. With her incredible skill, she could do anything a man could with his masculine strength. She joined the revolution because Porfirio Díaz's henchmen had assassinated her father. If she had wanted to, she could have married one of the most prominent Villista generals. She could have been one of the most famous women of the revolution. But Nacha Ceniceros returned quietly to her ravaged home and began to rebuild the wall and fill in the openings through which thousands of bullets had been fired against the murderous Carrancistas.

The curtain of lies against General Villa, spread by organized groups of slanderers and propagators of the black legend, will fall, just as will the bronze statues that have been erected with their contributions. Now I say—and I say it with the voice of someone who has known how to unravel lies, *Viva Nacha Ceniceros, Coronela de la revolución!*

Document 59. The Assassination of Emiliano Zapata[7]

On April 10, 1919, troops loyal to the federal government that had feigned their defection assassinated Zapata in the hacienda of Chinameca, Morelos. The following document is the best account of a heinous act of treachery that accomplished what nine years of military campaigns had not been able to do: the defeat of Mexico's beloved champion of land reform. This assassination not only made Zapata a martyr, but it also sullied the reputation of Carranza's primary general, Pablo González, who was widely held responsible for this plot.

Official Report
Liberating Army, Private Secretary of the General in Chief.
To General Gildardo Magaña, General Headquarters.

I am profoundly sorry to inform you that today, around half past one, General in Chief Emiliano Zapata was assassinated by troops of the so-called Colonel Jesús M. Guajardo, who carried out the cowardly act in San Juan Chinameca with complete premeditation, treachery, and opportunism. So that you are duly informed of the tragic event, I will relate the following details: As was communicated to you in a timely manner, we learned of deep antagonisms between Pablo González and Jesús Guajardo. General Zapata wrote to the latter inviting him to join the revolutionary movement. Guajardo answered this letter saying that he was inclined to collaborate with the chief "so long as he gave guarantees to him and to his soldiers." By the same post that brought this letter, the chief answered Guajardo, offering him every form of security and congratulating him for his attitude, "since he judged him to be a man of his word and a gentleman and [Zapata] was confident that he [Guajardo] would fulfill his promises to the letter." . . . On the second of this month the General in Chief, to definitively settle the matter, ordered Colonel Feliciano Palacios to go to Guajardo's headquarters in San Juan Chinameca. Palacios remained with Guajardo until yesterday at four in the morning, at which time he joined us, telling us that Guajardo had gone to Jonacatepec.

Here I must mention something that caused the General in Chief to lose confidence in Guajardo's "sincerity." So many stories were circulating about Guajardo's negotiation of his surrender to General Zapata, that people from some of the villages we visited asked the General in Chief to punish the followers of Victoriano Bárcenas—who at the time was under Guajardo's orders—for pillage, rape, murder and robbery that they committed in those villages. In view of this just petition, General Zapata wrote to Guajardo, by way of Palacios, asking him

---

7. Isidro Fabela, ed., *Documentos históricos de la Revolución Mexicana: Emiliano Zapata y el Plan de Ayala y su política agraria* (Mexico City: Fondo de Cultura Económica, 1970), 21:313–16. Translated by Timothy J. Henderson.

to investigate and punish the guilty. Guajardo took out 59 men who were under the command of "General" Margarito Ocampo and "Colonel" Guillermo López and ordered all of them shot by a firing squad in a place called "Mancornadero." This happened yesterday. Guajardo was in Jonacatepec, a place he said had been taken by the enemy. Upon learning this, we went to the Pastor Station, and from there, Palacios, on orders from the chief, wrote to Guajardo saying we would meet him in Tepalcingo. General Zapata was headed there with only thirty men, and he advised Guajardo to do the same. The chief ordered his people to withdraw, and with thirty men we set off for Tepalcingo, where Guajardo awaited us. He appeared at about four in the afternoon, not with thirty soldiers, but with 600 cavalrymen and a machine gun. When the column arrived in Tepalcingo, we went to meet him. There we saw for the first time the man who, the following day, would assassinate our General in Chief, a noble soul who received Guajardo with open arms: "My Colonel Guajardo, I greet you sincerely," he said, smiling. At 10 p.m. we left Tepalcingo, heading toward Chinameca, where Guajardo arrived with his column, while we spent the night in "Agua de los Patos." Around eight in the morning we went to Chinameca. Once there, the chief ordered that his people (150 men who had joined us in Tepalcingo) gather in the town square while he, Guajardo, Generals Castrejón, Casales y Camaño, Colonel Palacios, and myself discussed plans for the future campaign. A few moments later, rumors began to circulate that the enemy was approaching. The chief ordered that Colonel José Rodríguez (a member of his escort) take his people and explore around Santa Rita, and this order was followed. Then Guajardo said to the chief: "It is suitable, my General, that you go to 'La Piedra Encimada'; I will go by the plain." The chief approved this, and with thirty men we left for the place indicated. We had already left when Guajardo returned and said: "My General, you decide. Shall I go with the infantry or with the cavalry?" "The plain has many fences; go with the infantry," replied General Zapata, and we left. In "Piedra Encimada," we surveyed the field and, seeing no enemy movement, we returned to Chinameca. It was about half past noon. The chief had sent Colonel Palacios to talk with Guajardo, who was supposed to deliver five thousand cartridges, and, upon arriving at Chinameca, immediately asked for him. Then Captain Ignacio Castillo appeared along with a sergeant and, in Guajardo's name, he invited the chief to enter the interior of the hacienda, where Guajardo was with Palacios "dealing with the ammunition issue." We chatted with Castillo for about half an hour, and after that, the invitation was repeated and the chief accepted: "Let's go see the Colonel; no more than ten men shall accompany me," he ordered. And, mounting his horse—a sorrel that Guajardo had given him the day before—he went to the gate of the hacienda. On his orders, ten men followed, while the rest of us, feeling very confident, lounged in the shade of the trees with our carbines sheathed. The bugle sounded the call of honor, the final note fading just as the General in Chief passed under the lintel of the gate. Then, without giving us time to so much as grab our pistols, in a manner so treacherous, so cowardly, so villainous, they discharged their rifles two times point blank, and our General Zapata fell, never to rise again. His faithful assistant, Agustín Cortés, died at the same time. Palacios must also have been killed inside the hacienda. The shock was terrible. The soldiers of the traitor Guajardo, parapeted in the heights, on the plain, in the barranca, everywhere (nearly a thousand of them) shot at us with their rifles. Soon resistance was futile; on the one side were a handful of men distraught at the loss of their chief, and on the other a thousand enemies who took advantage of our natural bewilderment to beat us fiercely. . . . Thus was the tragedy. Thus Guajardo repaid the nobility of our General in Chief with treachery. Thus died Emiliano Zapata, thus died the brave ones, the men of honor, who confronted an enemy that resorted to treason and crime. . . . I present my deep and sincere condolences for the death of our General in Chief, and I repeat, my General, the assurance of my subordination and respect. Reform, Liberty, Justice and Law.

Revolutionary encampment in "Salsas," State of Morelos, 10 April 1919.

The private secretary,
Major Salvador Reyes Avilés

Document 60. Corrido on the Death of Emiliano Zapata[8]

Once again, popular lore weighed in with its own interpretation. The following corrido reveals Zapata's great grassroots appeal and also the messianic sense that he would return some day to redeem his cause.

Listen, gentlemen, hear the corrido
Of a sad turn of events
For in Chinameca, they killed in cold blood,
Zapata, the great insurgent
The date of April 19
You will remain with campesinos
Like a stain on our history
Bells of Villa Ayala,
Why do you ring so mournfully?
It's because Zapata has been slain
And Zapata was a brave man

---

8. "Ballad of the Death of Zapata," Letras, accessed March 1, 2021, https://www.letras.mus.br/corridos-mexicanos/corrido-de-la-muerte-de-zapata/. Translated by Jürgen Buchenau.

The great Emiliano loved the poor
He wanted to set them free
That is why all the men from all the small towns
Joined him in his fight
From Cuautla to Amecameca
Matamoros and the Ajusco
Men submitted by old Don Porfirio
Would ride with him
Campesinos dressed as mourners
From the meadows of Morelos
If they ask you for Zapata
Tell them he's gone to heaven

One day Zapata told Don Pancho Madero
When he was already President
If you do not give us the lands
The Indians will return to fighting again
He confronted Señor Madero
Then Huerta and Carranza
When they tried to turn their backs
On the Plan of Ayala
Run, run, little rabbit
Tell the news to your brothers
They killed Señor Zapata
He was on our side

Don Pablo González ordered Guajardo
To feign his surrender
And to shoot Chief Zapata
Upon arrival at his camp
Guajardo said to Zapata:
I will surrender to you with my troops
Meet me there in Chinameca
And we will have a drink

Little turbulent stream
What did the carnation say?
It said that the chief still lives on
And that Zapata will return

Emiliano embraced the felon Guajardo
To prove his friendship
The poor man did not foresee that
The Praetorian would sacrifice him
He marched calmly ahead of his troops
To the rendezvous in the hacienda
The traitors shot him in the back
From just a few feet away

Little morning nightingale
Flying above the sovereign hills
Look at the shameless way
Emiliano was finished off

Down from his horse fell Chief Zapata
And so did his assistants
And so in Chinameca
A handful of brave men lost their lives
Gentlemen, I bid you goodbye
For it is not further news
That Zapata died a hero
For giving land and liberty
From the side of a roadway
I took a white lily
To the tomb of Zapata
I brought it as an offering

Little turbulent stream
What did the carnation say?
It said that the chief still lives on
And that Zapata will return

Document 61. Public and Private
Morality in a Revolutionary General[9]

The revolution brought a new military elite to the fore, personified by General Obregón, the leader of the Sonoran faction whose armies helped turn the tide in favor of the Constitutionalists. Although Obregón did not hold any official position following his resignation as secretary of war, he was widely considered the most powerful man in Mexico. As Obregón prepared to run for president, observers reminded him of the need for presidential behavior, which did not include extramarital affairs, at least of the type that were public knowledge. Authored by a close associate of Obregón who would go on to become one of the architects of the ruling party, this document yields some insights into the code of honor surrounding the revolutionary generals.

Letter from Luis L. León to Alvaro Obregón

My dear and good friend, I have been able to ascertain this precisely because of my constant attention to you. You are going through a crisis in your private life at this moment, of which you are surely the one who is least able to understand the consequences. It is on this occasion that a true friend, whose opinion must be beyond reproach for you, comes to call your attention with all affection and sincerity. I am not going to discuss either the virtues or the personal attractions of the woman who has led your morals astray, but whatever these may be, they may be equally within your reach by following the path demanded of you by your own conscience and your honor as a married man. If you have made a mistake in your choice, and neither your wife nor your daughter can give you the happiness to which you are entitled, make her see it in the open, requesting that she break, before the law and society, the moral and legal bond that unites the two of you, and thus regain your freedom. If she is wicked and does not fulfill the delicate mission a wife needs to fulfill, denounce her before the Law and recover your freedom, but not to use it in debauchery, but so that you can unite your destinies to the woman who is most likely to make you happy.

If the woman whom you took as your wife—committed to her honor and your faith before society and before the Law—has given no reason for receiving the offense you have committed against her, your conscience and your honor as a man demand that you repair this failure, using the energies that you have applied to all the other acts of your life; putting an end to the disastrous deviation that is

9. León to Obregón, private letter, no date (1918 or 1919), Fideicomiso Archivos Plutarco Elías Calles y Fernando Torreblanca, Archivo Fernando Torreblanca, Fondo Álvaro Obregón, serie 050100, expediente 32, inventario 4828 "León, Luis L. (Ing.)." Translated by Jürgen Buchenau.

controlling your life; and returning to the side of that woman who is yours, who is the mother of your daughter, and to whom you owe your love and respect.

It defies sense, my good friend, that a man governed in his public life by an austere morality, which gives him all the moral strength required to retain the esteem and respect of his own and that of strangers, is governed by a diametrically opposite morality in his private life.

If we were to accept the fact that men who occupy public positions can detach their official from their private personality, being governed by different morals, we would reach the painful conclusion that they personally do not practice any morals, and that the morals they use in public life only pose for the apparent honor of the position, and that when they divest themselves of the official position, they automatically divest themselves of the morals with which they served that position.

Morality in men cannot be transitory. To deserve such a name, it needs to be part of personal nature and cannot be either relative or variant; it must . . . be applied equally in all the acts of our life, whether public or private.

I know I have gone on too long, but my conscience would not be clear if I did not present my points of view to you as clearly as my concepts allow; first, because of the great affection you have always so justly inspired in me, and second, to protect my conscience from any reproach I might be subjected to, if I do not act as I am doing at present.

Receive an affectionate embrace and I bid you farewell as always. Your friend who loves you very much.

Luis L. León

Document 62. Obregón Runs for President[10]

In June 1919, Obregón announced his candidacy in the elections scheduled for July 1920. According to his manifesto, Obregón announced his candidacy only out of a sense of duty. In fact, few Mexicans were fooled by what we might call a "Cincinnatus act," the self-fashioning of Obregón as a farmer who only reluctantly sought higher office. It also attacked Carranza's policy of economic nationalism and assured Mexican proprietors and U.S. investors that he would respect their privileges.

In recent months, even this hideout, where I wanted to consecrate my life to the activity of work and the tranquility of the home, has felt somewhat like the

---

10. Álvaro Obregón, *Manifiesto a la Nación lanzado por el C. Álvaro Obregón* (Hermosillo: Imprenta Moderna, 1919), 1–15. Translated by Jürgen Buchenau.

undertow that reaches the beaches when the depths of the seas are agitated. At first, this [sensation] seemed slight and unimportant, but it has grown until it has become a serious concern on my part in recent weeks.

In the beginning, there were a few letters, mainly from friends of mine, that suggested that I should abandon my withdrawal and prepare myself to enter the coming political contest. While I am writing this, an innumerable quantity of pleas are reaching me from friends, unknown persons, workers' groups, representatives of political groups, etc., etc. Finally, some political parties . . . have already launched my candidacy for the Presidency of the Republic in the next constitutional period.

The communications that I receive in this respect vary greatly in style. Some come in a tone of supplication, others in an imperative tone, some assigning me historical responsibilities if I declare my abstention from the contest, etc. They . . . speak to me in the name of the homeland, of democracy, of the group to which the leaders belong, in the name of the Revolution, etc.

The Path of Duty

. . . It has only been two years since constitutional order was restored to the nation, restoring all the rights to us taken away by usurpation. I wanted to be one of the first to enjoy them, since they signify the most legitimate triumph won with the sacrifice of all our comrades who died in the struggle, and I renounced in the most spontaneous manner the soldier's harness to which I had to submit myself for several years by duty's command, when it asked us to recover by armed force what with had been taken from us with arms in hand, in those memorable Ten Tragic Days. . . .

I have barely lived two years in the most legitimate well-being, and I have to open a new chapter of anxiety, responsibilities and dangers, so as not to break the ties that bind me to duty. . . .

I present myself, then, on the political stage to say to the nation by means of this manifesto:

I am a candidate for the Presidency of the Republic in the next electoral campaign. . . .

I am not going to dwell on formulating a program full of mirages that would serve as a call to action. I am convinced that the country no longer wants programs, which in the end turn out to be rhymed prose. The people want facts and yearn to find a successor to the current Chief Magistrate of the Nation who inspires confidence. My background is the only thing that should serve as a basis for those who believe it is necessary to support me and those who believe it is appropriate to fight me; and that background is the best guarantee that my rule will mean the most absolute respect for the law, to whose prerogatives all the inhabitants of the Republic will be entitled, regardless of their political or religious creed. . . .

The Economic Problem

The favorable resolution of this problem, which is of such great significance, cannot be achieved on the basis of an increase in taxes, but only by reducing budget expenditures; but such will not be practicable before the pacification of the country.

In turn, pacification will demand, as a basic condition, the favorable resolution of the two problems that I have previously pointed out as fundamental. . . .

The formulation of foreign policy will start from the following bases:

A. The inviolability of our sovereignty as an autonomous people.

B. Absolute respect for the sovereignty and institutions of the other countries that populate the earth.

C. Complete recognition of all rights that foreigners have legitimately acquired in our country, with absolute adherence to our laws.

D. Award all kinds of facilities to the capital that wants to invest in our country, for the development and promotion of its natural wealth, always seeking the most practical and equitable way of reconciling the advantages to be derived by capital, workers and the treasury.

E. See to it that all foreigners residing in Mexico may enjoy all the guarantees and prerogatives that our laws grant them, in the broadest manner.

F. An open and sincere tendency to reinforce and strengthen our international relations based upon the above-mentioned principles.

Nogales, Sonora, June 1, 1919

Document 63. The Plan of Agua Prieta[11]

In April 1920, a conflict between Carranza and the state government of Sonora precipitated the last violent change of government in Mexico to date. Over the past year, Carranza had made it clear that he would not support Obregón's candidacy for the presidency and had handpicked the civilian Ignacio Bonillas to succeed him. When Carranza dispatched troops to Sonora to intimidate Governor Adolfo de la Huerta, a staunch Obregón ally, the Sonoran alliance erupted in revolt, beginning with the manifesto below. A few weeks later, the rebels entered Mexico City, and Carranza was assassinated en route to Veracruz.

WHEREAS:

I. The National Sovereignty rests essentially and originally in the people; all Public Power emanates from the people and is instituted for its benefit; and the power

---

11. *FRUS*, 1920, vol. 3, doc. 165.

of public officials is only a partial delegation of the popular sovereignty, made by the same people.

II. The present President of the Republic, Venustiano Carranza, has constituted himself the leader of a political party and, pursuing the triumph of that party, has systematically made a mockery of the popular vote, has suspended, in fact, individual guarantees and has made repeated attempts against the sovereignty of the States thus radically weakening the political organization of the Republic.

III. These acts and this procedure, openly exposed, constitute, at the same time, flagrant violations of our Supreme Law, grave crimes of a common order and absolute betrayal of the fundamental aspirations of the Constitutionalist Revolution.

IV. All the peaceful means to direct the action of the aforementioned First Chief of the Federation into constitutional channels, having been exhausted without the achievement of such an end, the moment has arrived when the Mexican people resumes all its sovereignty, revokes the power which it has conferred upon this faithless agent and reassert[s] the absolute rule of its institutions and its laws.

In virtue of the above, we, the undersigned Mexican citizens in full exercise of our political rights, have adopted in all its parts and swear to sustain in its entirety the following:

ORGANIC PLAN OF THE MOVEMENT TO REVINDICATE
DEMOCRACY AND THE LAW

Article I. Venustiano Carranza ceases in the exercise of the Executive Power of the Federation.

Article II. Recognition is refused to the public officials whose assumption of office had its origin in the recent elections of local powers which took place in the States of Guanajuato, San Luis Potosí, Querétaro, Nuevo León and Tamaulipas.

Article III. Recognition is likewise refused to the citizens elected in the capacity of Councilmen of the Municipal Government of the City of Mexico during the last elections held in said capital.

Article IV. José Santos Godínez is recognized as Constitutional Governor of the State of Nayarit.

Article V. All the other legitimate authorities of the Federation and the States are also recognized. The Liberal Constitutionalist Army will sustain said authorities provided they do not combat nor molest the present movement.

Article VI. The Political Constitution of February 5, 1917 is hereby recognized as the fundamental law of the Republic.

Article VII. All the generals, military leaders, officers and soldiers seconding this plan shall constitute the Liberal Constitutionalist Army. The present Constitutional Governor of Sonora, Adolfo de la Huerta, shall temporarily have the character of Supreme Chief of the Army with all the faculties necessary for the military, political and administrative organization of this movement.

ARTICLE VIII. The Constitutional Governors of the States who recognize and adhere to this movement within the space of thirty days, reckoned from the date of promulgation of this plan, shall each name a duly authorized representative to the end that said delegates, assembled within sixty days after the present date, in the place designated by the man who is temporarily Supreme Chief, take measures for the definite appointment, by a majority of votes, of the Supreme Chief of the Liberal Constitutionalist Army.

ARTICLE IX. If in view of the circumstances arising from the campaign, the Assembly of Delegates of the Constitutional Governors referred to in the previous article does not secure a majority on the date set, the present Constitutional Governor of the State of Sonora, Adolfo de la Huerta, shall definitely remain the Supreme Chief of the Liberal Constitutionalist Army.

ARTICLE X. As soon as the present Plan is adopted by the majority of the Nation and the City of Mexico is occupied by the Liberal Constitutionalist Army, measures shall be taken to designate a Provisional President of the Republic in the manner provided by the following articles:

ARTICLE XI. If the movement should be consummated before the end of the present period of the Federal Congress, the Supreme Chief of the Liberal Constitutionalist Army shall convoke Congress to extra sessions wherever it may be able to meet and the members of both Chambers shall elect the Provisional President in conformance to the Constitution in force.

ARTICLE XII. If the case foreseen by Article VIII should arise after the end of the constitutional period of the present Chambers, the Supreme Chief of the Liberal Constitutionalist Army shall assume the Provisional Presidency of the Republic.

ARTICLE XIII. The Provisional President shall call elections of the Executive and Legislative Powers of the Federation immediately after he takes possession of his post.

ARTICLE XIV. The Supreme Chief of the Liberal Constitutionalist Army shall name Provisional Governors of the States of Guanajuato, San Luis Potosí, Querétaro, Nuevo León and Tamaulipas; of those which do not have a Constitutional Governor; and of all the other Federal entities whose administrators combat or refuse to recognize this movement.

ARTICLE XV. After the triumph of this Plan has been assured, the Provisional President shall authorize the Provisional Governors to call immediately elections of Local Powers in conformance to the respective laws.

ARTICLE XVI. The Liberal Constitutionalist Army shall rule in accord with the General Orders and Military Laws at present in force in the Republic.

ARTICLE XVII. The Supreme Chief of the Liberal Constitutionalist Army and all the civil and military authorities who second this Plan shall give guarantees to nationals and foreigners and shall give very special protection to the development of industry, commerce and all business.

Effective Suffrage—No Reelection. AGUA PRIETA, SONORA, April 23, 1920

VII. Consolidation, 1920–1928

Although the Sonoran triumph marked an important milestone as the final violent change of government in Mexico, the meaning of revolutionary reform—and particularly the scope of the new constitution—would not be fully defined for another two decades. Between 1920 and 1929, three major civil wars as well as a large number of regional rebellions wracked the country. We may look at those years as a period when the revolutionary regime slowly extended its authority in conflict and negotiation with regional warlords, the Catholic Church, the U.S. government, and the grass roots. This state still relied on patriarchy: it was major news when a woman was chosen as a member of the city council of Mérida in 1922 (doc. 66).

One of the first problems new president Álvaro Obregón addressed was land reform. A prosperous landowner, Obregón dreamed of a Mexico dominated by small farmers and had little interest in collective farming. His government used expropriation selectively to advance that aim (docs. 64–65). The effort was paltry, and the best land remained in the hands of hacendados.

To strengthen their rule, the Sonorans relied on the revolutionary army and ruthlessly weeded out those who opposed them, just as Carranza had done before then. For example, in July 1923, Pancho Villa was assassinated, most likely on the orders of Obregón and/or his secretary of the interior, General Plutarco Elías Calles (doc. 67). The two epitomized macho leaders who acted with impunity (doc. 68). On frequent occasions, the ambitions of these leaders clashed, most notably in what became known as the de la Huerta Rebellion (December 1923–May 1924), which featured a coalition led by the former secretary of the treasury and 60 percent of the Mexican army (doc. 69).

Those were violent years, yet they also saw reform in many areas. The federal government launched an ambitious rural education program (docs. 70–71). President Calles also vociferously defended Mexico's right to make its own laws against the aggressive posturing of U.S. secretary of state Frank B. Kellogg (docs. 72–73). Calles aligned with a major labor movement, the Confederación Regional Obrera Mexicana (CROM) led by Luis N. Morones, one of his cabinet members. As observers noted, the CROM was an arm of the government rather than an independent advocate for the workers (doc. 74).

A decade that many historians have called "postrevolutionary" also featured the most significant confrontation between church and state. Opposed to the cultural, social, and political role of the Catholic Church, Calles decreed enforcement of the anticlerical articles of the constitution as part of a reform of the penal code. In November 1926, Pope Pius XI issued an encyclical decrying the government's treatment of the Church (doc. 75). The Church was not blameless in the controversy, as the primary French diplomat in Mexico observed (doc. 76). But devout Mexicans remember this conflict as the time when the government arrested their priests (doc. 77), and many joined the Cristero Rebellion. In July 1928, when Obregón prepared to return to the presidency, Mexico's future looked as uncertain as in 1920.

Document 64. Obregón on Land Reform[1]

Shortly before his inauguration, Obregón addressed a group of members of Congress that included the noted Zapatista Antonio Díaz Soto y Gama on the subject of land reform in a much-anticipated speech. As we have seen, the president-elect's platform had focused on political reforms and the reestablishment of diplomatic relations with the United States, and Obregón himself ran a growing privately owned agribusiness. However, the caudillo's strategic alliance with the Zapatistas in the waning days of the Carranza administration impelled him toward a more agrarista position. His remarks appeared to straddle the fence between his commitment to the Zapatistas and his own belief in privately held land.

In our country, a majority of landowners have unfortunately remained entirely oblivious to the evolution of agriculture. They have followed their routine procedures so closely that they have not been able to compete with similar products from other countries in the world, and they always ask for protectionist tariffs in order to obtain a price that allows them to sell their products.

. . . Agriculture in other countries has three factors: Capital, translated into property, modern machinery, implements that simplify work; intelligence, which means organization and direction; and work, which is what the day laborers are involved in. Under those conditions, Capital can obtain sufficient return to satisfy its needs, and the day laborer can have a salary that allows him to live with some well-being . . . perhaps greater than what he would have obtained with his personal effort and with traditional planting techniques.

. . . The farm laborers began to observe that . . . years went by, and the painful inheritance of hunger passed on from generation to generation. . . . Relying on old techniques, the bosses expected the profit that their capital demanded, not out of . . . their skill, machinery, or capital, but out of the personal effort of their own day laborers. Every one of those men longed for a piece of land where to build his

---

1. Álvaro Obregón, *El problema agrario: Versión taquigráfica del cambio de impresiones tenido por el Presidente electo con un numeroso grupo de Diputados al Congreso de la Unión, Octubre de 1920* (Mexico City: n.p., 1920), 4–25. Translated by Jürgen Buchenau.

house of maguey stalks, and to obtain for his own benefit the total product of his personal effort, because the bosses claimed a part of it, and the rest was not enough to feed his children.

I am entirely in agreement with the agrarian principle, but we must proceed with absolute discretion; we must proceed with such tact that we can solve this problem without endangering our well-being.

If we begin by destroying large property in order to create smallholdings later on, I sincerely believe that we have made a mistake. Whenever the government promulgates a law fixing the maximum area [of landholding], it will no longer have the right to collect taxes or contributions for the entire area of the ranch, and it has not yet created the small property.

If we make a law that subjects farmers to use primitive techniques to continue to cultivate land, we will come to this painful conclusion: a man with primitive [farming techniques] can cultivate, at maximum, helped by his small children, and in some cases by his wife, five to six hectares.

. . . Mexico has 50,000,000 hectares of arable land. Mexico has 16,000,000 or . . . 15,000,000 inhabitants; Out of the 15,000,000, there will be 3,000,000 heads of families, from which we will have to subtract . . . workers, [members of the] Army; . . . public and private employees . . . merchants, industrialists, and bankers. We will be left with a million heads of household who could direct all their efforts to the development of agriculture. If we condemn our agriculture to live eternally governed by primitive [techniques], . . . a million men dedicated to agriculture could cultivate by those means a maximum surface of six million hectares.

A surplus of forty-four million hectares would remain without cultivation, and Mexico, gentlemen, would appear the most formidable landowner before the rest of the world.

Why?

Because it would only cultivate a tenth of the arable land, and at a time when the whole world needs maximum agricultural production, in order to silence the cries of hunger . . . felt by the masses, especially in European countries.

Let us therefore solve the agrarian problem without ignoring the fact that our country has much more land than what is needed to solve it. We should not destroy large estates before creating smallholdings because doing so would lead to an imbalance of production that could perhaps lead us to a period of famine. . . .

I am of the opinion that a law should be passed . . . creating an ownership right for every man capable of cultivating a piece of land; that the maximum area to which that man was entitled be fixed, and that all the land necessary to satisfy all the claims presented be requested from the large landowners, in such a way that smallholdings will have already been created at the moment of destruction of the large estate, substituting its production.

This is, in my opinion, . . . fundamental . . . ; to avoid an imbalance in production, to avoid an economic imbalance that could lead us to a period of hunger. It would be ironic if we were to create a period of hunger as the only country, or perhaps one of the countries that is most prepared to banish forever from its surface the ghost of hunger. . . .

. . . Once property and agrarian credit have been destroyed, we will chase away the foreign capital we need more than ever. We will have created an economic disequilibrium as there will not be anyone from whom to collect taxes, just because there is law that does not allow anyone to own more than 50 hectares of land.

Document 65. Confronting Agrarian Reform[2]

The following selection from the letters of Rosalie Evans, a U.S. landowner in western Puebla, paints a different picture of land reform. The owner of a hacienda of some 800 hectares, Evans confronted an agrarian cacique allied with Obregón, Manuel P. Montes. In a drawn-out conflict that involved U.S. and British diplomats as well as the Mexican national government, Evans fought agrarian reform—an effort that ended in her own death in August 1924. This selection from a letter to Evans's sister reflects her initial impression of Montes.

San Pedro
May 21, 1921

About four I forced myself to dress and go in my little buggy to San Martín [Texmelucan] to see Don P_____. At the moment of getting in the buggy I was stopped by the arch-devil of the valley, whom the Indians have elected as their "member of Congress." Manuel Montes being his name, so you will rejoice with me if he meets his death before I do mine. He was dressed in a black frock coat, and a bull fighter hat; is short and square, with the cruelest little black eyes, like a snake ready to strike. So dressed to impress, I suppose. With him another deputy with a stooping frame and a long beard, also to cause respect. Back of them the usual rabble, but only one man caught my eyes; he had a wooden leg.

He with the beard began with a pompous address and handed me an order from Obregón and [Minister of Agriculture Antonio I. Villarreal] . . . which, to my utter astonishment, was entirely in my favor. I said, with real surprise: "This paper tells you to respect me and my property."

---

2. Rosalie Evans, *The Rosalie Evans Letters from Mexico* (Indianapolis: Bobbs-Merrill, 1926), 148–51.

"Yes," replied he with the long beard, "but I bring an oral message from the Minister Villarreal to deliver over all of your crop, at once, to these gentlemen (the rabble rout) and he will indemnify you afterward."

I said: "Do you think that on an oral order I would give you my crop?"—and the riot began.

Manuel Montes got leave from "Congress" to come down and speak to the people, so you can appreciate my danger and that of my men. It was he who had arranged the simultaneous killing of administrators that I told you of and who at eleven the same morning had made the people attack San Juan Tetla—perhaps you will remember it, a place we once wanted to buy, now owned by [William O.] Jenkins and Arrismondi, brother of the administrator killed two years ago. Montes said that he would lead his people on San Pedro himself, and make the señora listen to reason. He leads all the strikes and if you once let him speak, rouses the people to madness.

I determined that he should not speak on my place. He tried to harangue them and "all my rage arose," I am told, for really I did not realize it. I outspoke him, calling him a coward, assassin, and my whole wicked vocabulary of insults. He trembled with rage, but I got my hand on my pistol and *he* ran—I standing up in the buggy, [hacienda administrator] Iago by the mule (which they tried to unharness). Montes was followed by the bearded hypocrite. They mounted their little ponies as fast as they could, calling to their people to take the crop by force. Iago had his pistol ready and whistled for the soldiers who were sleeping somewhere inside. There was much shouting and confusion, the man with the wooden leg making an awful stumping sound in front of the mule, when the boy captain of my soldiers ran into the midst of them crying out: "Insult me, not the señora. I will not fire yet, you are too few for me." (There were about twenty.) I saw we had won the day. They were not armed, so I forbade firing, and "Satan fled murmuring" that he would be back in the morning.

I left the captain on guard. He really is a perfect little devil, about twenty-three, but does my bidding. He asked that I should bring him permission from San Martín to fire if necessary, so far he has only police authority. We then drove to San Martín. As usual, no support! We did not ask for more men, we had seven and with the three of us armed we were quite enough.

Document 66. A Woman in Public Office[3]

Mexican women were slow to gain additional rights as a result of the revolution, and especially regarding the right to vote. At a time when the United States approved women's suffrage at the national level through the Nineteenth Amendment (1920), the voting rights of women in Mexico only advanced slowly and at the state level. Only two southeastern states—Yucatán and Chiapas—elected women representatives during that time. One of these representatives, Yucatán's Rosa Torre González, recounted her days as a councilor in the state capital of Mérida. The excerpt not only relates Torre González's pioneering work but also the towering and charismatic figure of her political mentor, Yucatán governor Felipe Carrillo Puerto, who was the leading exponent of Southeastern "socialism," which emphasized popular mobilization in resistance leagues and statewide revolutionary parties, women's rights, anticlericalism, and economic justice.

As the first woman to reach the rank of a Councilor in our Republic, I find myself unavoidably obliged to report on my performance in the Ayuntamiento of Mérida to all of the women's organizations and also the people interested in those problems, in the expectation that I will dispel certain prejudicial notions from those who maintain that women should neither interfere in administrative matters nor occupy posts filled by a popular election.

But before turning to that subject, undying gratitude compels me to pay a just tribute to the late and never well-mourned former governor of Yucatán, Felipe Carrillo Puerto, who, motivated by noble and disinterested ideals, carried out the greatest work of redemption that Yucatán has ever seen. That man, whose lordly figure withstood all the wrath of his enemies, knew how to break the chains of tradition and social prejudice. He distinguished himself for his struggle in favor of the working classes, both as a federal deputy and as governor of the State of Yucatán. He legislated in favor of the workers and campesinos. He strongly supported women, attending to their needs and supporting them in popularly elected positions where the true Yucatecan people chose them. . . .

In October 1922, through the efforts of Compañera Elvia Carrillo Puerto, President of the group "Rita Cetina González," the Central Resistance League, which was the social and political organization of the Party of the Southeast, requested a finished slate from the Feminine League so that a woman would appear on the slate running to make up the next city council. A great meeting held in the building of our Association set up said slate with the following names: Elvia Carrillo Puerto, Eusebia Pérez, and Rosa Torre G.

---

3. Rosa Torre González, "Mi actuación en el H. Ayuntamiento de Mérida en el año de 1923," *Revista de la Universidad Autónoma de Yucatán* 230 (2004): 3–9, https://www.revistauniversitaria.uady.mx/pdf/230/ru2302.pdf. Translated by Jürgen Buchenau.

The Socialist Party of the Southeast and its Chief, Felipe Carrillo Puerto, selected me as a candidate on the slate that the aforementioned Socialist Party of the Southeast was to nominate one afternoon in October, Don Felipe Carrillo Puerto held a meeting with the presumptive candidates.

At the aforementioned meeting, he expressed his desire that women . . . should be included on a ballot to exercise their right granted by law to vote and be elected. That is how comrade Carrillo Puerto explained and supported my inclusion in the proposed municipal slate. What is more, he asked my comrades to treat me with the utmost consideration and to provide me with all kinds of facilities to carry out the propaganda work in the towns and villages included in the Municipality.

After the socialist ticket triumphed in the elections held on November 1, 1922, I took possession of my post on January 1, 1923. . . . Conscious of the responsibility that weighed on my shoulders from that moment on, I responded enthusiastically to the congratulations. Carrillo Puerto encouraged me and, with paternal affection, advised me and instilled in me the strength and decisiveness to take action.

How painfully I still remember the generosity of the noble ruler who did so much to protect the woman, the child and the people in general, and I understand the mourning and sadness that covers the proletarian homes of Yucatán. He preached by example rather than by word.

Lic. Manuel Berzunza was elected Municipal President. I always received endless attention from him, both because he was an excellent person, and because Don Felipe Carrillo Puerto continually requested of him that I would be very well treated. In accordance with municipal law, Lic. Berzunza appointed me to the Press and Welfare Commission. Since the City Council wanted a newspaper as a mouthpiece of the Administration, I began to publish the Boletín Municipal that consisted of the Minutes of the Sessions and the Notices to the Public. . . .

The Municipal President—a great soul—always tried to ensure that the proletarian people had health care facilities, and as required by law, in addition to what I have said, I attended to the welfare aspect by providing emergency medical services to the towns and villages of the Municipality.

By virtue of the fact that the Commissions rotated within the City Council, I was in charge of the Entertainment Commission. I always censored the movies in a timely manner in order to avoid economic damages to the entrepreneurs; but mainly, to eliminate everything that was immoral or could influence the public as a bad example, in my opinion: movies with plots that included robberies, murders and other immoralities. I rejected all of this strongly. I ordered the shows to begin at the hour fixed in the program, for the benefit of the public and keeping to the established regulations. . . . I banned the resale of tickets because it appeared to me a real exploitation of the people. I also presided over the bullfights of the famous Spanish bullfighter "El Gallo."

When I was entrusted with the Health and Hygiene Branch, I considered the sensitive nature of a problem involving the health of the people. That is why I put great effort into the elaboration of a program of work that I developed and carried out to the extent of my abilities. With the objective of fulfilling my task as well as possible, I conducted several interviews with the Chief Physician of the Superior Board of Health and Hygiene in order to correct certain irregularities I had found in the sale of foodstuffs such as meat, fish, milk, etc.; removing from it everything that could harm public health for any reason. . . .

Having overcome many economic difficulties, I tried to satisfy the demands of the teachers as far as my powers allowed me, since I am well aware of the idea that the school is the pedestal upon which to build social reforms. I was in charge of the children's regular attendance in schools; and I promoted and successfully carried out a literacy campaign. At the same time, I undertook an energetic fight against hard drugs while also attending to women's issues in prisons.

I paid special attention to the specific problems of my gender, solving those within my reach and trying to improve their situation. Women who fell into the abyss of vice were the object of my careful attention, and I had great satisfaction in convincing many of them to abandon the thorny path in which cruel destiny had placed them. They could always count on my advice and words of encouragement.

I promptly attended to all the complaints that came to me, for election by the people obliged me to watch over them. . . .

This account has briefly related my work as Regidora in the Municipality of Mérida, Yucatán, Mexico, and especially for women, with the aim that those who read it might see the enormous possibilities of the Mexican woman to benefit others, children and the people in general, from posts of popular election. . . .

I hold out hope that the Mexican woman, convinced of her true intrinsic value and her patriotism, may be able to occupy the place that belongs to her to guide the State in the process of growth of our beloved Mexico.

Mérida, Yucatán, México, March 1924
Rosa Torre G.

Document 67. Corrido on Pancho Villa's Murder[4]

Just like the cowardly assassination of Emiliano Zapata in 1919, Pancho Villa's murder in July 1923—most likely on the orders of people in high positions in the government— prompted outrage throughout Mexico. It also spawned a corrido less lyrical than the one decrying Zapata's death, but just as interesting, as it highlights the government's continuing fear of Villismo so long as the great caudillo remained alive.

When They Killed Pancho Villa

I will sing to you, gentlemen,
What happened in Parral
In a cruel ambush, gentlemen
Francisco Villa died

He had already given his soul, gentlemen,
To the chief executive of the nation.
But because he was dangerous, gentlemen
The government killed him.

They killed Francisco
They killed him in an act of treason
For as long as he lived
The nation would not have peace
So he died in an ambush
With nine bullets in his heart

With his best soldiers, gentlemen
Francisco Villa died
His blood no longer floated, gentlemen,
From the roof of men of honor
In his automobile, gentlemen,
They were all left in a heap.
So died the great caudillo, gentlemen
Great revolutionary

---

4. "Cuandomataron a Villa" Cultura Colectiva, accessed May 1, 2021, https://culturacolectiva.com/historia/pancho-villa-corridos-sobre-su-vida-y-muerte. Translated by Jürgen Buchenau.

They killed Francisco
They killed him in an act of treason
For as long as he lived
The nation would not have peace
So he died in an ambush
With nine bullets in his heart.

Document 68. Portrait of a Macho General[5]

The first nine years of the Sonoran era (1920–1929) were rife with civil wars and political intrigue. Nowhere is this intrigue captured better than in Martín Luis Guzmán's famous novel La sombra del caudillo *(The Caudillo's Shadow). In Guzmán's mind, militarism lay at the heart of the conflict and instability of those years. Inspired by General Francisco R. Serrano, later assassinated on the orders of Calles and Obregón, the following selection from the opening chapters describes the archetypal military leader, and specifically his attitude toward women.*

General Ignacio Aguirre's Cadillac crossed the streetcar rails of the Calzada de Chapultepec and, making a sharp turn, came to a stop, a short distance from the Insurgentes stop.

The chauffeur's assistant jumped from his place to open the passenger door. Bright reflections of the early afternoon cityscape—the outline of houses, trees on the avenue, blue sky covered at intervals by large, white cumulus clouds—slid across the dark bluish window as the door opened.

Several minutes elapsed.

Inside the car, General Ignacio Aguirre, minister of war, and his inseparable, irreplaceable, intimate friend, Representative Axkaná, continued to talk with the characteristic animation of young Mexican politicians. The slight tone of detachment in which Aguirre spoke immediately distinguished him as one of the important public officials in Mexico. The nuances of his speech marked him as a man of authority even when he wasn't giving orders. Axkaná, on the contrary, let his words flow, sketched out theories, and explored generalizations. Though his gestures made him appear feeble, his arguments were stronger than his colleague's; he was clearly not a powerful man himself but an advisor to such men. Aguirre was the military politician; Axkaná the civilian politician. The former acted at critical

---

5. Martín Luis Guzmán, *The Shadow of the Strongman*, trans. Gustavo Pellón (Indianapolis: Hackett Publishing, 2017), 3–9.

moments in public affairs; the latter believed he guided those events, or at least explained them....

Aguirre said:

"Then we agree you'll convince Olivier I can't accept the nomination to the presidency of the republic."

"Of course."

"And he and everyone else should support Jiménez, who is the Caudillo's candidate...."

"That, too."

As Axkaná put out his hand, Aguirre insisted:

"Using the same line of reasoning you just used?"

"The same."

The hands clasped.

"For sure?"

"For sure."

"See you tonight, then."

"See you tonight."

And Axkaná nimbly jumped out of the car.

His slim figure emerged golden and splendid into the afternoon's enveloping glow. On one side he was bathed by the sun, on the other his body's reflection danced on the surface of the impeccably polished car. His warm face shone above his dark blue suit; his eyes were the same green as the light descended from the tree branches....

Facing the car, he took a step back to allow the chauffeur's assistant to close the door. Then, drawing closer again, he opened the door once more and, putting his head into the car, said:

"I remind you again of the recommendation I made this morning."

"This morning?"

"Come on now, don't pretend."

"Oh yes! About Rosario."

"Yes, about Rosario ... I feel sorry for her."

"Sorry? Why? Don't be a child!"

"Because she's totally defenseless, and you're going to drag her through the mud."

"Please, I'm not mud!"

"Of course you're not, but the mud will come later."

Aguirre reflected for a second, then said:

"Look, I promise you one thing: I, for my part, will do nothing to bring about what you fear. Now, if 'things' just happen, I wash my hands."

"'Things' won't just happen."

"Very well. Then my promise is enough."

"I don't think so."

"Yes, my friend, yes. In this case I really promise you."

"Really, how?"

"Really . . . I give you my word of honor."

"Honor."

The two friends were silent for an instant and held each other's gaze. The same fatigue that, shortly before, was noticeable in Ignacio Aguirre's voice now passed a veil over his dark pupils. Axkaná's intense, clear eyes suddenly gave Aguirre a penetrating, inquiring look.

Axkaná was the first to speak:

"Fine," he smiled. "I'll settle for that. Although, to call a spade a spade, among politicians, 'honor' is hardly a guarantee."

Aguirre tried to reply, but there wasn't time. Axkaná, his smile turning into laughter, had already slammed the door and was heading for the Ford taxis lined up on the other side of the street.

The Cadillac then got moving, advanced to the corner of Avenida Veracruz, and, turning there, sped along in the direction of the horsetrack. . . .

At that very same time, under the towering treetops of the Calzada de Insurgentes, Rosario awaited the moment of her meeting with Aguirre. Since this was a custom that had been going on for more than a month now, the brilliant light of siesta-time felt free to do as it pleased with Rosario. The light pursued Rosario as she strolled along; it acted as if she were another feature of the landscape, included her in the play of humid brilliance and transparent radiance. She was, for instance, lit from above by the fiery glow of her red umbrella as she passed through sunlit areas. And later, as she passed the shady spots, she was dappled with golden glitter, covered by tiny disks of gold that rained from the branches of the trees. The shards of light, like liquid jewelry, fell first on the bright red umbrella, then slid to the pale green of her dress, and finally puddled—aglow and shimmering—on the ground where her foot had just stepped. From time to time one of those luminous drops touched her shoulder until it dripped, backwards, down her naked arm, moving in time to the rhythm of her steps. Other drops stuck to her ankle, illuminating its suppleness in the fleeting moment when her foot was about to lift from the ground. Yet if Rosario turned her face, other drops of light were caught, trembling intensely, in the black curls of her hair.

A star came to rest on her forehead as she turned to look at Aguirre's Cadillac, which was now approaching. Her umbrella, sprinkled all over with similar stars, created a background for her beautiful head, turning her, for a moment, into a Virgin in a niche. Giving her a golden-pink glow, the luminous aura enhanced the oval of her face, enriched the darkness of her eyelashes, the outline of her eyebrows, the contours of her lips, the freshness of her complexion.

Ignacio Aguirre observed her from afar: she radiated light and beauty. And as he drew near, he felt a vital force, something impulsive, impetuous, that his body somehow communicated to the Cadillac: the automobile expressed this with a series of quick, nervous jolts to the brakes. The driver, who knew his master, sped on and, like a horseman bringing a virile horse to a dramatic halt at the end of a race, suddenly stopped the car in exactly the right spot. The car's body shook, the axles vibrated, and the screeching wheels left black and pungent tire tracks on the road.

Youthful, eager, smiling, Aguirre opened the door. His manner did not indicate he was about to get out but rather that he wanted to invite Rosario in.

"Are you getting in," he said, "or do I get out?"

By way of an answer, Rosario lifted her head and leaned it on the shaft of her umbrella. Her pose was clearly taunting. The star on her forehead came to rest on her breast.

"You get out, of course. When are you going to stop asking me the same thing?"

"The day you agree to get in."

And Aguirre stretched his leg out onto the running board.

"Is that so? That will never happen."

He jumped to the ground and held out his hand. Rosario accepted it in the very feminine, suggestive way in which she liked to shake hands: with a graceful twist, her head and bust facing in slightly opposite directions, twisting her wrist and lifting her shoulder so as to show the dimples in her elbow as the hand surrendered.

Aguirre, as he squeezed her fingers with a slightly brutal force, asked, stressing each syllable:

"Never, you say?"

The rude pressure of the hand was offset by the caressing softness of the voice. Aguirre knew from experience the amorous effects of such contrasts.

"Never!" she repeated, also stressing both syllables. Without blinking she held Aguirre's gaze, which hit her full in the face.

But the mute challenge ended quickly, because Aguirre, as always when he looked into Rosario's eyes, fled swiftly from them to avoid getting dizzy. As a good soldier, he knew the only reason to enter into amorous battles is to win them—otherwise, victory lies in retreat. In Rosario's case, furthermore, all retreats were roads to glory. Rosario had just turned twenty: her bust was shapely, her legs well-turned and her head was endowed with a grace and elegance of movement that enhanced, with a remarkable active radiance, the beauty of her features. Her eyes were large, brilliant, and dark; her hair black; her mouth precisely drawn and sensual, her hands and feet small and agile. To behold her was to feel that all the yearnings of adult vigor and all the desires of youth were suddenly churned up like a sea in a storm—at least, that is what Aguirre felt. When she spoke, her speech—a little common, a bit timid—revealed a lively and promising (though somewhat lacking) intelligence and a candid spirit enhanced by her well-groomed body and her good taste in clothes. When she smiled, the fineness of her smile fully indicated what the qualities of her spirit might have been with greater cultivation.

"Very well," agreed Aguirre, "then, it's never. We'll have to settle for strolling under the trees of the boulevards as we have up to now." . . .

And thus, they walked and talked for a long while.

At Rosario's side, Ignacio Aguirre did not in any sense appear inferior, neither in terms of his good looks nor his manners. He was not handsome, but his build combined slimness and vigor in an extraordinary way, and this favored him. His bearing was decidedly masculine, and the grace, directness, and ease in his manner compensated for the deficiencies of his incomplete education. His athletic, muscular build was evident beneath the cloth of his civilian suit, although to a lesser degree than when he wore his more form-fitting uniform. And even in his face, which in itself was imperfect, there was something that made the whole of his features not only pleasant, but even attractive. Was it the smoothness of the line from his temples to his chin? Was it the meeting of his forehead and nose at the double brushstroke of his eyebrows? Was it the fleshiness of his lips that enhanced the fading, curving lines toward the corners of his mouth? His matte complexion, and the even shadow of his cleanly shaven chin and upper lip, compensated for his unhealthy color, in the same way that he compensated for his incipient near-sightedness by making a particular gesture when trying to see into the distance.

As they walked and talked, Rosario, shorter than him, did not see his face as much as his shoulder, arm, chest, and waist. That is to say she felt attracted, perhaps without realizing it, by the principal source of Aguirre's physical charm. And sometimes, too, as she spoke to him or listened, Rosario gave herself over to imagining the masculine movements of her friend's legs under the capriciously moving pleats of his pants. Aguirre's legs were vigorous and full of energy.

Document 69. The Plan of Veracruz[6]

The Sonoran group shattered in 1923, bringing about yet another devastating civil war. Obregón and his finance minister, the fellow Sonoran Adolfo de la Huerta, had increasingly sustained differences in a number of areas, including the treatment of political opponents, federal interference in state elections, and relations with the United States. In the fall of 1923, just weeks after the United States finally recognized the Obregón administration, these differences resulted in an open break, and de la Huerta challenged Obregón's handpicked successor, Plutarco Elías Calles. On December 7, the

---

6. "Declaración revolucionaria de Adolfo de la Huerta," reproduced in Pedro Castro, *Adolfo de la Huerta y la Revolución Mexicana* (Mexico City: INHERM, 1992), 161–64. Translated in RG 165: Military Intelligence Division, file 2657-G-432, National Archives, College Park, MD.

Plan of Veracruz laid out the program of a disparate coalition of rebels who agreed on little else than Calles's and Obregón's removal.

Soon after arriving in Veracruz, the true soldiers of the Republic, under the worthy and patriotic leadership of General de División Guadalupe Sánchez . . . who have interpreted the profound desire of the Mexican people never to consent to the lowering of their sovereignty, repudiated the government of General Alvaro Obregón for infringing upon our political liberties.

Never in the annals of our political history has the collective conscience expressed itself more precisely or with greater justification, and never has the violation of the people's sovereignty been more odious and intolerable. The standard bearer of the Nation defending its freedoms against a coarse imposition less than three years ago today . . . injures the nation, exerting the power against the people who gave that power to him.

General Obregón has violated the sovereignty of the States of the republic; witness the electoral fraud in the state of Veracruz which consolidated the tyranny of Governor Tejeda; the denial of the support of the Federation to the Constitutional Governor of Michoacán, apprehended and jailed by forces of the Army; the deposing, by force of arms, of legitimate *ayuntamientos* in San Luis Potosí, fomenting thus the most dangerous anarchy; the repudiation of the genuinely elected Congress of Zacatecas, only to support a despotic Governor who seconded unscrupulously his imposition plans; the use of pressure on the authorities of Nuevo León to block the duly elected governor, creating thus a situation favorable for his illegal projects; the expulsion of the Constitutional Governor of Coahuila, substituting for him authorities sprung from the Callista imposition.

To kill the independence of the Legislative power of the Nation, he has organized, with the Praetorians who stain the honor of the Army and with most of his department heads, plots to assassinate deputies; has used threats to subjugate timorous deputies; has bribed indecorous deputies and senators with sinecures and gifts and has even had recourse to kidnapping some in order to make impossible the free functioning of the Legislative Power; he surrounded himself with political mercenaries to prepare the formation of servile chambers to consummate the imposition of a candidacy unpopular with the people from the start.

The Supreme Court of Justice of the Nation, which has the prerogative of deciding conflicts that arise between the Federation and the States, has seen nullified its supreme decrees which protect and recognize the Constitutional Governments of Michoacán and San Luis Potosí.

He has employed the immense power which the people placed in his hands to restrict its liberties, becoming the political leader of the unpopular candidacy of General Plutarco Elías Calles. He has instructed civil authorities and corrupted military chiefs until they failed in their civic duties through systematic calumny of the people's candidate.

Accepting provisionally, as an honor, the leadership of the movement for liberty initiated by patriotic soldiers, I issue this manifesto, making known to the Nation the basic principles which will guide me:

1)   Absolute respect for the life, the liberty, and the property of all native and foreign inhabitants.

2)   Immediate regulation of Article 123 of the Federal Constitution, securing equitable definition of the prerogatives of workmen and of the obligations of the employers.

3)   For the solution of the most intense national problem: LAND AND JUSTICE for all, constituting and organizing the small agricultural property for everyone who really desires to cultivate the soil. Fractioning of the large estates with strict adherence to the spirit of Article 27 of the Constitution, the Government mediating between landowners and those acquiring the land. Endowment of *ejidos* (public lands) for those towns which have not even come out of the communal state, and only until after the development of these same communities and on their petition, they wish to enter the system of individual property. Indemnization, on account of expropriation, for the communal endowment, will be fixed by means of a Federal registry. For the cash payment of these indemnizations, there will be imposed a tax of 50 million pesos which was already proposed by the undersigned when he was Secretary of the Treasury and Public Credit. In order to relieve the small land-holders, there will be established, throughout the country, institutions of Agricultural credit which will facilitate cultivation and increase production. The bonds of the Agrarian property will be floated on the home and foreign markets, with the direct intervention of the Federal Government, in order to secure the payment of indemnifications in cash.

1)   Unshakable respect for the suffrage.

2)   Constitutional reform to establish the effective abolition of the death penalty, with the sole exception of traitors during a foreign war.

3)   Duly regulated Women's suffrage.

4)   Intensification of education.

The Governors of States and representatives in the Congress of the Union, who have seconded and may second the ruthless imposition by the President of the Republic, are repudiated.

Repudiated, likewise, are all the other officials, elected by popular vote, who do not protest their adhesion to the present movement before the 15th.

Document 70. The Rural Maestra[7]

During the Obregón administration (1920–1924), Secretary José Vasconcelos endeavored to build a strong education system, thus implementing Article 3 of the Constitution. According to this article, education was to be free and secular. To help with this effort, in 1922, he enlisted Gabriela Mistral, born Lucila Godoy y Alcayata in 1889 in Vicuña, Chile, who became one of his closest advisers. Like Vasconcelos himself, Mistral did not share the anticlerical vision of the constitution. Titled "La Maestra Rural," or "The Rural Woman Schoolteacher," the following poem expresses her vision of the role of women in rural education. Mistral won the Nobel Prize in Literature in 1945 and is considered one of Latin America's greatest writers of the twentieth century.

The Teacher was pure. "The gentle gardeners," she said,
"of this estate, which is the property of Jesus,
must keep their eyes and hands pure,
and keep their oils clear, to give bright light."

The Teacher was poor. Her kingdom is not human.
(Thus is the sorrowful sower of Israel).
She wore brown sack cloth, she did not bejewel her hand,
and her entire spirit was a magnificent gemstone!

The Teacher was cheerful. Poor wounded woman!
Her smile was a way to weep with kindness.
Over the tattered and reddened sandal,
such a smile, the outstanding flower of her sanctity.

Sweet being! In her river of flowing honey
long did grief nourish its tigers!
The irons that pried open her generous chest
Left wider still the basins of her love!

Oh, farm laborer, whose son learned from her lips
hymn and prayer: you never saw the gleam
of the captive star that burned in her flesh.
You passed without kissing her blossoming heart!

---

7. Gabriela Mistral, *Desolación: Poemas de Gabriela Mistral* (New York: Instituto de las Españas en los Estados Unidos, 1922). Translated by Jürgen Buchenau.

Campesina, do you remember that you once attached
her name to a brutal or petty remark?
A hundred times you looked at her, not once did you see her
And in your son's plot, there is more of her than of you!

She passed her fine and delicate plowshare through it
To open furrows and lodge perfection there.
The morning of virtues from where the seeds drop like snow
is yours. Campesina, won't you ask for forgiveness?

Her split oak tree gave shade to a forest
the day when death invited her to leave.
Thinking that her mother was waiting for her asleep,
Without resistance, she gave herself to the One with Deep Eyes.

And she has fallen asleep in her God, like a moon-lit cushion;
pillow of her temples, a constellation;
the Father sings his lullabies for her
And peace rains hard upon her heart!

Like a filled vessel, she brought her soul,
made to pour small pearls over humanity;
and her human life was the wide breach
that the Father usually opens to shed light.

That's why even the dust of her bones nourishes
purple rosebushes of violent flame.
And the caretaker of tombs tells me he can smell
the plants of the ones from these bones, as he passes by!

Document 71. The House of the Indigenous Student[8]

One of the most important programs of the revolutionary regime was the provision of rural education, designed to Hispanize the indigenous population, teach literacy, and inculcate the regime's modernist and secular values. Beginning with the leadership of Obregón's secretary of public education, José Vasconcelos, the state greatly expanded rural education in the 1920s. The following selection from the Secretariat's report on its Casa del Estudiante Indígena *(House of the Indigenous Student) illustrates the values and strategies behind the education reform as regards Mexico's sizable indigenous minority.*

. . . For the selection of the Indians . . . the following requirements and conditions will apply: 1) be a male Indian of 14 to 18 years of age at the time of enrollments. . . . Preferably having studied the first and second rural grade; but if [students who meet this condition] cannot be found, they can come without knowledge acquired in school of any kind. 2) Show characteristics of intelligence, physical vigor, and health necessary to not make their presence in the house in vain. 3) Be natives of areas of a dense Indian population. 4) Reside permanently outside medium-size or large population centers. 5) Speak and understand the local Indian language with relative perfection. 6) Discard those Indians who can integrate themselves into the Mexican social community without needing official assistance. . . . 7) It is best if at least two Indians arrive from each region who speak the same language. . . .

The primary objective of the Institution is to eliminate the evolutionary difference that separates the Indians from the current era, transforming their mentality, tendencies, and customs, in order to have them join modern, civilized life and to integrate them wholly within the Mexican social community. To that end, the boarders will enjoy the optimal material conditions that the national treasury can afford. . . . It will make them participants in the fundamental culture; it will impart knowledge in menial, agricultural, and industrial skills, and, in sum, it will give them a holistic education that will make them progressive elements per se. *Under no circumstances* . . . will it leave them isolated; on the contrary, it will inspire a vigorous feeling in the young Indians that they are members of the great national family. . . .

Another one of the essential aims of the House of the Indigenous Student consists in the rapprochement and spiritual fusion of the diverse autochthonous families that populate the national territory, bringing about reciprocal knowledge, sincere friendship, lasting cordiality, school camaraderie, and esprit de corps among the Indian boarders. In sum, it will seek indigenous racial solidarity. . . . For the social benefit work that we hope the Indian students . . . will carry out in their

---

8. Secretaría de Educación Pública, *La Casa del Estudiante Indígena: 16 meses de labor en un experimento psicológico colectivo con indios* (Mexico City: SEP, 1927), 35–37, 122. Translated by Jürgen Buchenau.

pueblos of origin, it is indispensable that they keep proficiency in their language so that they will not lose this weapon that will help them establish a firm connection, based upon trust, with their brothers.

The Indian is not inferior to the white or the mestizo, and neither is he superior. He simply has the same aptitude for improvement as the other two. His current backwardness is not his fault. . . . These boys . . . have completely annihilated the old cliché that the privileged classes have tried to perpetuate by stereotyping the notion of an indigenous race that is completely indifferent to comfort, lazy, vicious, passive, aware of its own inferiority, servile, mentally incapable of advancement; in sum, irredeemable. In the face of the proud, selfish and conceited city, these Indians have demonstrated their commendable industriousness, incomparable morality, racial pride, spirit of service, unlimited capacity of ascent, and an extraordinary power of adaptation to the new environment that surrounds them. . . .

Document 72. Mexico on Trial before the World[9]

While Obregón was careful not to antagonize the U.S. government at a time when his administration was seeking U.S. diplomatic recognition, President Plutarco Elías Calles (1924–1928) decided to assert his country's sovereignty, specifically the economic nationalism expressed in Article 27 of the Constitution. His government ended payment on U.S. claims and took on the powerful foreign-owned oil industry. Published by the press, the following selection from the statement of U.S. secretary of state Frank B. Kellogg warned Calles of the consequences of challenging foreign investors. The excerpt reveals an imperious attitude with regard to the right of the U.S. government to interfere in the internal affairs of other nations, and it recalls the attitude of the Taft administration and its ambassador, Henry Lane Wilson, in the Tragic Ten Days in 1913.

Kellogg to the Chargé d'Affaires in Mexico

WASHINGTON, *June 12, 1925—2 p.m.*

The Secretary desires you to know that he has made the following textual statement to the press:

"I have discussed Mexican affairs with Ambassador Sheffield at great length. He has gone over the entire situation. It will be remembered that we entered into two Claims Conventions with Mexico under which Joint Claims Commissions were

---

9. U.S. Department of State, *Papers Relating to the Foreign Relations of the United States, 1925*, vol. 2, doc. 408 (Washington, D.C.: U.S. Government Printing Office, 1940). Hereafter cited as *FRUS* with year and document number.

appointed to adjust claims of American citizens for properties illegally taken by Mexico and for injuries to American citizens of their rights. These Commissions are now sitting and will, in due time, adjudicate these claims. Conditions have improved and our Ambassador has succeeded in protecting American, as well as foreign, interests. Our relations with the Government are friendly but, nevertheless, conditions are not entirely satisfactory and we are looking to and expect the Mexican Government to restore properties illegally taken and to indemnify American citizens.

A great deal of property of Americans has been taken under or in violation of the Agrarian Laws for which no compensation has been made, and other properties practically ruined and, in one instance, taken by the Mexican Government on account of unreasonable demands of labor. Mr. Sheffield will have the full support of this government and we will insist that adequate protection under the recognized rules of international law be afforded American citizens. We believe it is the desire of the Mexican Government to carry out the Conventions and to indemnify American citizens for property taken. So long as we are satisfied that this is the policy of the Mexican Government and this course of action is being carried out with a determination to meet its international obligations, that Government will have the support of the United States. I cannot go into the details of the many cases which Mr. Sheffield has taken up with the Mexican Government but they will be worked out as rapidly as possible.

I have seen the statements published in the press that another revolutionary movement may be impending in Mexico. I very much hope this is not true. This Government's attitude toward Mexico and toward threatened revolutionary movements was clearly set forth in 1923 when there was such a movement threatening the constituted Government of that country, which had entered into solemn engagements with this Government and was making an effort to meet those obligations at home and abroad. The attitude taken by this Government at that time has since been maintained and it is now the policy of this Government to use its influence and lend its support in behalf of stability and orderly constitutional procedure, but it should be made clear that this Government will continue to support the Government in Mexico only so long as it protects American lives and American rights and complies with its international engagements and obligations. The Government of Mexico is now on trial before the world. We have the greatest interest in the stability, prosperity and independence of Mexico. We have been patient and realize, of course, that it takes time to bring about a stable government but we cannot countenance violation of her obligations and failure to protect American citizens."

The above is telegraphed to you for your information and guidance and for informal communication to the Mexican Foreign Office.

Document 73. Defending Mexican Sovereignty[10]

In response, Calles wasted no time asserting Mexico's right to make its own laws. His statement brought him much support in Mexico at a time when the president was also gearing up to confront the Catholic Church.

Statement Issued to the Press on June 14, 1925

Declarations of the State Department have been published in which Mr. Kellogg, answering some questions relating to the visit of Ambassador Sheffield to said department, affirms that some properties of American citizens have been illegally taken in Mexico for which no compensation has been made and in one instance taken by the Mexican Government on account of unreasonable demands of labor. At the same time he refers to the Joint Claims Commissions stating that he is convinced that the Mexican Government wishes to comply with the conventions and indemnify for the properties taken from American citizens; that he has seen the statements published in the press that another revolutionary movement may be impending in Mexico and that the Department of State very much hopes this is not true, the attitude of said department being to use its influence and lend its support in behalf of stability and orderly constitutional procedure in Mexico, but it makes clear that the American Government will continue to support the Government in Mexico only so long as it protects American lives and American rights and complies with its internal engagements and obligations. He adds that the Government of Mexico is now on trial before the world.

It is a duty for my Government to rectify said statements as required by truth and justice. The best proof that Mexico is willing to comply with her international obligations and to protect the life and interests of foreigners lies in the fact that although, according to international law, she was not bound to do it, she invited all the nations whose citizens or subjects might have suffered damages through acts executed during the political upheavals that have taken place in the country with a view to conclude with them a convention to establish joint commissions that might consider said damages in order to grant due indemnizations. Besides that another convention was entered into with the United States to adjust claims of citizens of both countries against the other and in said convention are included all cases in which properties or rights might have been affected in disagreement with the Mexican laws. Therefore, so long as the aforesaid commissions do not adjust the cases submitted to their decision, it is irrelevant to charge Mexico with failure to protect American interests and violation of her international obligations.

---

10. *FRUS*, 1925, doc. 409; reprinted from *The New York Times*, June 15, 1925.

The application of the Agrarian laws cannot be a subject of complaint because Mexico has issued them in the exercise of her sovereignty, and apart from that the State Department, in behalf of the American citizens, has accepted the form of indemnification prescribed by Mexican laws.

It is to be regretted the contradiction found in Mr. Kellogg's statement, when he declared that the United States have the greatest interest in the maintenance of order in Mexico and in the stability of her Government and at the same time stated that he had seen news of revolutionary movements since this last affirmation, tends to cast some alarm in the world in regard to the conditions of my country. And finally the statement that the Government of the United States will continue to support the Government of Mexico only so long as it protects American interests and lives and complies with its international engagements and obligations embodies a threat to the sovereignty of Mexico that she cannot overlook and rejects with all energy because she does not accord to any foreign country the right to intervene in any form in her domestic affairs nor is she disposed to subordinate her international relations to the exigencies of another country.

The statement under reference affirms also that the American Ambassador has succeeded in protecting American as well as foreign interests, and if he has thus succeeded he has no right to charge Mexico with failure to protect said interests, and attention should be called to the fact that said Ambassador does not represent any other foreigners but his own fellow citizens, and Mexico could not admit that without her previous authorization the American Ambassador should act in behalf of persons or interests alien to those of his country.

If the Government of Mexico, as affirmed, is now on trial before the world, such is the case with the Government of the United States as well as those of other countries. But if it is to be understood that Mexico is on trial in the guise of a dependent, my Government absolutely rejects with energy such imputation, which in essence would only mean an insult.

To conclude, I declare that my Government, conscious of the obligations imposed by international law, is determined to comply with them, and therefore to extend due protection to the lives and interests of foreigners; that it only accepts and hopes to receive the help and support of all the other countries based on a sincere and loyal cooperation and according to the invariable practice of international friendship, but in no way it shall admit that a Government of any nation may pretend to create a privileged situation for its nationals in the country, nor shall it either accept any foreign interference contrary to the rights and sovereignty of Mexico.

Document 74. Labor in Revolutionary Mexico[11]

Luis Araquistáin Quevedo, a Spanish socialist, visited Mexico in 1927 to see its revolution up close. Like many other "revolutionary tourists," Araquistáin viewed the revolution sympathetically and supported the rhetoric of the Mexican government. For this visitor, Mexico offered hope and could serve as a model for other Spanish-speaking countries. Nonetheless, his account is not free from the stereotyping that characterizes other travel accounts. The following passage provides Araquistáin's perspective on organized labor.

The Mexican Revolution is fundamentally agrarian. The land is its principal scene, and the peasant is its protagonist. But it . . . also affects the world of large industry, perhaps the most modern of Hispanic America. In Mexico, there are almost 150 textile and garment factories, numerous mines, and industrial plants producing metal, shoes, paper, tobacco, beer, etc. This industry employs approximately 300,000 skilled workers. Apart from the peasant, the industrial worker has been the most decisive force in the . . . Mexican Revolution.

While the rural worker fought for the right to land, the urban worker fought for the right to unionize. Until 1910, this right had been virtually nonexistent in Mexico. . . . A strike was a criminal offense sanctioned in the Penal Code of 1872. The following saying was very popular in Mexico: "The wealthy only need to abide by the Civil Code, but the poor, by the Penal Code." Especially if they timidly dared to declare a strike. In 1907, Porfirio Díaz ordered the armed suppression of several strikes that broke out in Veracruz and Puebla.

The fall of the Porfirian regime encouraged the emergence of workers' associations that were tolerated by the government headed by Madero. In 1912, the Casa del Obrero Mundial was founded, school of propagandists that brought forth the most notable leaders of the workers' movement in Mexico. In 1914, after the few men who remained in Casa del Obrero Mundial had publicly accused Victoriano Huerta of Madero's assassination, [the dictator] ordered it closed in 1914. When Carranza began his uprising against Huerta, the workers organized Red Battallions to defend the Constitutionalist cause. But Carranza never favored the growth of workers' organizations, except when these organizations were helpful to him. In 1916, there was a strike to protest the unbearably high cost of basic necessities brought about by the fraudulent depreciation of the currency. Every military leader printed mountains of paper money, the value of which naturally fell to almost zero. The result was that the prices of consumer goods reached almost astronomical figures. . . . Carranza shut down the trade unions and imprisoned the strike leaders.

---

11. From Jürgen Buchenau, ed., *Mexico OtherWise: Modern Mexico in the Eyes of Foreign Observers* (Albuquerque: University of New Mexico Press, 2005), 182–85. Reprinted by permission.

He wanted to have them shot, but the military tribunal charged with the task of trying their case absolved them two times. For Carranza, just like for don Porfirio, a strike was a crime worthy of the death penalty. . . . Finally, the Constitution of 1917 fully guaranteed the right to unionization in Article 123. . . . Among other provisions notable for their just and humanitarian character, Article 123 establishes a maximum work day of eight hours, and the obligation to submit all unresolved conflicts between capital and labor to a Council of Mediation and Arbitration.

Within limits, [the law] also recognizes the right to strike and picket. . . . The Constitution . . . defines as illicit those strikes in public services that are not announced ten days in advance of their effective date . . . , those in which a majority of the strikers commit acts of violence against people and property, and, in case of war, those in which the strikers work in companies dependent on the government. . . . Licit strikes are those that seek an improvement in working conditions, as well as solidarity and protest strikes (as long as they are brief) against government decrees that either harm the legal status of the labor unions or provoke, for whatever reason, the opposition of the workers as professionals.

The restrictive spirit of the Mexican legislation that governs the right to strike evidently tends to moderate the influence of the more intransigent and irresponsible elements of the workers' movement in order to minimize the conflicts that can be avoided by mediation and arbitration. These conflicts can cause considerable unnecessary damage to both parties as well as indirectly to industry itself and to the nation. In addition, it is often the unions themselves that condemn a strike movement. . . .

A Mexican strike is one of the most original spectacles of its kind. I got to witness one in Mexico City. It was not a very important one, but very much typical. The employees of a store in a downtown street had declared a strike, and in front of the closed door [of the store], the workers of both sexes held a constant vigil, day and night, flying the black flag as the strike symbol. Large placards leaning against the wall explained to the public the reasons of the [strikers'] position, which were, as one might understand, unflattering to the merchant house. The owner of the store could do nothing to avoid being discredited within his own sight, as in a picket. A couple of police officers were also present in constant guard in order to protect the workers' right to formulate their grievances and to unfurl the infamous black color of their flag. The only thing permitted [to the owner] was to defend himself against the charges of his workers by means of another placard.

A curious detail: since the strike had not been declared unanimously, the dissident minority presented on other placards—also protected by the police—the reasons why, in their opinion, the employees should go back to work. The strike had already lasted for a long time, and the public, curious about this peaceful battle of manifestoes between capital and labor, weighed the pros and cons of the antagonistic positions and hoped in their inner souls for the triumph of the most just cause. A beautiful lesson in civility that shows abiding respect for the contending groups. I have never seen this lesson applied in many of the European and American countries that consider themselves very civilized and that do not tire of maintaining that all Mexicans are incorrigible savages. As everywhere, there may be savagery; but there is so much more, and much that does not exist in the rest of the world.

Document 75. The Pope Speaks Out[12]

The final three selections in this section discuss the controversy between church and state, which erupted fully in the summer of 1926, when the so-called Calles Law imposed strict requirements on priests in Mexico. This passage from a November 1926 encyclical of Pope Pius XI provides the Holy See's official position on the conflict and its rejection of the religious restrictions imposed by the Calles government.

Iniquis Afflictisque (Unjust and Sad). Encyclical of Pope Pius XI on the persecution of the Church in Mexico. Nov. 18, 1926

5. It is scarcely necessary, Venerable Brothers, to go back very far in order to narrate the sad calamities which have fallen upon the Church of Mexico. . . .

8. In the first place, let us examine the . . . "Political Constitution." . . . The civil authority is given the right to interfere in matters of divine worship and in the external discipline of the Church. Priests are put on the level of professional men and of laborers but . . . must be not only Mexicans by birth and cannot exceed a certain number specified by law, but are at the same time deprived of all civil and political rights. They are thus placed in the same class with criminals and the insane. . . . The vows of religious, religious orders, and religious congregations are outlawed in Mexico. Public divine worship is forbidden unless it takes place within the confines of a church. . . . All church buildings have been declared the property of the state. . . . As a matter of fact, the Church can no longer own property of any kind. . . .

9. Education has been declared free, but with these important restrictions: both priests and religious are forbidden to open or to conduct elementary schools. It is not permitted to teach children their religion even in a private school. Diplomas or degrees conferred by private schools under control of the Church possess no legal value and are not recognized by the state. . . . How was it possible for the Archbishops and Bishops of Mexico to remain silent in the face of such odious laws?

---

12. Pius XI, "Encyclical of the Persecution of the Church in Mexico," Vatican, accessed May 1, 2021, http://w2.vatican.va/content/pius-xi/en/encyclicals/documents/hf_p-xi_enc_18111926_iniquis-afflictisque.html.

10. Immediately after their publication the hierarchy of Mexico protested in kind but firm terms against these laws, protests . . . approved as well by the whole hierarchies of other countries, as well as by a great majority of individual bishops from all over the world, and which finally were confirmed even by Us in a letter of consolation of the date of the second of February, 1926. . . . The Bishops hoped that those in charge of the Government, after the first outburst of hatred, would have appreciated the damage and danger which would accrue to the vast majority of the people from the enforcement of those articles . . . and that, therefore, out of a desire to preserve peace they would not insist on enforcing these articles to the letter, or would enforce them only up to a certain point, thus leaving open the possibility of a modus vivendi. . . .

11. In spite of the extreme patience exhibited in these circumstances by both the clergy and laity, . . . every hope of a return to peace and tranquility was dissipated . . . as a direct result of the law promulgated by the President . . . on the second of July, 1926, by virtue of which practically no liberty at all was left the Church. As a matter of fact, the Church was barely allowed to exist. The exercise of the sacred ministry was hedged about by the severest penalties as if it were a crime worthy of capital punishment. . . .

12. The most recent law . . . is much worse than the original law itself and makes the enforcement of the Constitution much more severe, if not almost intolerable. The President . . . and the members of his ministry have insisted with such ferocity on the enforcement of these laws that they do not permit the governors . . . , the civil authorities, or the military commanders to mitigate . . . the rigors of the persecution of the Catholic Church. Insult, too, is added to persecution. Wicked men have tried to place the Church in a bad light before the people; some, for example, uttering the most brazen lies in public assemblies. But when a Catholic tries to answer them, he is prevented from speaking by catcalls and personal insults. . . .

14. All foreign priests and religious men have been expelled from the country. Schools for the religious education of boys and girls have been closed. . . . Many seminaries likewise, schools, insane asylums, convents, institutions connected with churches have been closed. In practically all the states of the Republic the number of priests who may exercise the sacred ministry has been limited and fixed at the barest minimum. . . . Certain regulations demand that priests must be of an age fixed by law, that they must be civilly married, and they are not allowed to baptize except with flowing water. . . .

16. But the cruel exercise of arbitrary power on the part of the enemies of the Church has not stopped at these acts. Both men and women who defended the rights of the Church and the cause of religion, either in speeches or by distributing leaflets and pamphlets, were hurried before the courts and sent to prison. Again, whole colleges of canons were rushed off to jail, the aged being carried there in their

beds. Priests and laymen have been cruelly put to death in the very streets or in the public squares which front the churches. . . .

30. . . . those who now in Mexico persecute their brothers and fellow citizens for . . . keeping the laws of God, must recognize . . . that whatever there is of progress, of civilization . . . in their country is due solely to the Catholic Church. In fact every man knows that after the introduction of Christianity into Mexico, the priests and religious especially . . . worked without rest and despite all the obstacles placed in their way, on the one hand by the colonists who were moved by greed for gold and on the other by the natives who were still barbarians, to promote . . . both the splendor of the worship of God and the benefits of the Catholic religion, works and institutions of charity, schools and colleges for the education of the people and their instruction in letters, the sciences, . . . in the arts and crafts.

Document 76. A French Diplomat's Perspective on the Church-State Conflict[13]

Among the documentation of the church-state conflict in Mexico, a long report from the French minister in Mexico, Ernest Lagarde, stands out for its thoroughness as well as its scathing critique of all parties involved in the conflict. In more than seventy pages, Lagarde laid out the political and social landscape to his superiors, offering little hope of settlement of a conflict in which, as the diplomat believed, all parties acted in bad faith. The following excerpt summarizes the outbreak of the most virulent phase of the conflict in 1926, as well as Lagarde's assessment of the Mexican government and the high clergy, especially the episcopate.

The conflict burst forth with unusual violence in February 1926. On February 5, the anniversary of the enactment of the Constitution of 1917, the newspaper *El Universal* published a statement of the Archbishop of Mexico, which Mr. Mora had made the day before and in which stating that he was in agreement with the episcopacy, the clergy, and the believers, the primate renewed the protest which the Mexican prelates had raised in 1917 against Articles 3, 5, 27, and 130: he refused to recognize them and said that he was ready to fight them. *El Universal* in the following days republished this protest twice. The Government immediately ordered legal action to be taken against the Archbishop, who was accused of rebellion against the laws and institutions of the country. But as Mr. Mora denied the statements to

---

13. Report by French chargé Ernest Lagarde, RG 59: General Records of the Department of State, 812.404/867 translated and enclosed in Morrow to Secretary of State, Mexico City, February 27, 1928, pp. 25–30, National Archives, College Park, MD.

which objection was made and affirmed that he had merely alluded to the protest of 1917, and stated that the publication had been made without his authorization, the court, although skeptical as to the worth of the amended statements of the prelate, decided to throw out the indictment. But forthwith, Calles, backed by the radical parties which attributed the arrogance of the clergy to the tolerance with which the Government had, until then, applied the law, decided to take steps to insure complete deference to the Constitution. According to the President, the clergy, steadfast enemy of the social reforms, refused to accept the law: there was no religious problem inasmuch as the Constitution allowed freedom of conscience and limited only the action and the powers of the clergy; under pretext of defending the freedom of the Church, political ends, the acquisition of power, were aimed at. Still further, the Government claimed to have seized correspondence between Rome and the bishops, and between the latter and certain agitators, which proved that a rebellious movement was being organized. The rebels de la Huerta and Estrada, who had fled to the United States, were furthering these attempts, and were ready to take advantage of them; the episcopacy, faithful to its traditions and counting on American support, tried to provoke an insurrection and endeavored to keep on good terms with persons in the governmental parties at the very moment that a very serious tension, caused by the new legislation with regard to foreign ownership of land and petroleum rights, threatened the relations between Mexico and the United States, and, pleased with the difficulties of their country, they made direct appeals abroad; the professional agitators, always ready to start civil war, had already begun to make plans and public order once more became uncertain. As a matter of fact, an uprising was organized for the first days of January 1926, but the authorities, warned by one of the many spies whom they maintained in all spheres, were able to forestall the plot and they had seized documents which were very compromising to certain members of the Mexican and foreign clergy.

Thus started, the struggle was necessarily to be long and desperate. It began on February 10 by the arrest of 17 Spanish priests, officiating in various churches of the capital, and by their brutal expulsion, without even giving them time to secure the means to travel. Throughout the country the authorities have undertaken a real hunt for the ecclesiastics of foreign nationality who were officiating; a number of Catholic welfare organizations (orphanages, workshops, asylums, etc.) are closed and their non-Mexican personnel is [*sic*] expelled from the country. A circular directed by the Minister of the Interior to the Governors on February 23 and commands the latter to enforce the law strictly and, for this purpose, to use all methods which they may deem convenient and effective. Accusations, breaches of word, false pledges, searches, persecutions, assaults, arrests, expulsions . . . and even executions—thus is the conflict despotically begun, marked, here and there, by sanguinary incidents. The police which carries out these orders is the political police dependent upon the Confidential Department placed directly under the authority of the Minister of the Interior: they seem to have received instructions to aggravate the odious character of these measures by the brutality of their behavior and by their bad faith reaching to the point of willful and malicious injury. What is more, the Government refuses to discuss or to explain and, in order to render all the discussion impossible, those of its officials who bear the responsibility for carrying out of this policy leave the capital.

The violence and the unexpectedness of the action of the public authorities had stupefied the clergy. In Catholic circles, the confusion was complete. Between the various associations—the Knights of Columbus, the National League for Religious Defence, the Union of Catholic Ladies, the Catholic Labor Confederation, the Mexican Association of Catholic Youth, the National Association of Heads of Family—there was less cohesion than rivalry; the Catholic forces were unorganized and weak, unfit and not prepared for resistance, they could not lay claim to the support of public opinion, non-existent here, or of the press, gagged; even earnestness of faith was lacking in this country where everyone is nominally Catholic but where, in reality, indifference is widespread and where, according to the statement of Mgr. Leopoldo Ruiz, Archbishop of Morelia, at the Apostolic Congress of Amsterdam in 1924, not more than twenty per cent of those who have been baptized are true Christians; in a word, in the ranks of the believers, neither civic courage nor devotion nor benevolence, except among the women, and not a single person capable of undertaking real leadership in politics. Such are the forces, such the leaders. The episcopacy, not to speak of the remainder of the clergy, is indiscreet, restricted in vision, intransigent, vain, thoroughly disunited: the Archbishop and Primate of Mexico, a decrepit old man, an opportunist without willpower, a believer in political intrigues, who has not had for a long while any real voice in the conduct of the affairs of the Church: Mgr. Vera, Archbishop of Puebla, and Mgr. Danegas, Bishop of Querétaro, two men fitted for meditation, not for strife; Mgr. Herrera, Archbishop of Monterrey, Mgr. Manrique, Bishop of Huejutla, Mgr. Castellana, Bishop of Tulancingo, three fanatical, impulsive prelates; Mgr. Quizar, Bishop of Veracruz, Mgr. Fulcheri, Bishop of Zamora, Mgr. Urarga, Bishop of Cuernavaca, all three moderate and conciliatory; finally, the real heads of the Mexican Church, the Archbishop of Morelia, Mgr. Leopoldo Ruiz, a remarkable theologian, an energetic man and of very high morals; the Bishop of San Luis Potosí, Mgr. de la Mora, courageous and untiring organizer, both of whom made their dioceses the best in Mexico; the Archbishop of Guadalajara; Mgr. Orozco, a fighter; ambitious, heedless, so hostile to any conciliation that Rome has often had to reprove him; the Archbishop of Durango, Mgr. González, a very well-informed man, but given the mitre too young, having the temperament of a political leader, but domineering, blundering, restless, inconsistent; the Bishop of Tabasco, Mgr. Pascual Díaz, an intelligent Jesuit, ambitious, intriguing, intolerant, who, as Secretary of the Committee of the Episcopacy, which he has been since the forced abandonment of his see, plays a part in religious affairs which tends each day to become more important; but all five virtually open candidates to succeed the primate and, because of that, rivaling one another in their irreconcilability in order to make their influence stronger.

On the other hand, the group of the authors of the Revolution, with interests and ambitions often conflicting but united in their hatred of the Church: solidly established parties, rich in men and means, accustomed to power and government, supported by and obeying the suggestions of the labor and agrarian unions organized in the CROM, the all-powerful Regional Confederation of Mexican Workers which have always considered the clergy and their allies, the landed aristocracy, as their most implacable enemies. Finally, the President [Plutarco Elías Calles], with a will of steel, allowing neither discussion nor advice nor half-measures, and who has made the fight against the clergy his own personal policy. At his service, the officials of the Government obliged, under the threat of dismissal, to act ruthlessly; the army, well paid and well trained, stronger and better disciplined than ever; good finances; a police force thoroughly informed by a swarm of spies; a servile press, both by nature and through fear; the reputation of being determined on cruelly punishing any disorder and any breach of the law; in a word, a regime of autocracy and terror.

Document 77. When They Came for the Priest[14]

The final document in this section is the oral history of a campesina woman who remembered the arrest and removal of the priest in her town, Xalatlaco in the state of Mexico, located on the western slope of the Ajusco volcano. It provides a view of the church-state conflict at the grass roots, pointing out the significant role that priests played in Mexico's local society, politics, and economy, particularly in the country's heartland.

They Came for the Priest and Took Him Prisoner

I remember when Carranza[15] ordered the closure of the temples; He wanted to remove religion. This year we went on a pilgrimage afraid that they were going to catch us, to grab us, because that year was when the [church] services were closed. With the priest we went afraid. We went to stay at an inn in Santa Fe. We didn't go through the center, but through Chapultepec. We went through a small town

---

14. *Memoria campesina: La historia de Xalatlaco contada por su gente*, eds. Soledad González Montes and Alejandro Patiño Díaz (Toluca: Instituto Mexiquense de Cultura, 1994), 139–41. Translated by Madison Green.
15. Based on the context, the author means "Calles," not "Carranza."

nearby called Atzcapotzalco. We even went as far to go around; we entered from the side of the Basilica, we didn't go in from the front because of the danger.

The priest was Nemesio González from Calimaya. He was the one who started that, I believe for two years, but by the second year we were already free. For one year we watched our backs, we were afraid. Surely the priest was afraid as well. No more than a year did Carranza want to remove religion., I believe that it was because he was not Catholic, and because of that he wanted to close the churches. That year they came for the priest and they took him prisoner. They came for him one morning and arrested him in Toluca, as a prisoner, but kept him in a private home.

It was still just me. We got a lot of people together because we were members of the A.C.J.M.;[16] there were young people and they were the ones in charge of the agreement. When they came to bring [take away] the priest, they went immediately calling out to the people. Then word spread and we followed the priest. I think he went on horseback, the people walking. The soldiers on horseback but the infantry on foot. This is how they took the priest. I remember well, it was a sad thing. At Atenco's hacienda (farm) they stopped to have lunch; even for that they had sympathy. Then the people saw and ran to give the priest breakfast. They left the people alone, they did not offend anyone, only the priests. Those who wanted to go went, men and women.

From Atenco we went to Toluca. To a house that I believe was a barrack, it was then that the priest arrived there. They gave him a room for himself, they weren't that barbarian, and the people stayed where they could. The next day they took him out to testify, they walked him from one place to another. What I don't know is what they accused him of, I do not agree with you there. But what are they going to accuse him of? Nothing more, I believe, because he served the church; what else would they want? The people ran, went from here to there, seeing how it was arranged. We didn't take off; wherever the priest went, everyone went with him. The next day they took him out to another place, to San Juan de Dios; they took him to I don't know what and everyone followed him there behind him. They were many.

It made me feel a lot of pain and when I remember it gives me [pain] . . . because they took him like a criminal, just like a criminal I say, with soldiers in the back and soldiers in front and on the sides, as if they were going to run away. I remember this day and it makes me very sad. If the priest wasn't bad, only that Carranza made it that he wanted to remove religion. That is why he imprisoned many priests, such as our parish priest from Calimaya, Nemesio González.

The priest worked a lot; he was good. If he had stayed here, the town would have progressed a lot. He ordered the purchase of blackberry so that there would be silkworm; he had a soap kiln built, so that people could work making soap. He brought teachers, he brought ladies so that they could show the women how to make shawls;

---

16. Association of Mexican Christian Youth.

they showed the men how to make bricks. On Sundays the children were called for the doctrine. In the afternoon, he would teach us the doctrine for a while and then he would take us to the ravine near San Bartolito, there was clay in this river. He would take us to bring mud and sand from elsewhere for the soap and the brick kiln. He also taught the cultivation of bees and distributed [it] so that there would be wax. It was when they began to do something for the church. I don't remember what he looked like, but he was probably an old man. That priest didn't last.

VIII. Toward the "Institutional Revolution," 1928–1940

On July 17, 1928, the bullets of a Catholic assassin claimed the revolution's last high-profile victim: General Álvaro Obregón (doc. 78). Obregón's murder and the reorganization of the revolutionary elite under the aegis of a national ruling party substantially strengthened the authority of a state that still called itself revolutionary. In the words of President Calles, Mexico passed from a being a country "ruled by one man" to a "nation of institutions and laws" (doc. 79). The new regime ultimately withstood substantial challenges from the Cristero rebels (doc. 80) and disaffected Obregón supporters (doc. 81).

After Obregón's assassination, Calles continued to exert substantial power from behind the scene as *jefe máximo*, or supreme chief, of the revolution. While the Great Depression wracked Mexico, and agrarian reform all but disappeared as the nation faced a food shortage, substantial reform movements continued to challenge the status quo. The state government of Tabasco published a primer that outlined the priorities and ethics of "socialist" citizens (doc. 82), and women pushed for full enfranchisement, aware of the recent implementation of women's suffrage in the United States (doc. 83).

In 1934, the revolutionary regime veered left under President Lázaro Cárdenas. The new administration reinvigorated the agrarian reform program (doc. 84) and distributed 42 million acres of land. To an unprecedented degree, Cárdenas also made himself available to ordinary citizens (doc. 85), allowing each Mexican to send the government a telegram per week free of charge. A newly radicalized labor movement pushed the Cardenistas to significant reforms (doc. 86), and most significantly, the expropriation of the foreign-owned oil industry after its owners refused to follow court orders in favor of the oil workers and their union (docs. 87–88).

Cardenismo had its limits. Women were disappointed not only in the failure of legislation to ensure women's suffrage but also in the persistence of patriarchal structures (doc. 89). Soviet émigré Leon Trotsky observed the weakness of the labor movement (doc. 90). However, the greatest challenge to the government came from the right, in 1940, from disaffected supporters of General Juan Andreu Almazán, the loser of the presidential elections to choose Cárdenas's successor (doc. 91). After that election, the revolution ran out of steam, giving way to a close wartime collaboration between Mexico and the United States and the ascent of a new generation of politicians.

Document 78. The Trial of José de León Toral
and Madre Conchita[1]

On July 17, 1928, José de León Toral assassinated General Álvaro Obregón at a banquet given in honor of his election to another presidential term. The investigation led the government to a religiously motivated network that included "Madre Conchita" (née Concepción de la Llata), the Mother Superior of the "Convento de las Hijas de María." Madre Conchita had organized a series of clandestine meetings with Toral in attendance following the execution of Father Miguel Pro, and his brother, Humberto, on trumped-up charges after the failure of an earlier assassination attempt against Obregón. On November 2, 1928, Toral and Madre Conchita were put on trial. The following excerpt from the trial's transcript reveals much about the mindset of the group. Toral was executed in February 1929. Madre Conchita was sentenced to twenty years imprisonment in a penal colony but was pardoned two years later.

—Toral: Humberto Pro had been my comrade since 1920 . . . I went to his house when they took his dead body there, and I stayed a long while looking at Humberto's cadaver. . . . I consider the assassination of Obregón the fruit of his death alone.

I sometimes imagined this: if we lived in another world, or if the afterlife were Europe, for example, I could say to Sr. Obregón with a friendly voice: "Look, things can't work out here unless you are no longer here. Let's go to Europe; I promise to accompany you. I have a friend there who will supply all of our needs, who will lodge us in a palace. In the end, the only sacrifice is for you to leave Mexico and your wife and never to be in touch with them again. But we will be very fine there. I offer to accompany you so that you are not alone, and so that you do not even have to make the trip by yourself.

. . . In that fashion I asked this of God: "May he save himself; move his heart . . . so that one of my bullets may strike him in the heart, and that this may be the signal that he has repented; and that you have touched him and forgiven him. When I heard that two of my bullets had hit his heart, it made a marvelous impression upon me.

. . . Shots still rang out when I heard "don't kill him, don't kill him."[2]

. . . I pursued these activities and dedicated the entire day to them. It was not difficult to imagine that they would apprehend me one day and send me to the Islas

---

1. Héctor, Rodríguez Espinoza, "Assassination of Alvaro Obregón, 1928," August 22, 1916, Primera Plana, accessed April 5, 2021, https://www.primeraplanadigital.com.mx/2016/08/22/asesinato-de-alvaro-obregon-1928-relato-del-juicio-historico-de-toral-y-la-madre-conchita/. Translated by Jürgen Buchenau.
2. Obregón's friends wished to see the assassin captured alive so they could interrogate him.

Marías or kill me. I told Madre Conchita this, and she could not conceive of me in any other way.

. . . They arrested my father on the morning of the next day; and my own father criticized me. He was crying and said "But what is this? What happened?" Afterward, he told someone else: "He can't have acted alone; someone made him do it; tell all, what do you have to gain from keeping it a secret?" . . .

—Ortega:[3] Do you consider Madre Conchita a woman who is superior in terms of her intelligence, her teaching, her religious faith, and in leading an exemplary life?

—Toral: Of course.

—Ortega: Do you regard her as better than you?

—Toral: Yes, I do.

—Ortega: Did you visit her when she was in Chopo Street, two or three times per week?

—Yes, sir.

—President asks Madre Conchita: You were naturally not in agreement with the state of things regarding religion.

—Madre Conchita: Yes, I agree, because I believe it is a trial from God, and God so commands. There were never any seditious meetings [in my convent]; I deny it.

—President: How can a meeting not have been seditious in which a person received poison so that he could go kill General Obregón?

—Madre Conchita: . . . The fact that other elements that . . . partook in other activities entered my house was a random event. . . .

—President: A random event repeated with great frequency.

—Madre Conchita: No, sir.

—Was it a coincidence that you watched the making of bombs?

—Madre Conchita: I did not see that.

—President: But you knew about it.

—Madre Conchita: No, sir.

—President: Well, according to some existing testimony, you seem involved in this.

—Madre Conchita: But I wasn't present at their activities.

—President: In your presence they changed their story; when they were alone, they told the truth. Because it is strange that they would give a deposition to the . . . police sworn before the judge, where they have all of the guarantees provided by law, and nevertheless, they change their minds when you are there.

Why did these men go to the convent? They could have gone to look for another house for their meetings.

—Madre Conchita: They were more afraid in other houses but my own.

---

3. Fernando Ortega, Toral's defense attorney.

—President: How come you didn't decide to dissuade Toral from killing General Obregón?

—Madre Conchita: How can I dissuade someone who hasn't told me what he's trying to do? How can I tell Your Excellency that you shouldn't become a monk if you don't intend to do so? (Laughter)

—Procurador Ezequiel Padilla: When their attempt at Celaya failed, you started to train José de León Toral adequately.

—Madre Conchita: I will train you to be a priest.

—Padilla: When I come to seek your advice, you can go ahead. . . . For you, crimes do not exist.

—Madre Conchita: Yes, crimes do exist.

—Padilla: But everything is the will of God.

—Madre Conchita: Because there are things that God commands and things that God allows.

Document 79. A Nation of Institutions and Laws[4]

Obregón's assassination removed Mexico's primary political and military leader from the scene. With the help of President Calles, Obregón had ruthlessly shoved aside his opponents, an effort highlighted by the killings of presidential hopefuls Francisco R. Serrano and Arnulfo Gómez in 1927. Therefore, Obregón's murder cast suspicions upon the political class, including President Calles himself. Calles's final state-of-the-nation address to Congress definitively quashed rumors that he would extend his time in office and called for institutionalization and the removal of the military from political life. Not surprisingly, however, as the so-called jefe máximo of the revolution, Calles would retain great political influence after his term expired.

The death of the president-elect is an irreparable loss which has left the country in an extremely difficult situation. There is no shortage of capable men: indeed, we are fortunate to have many capable individuals. But there is no person of indisputable prestige, who has a base of public support and such personal and political strength that his name alone merits general confidence.

The general's death brings a most grave and vital problem to public attention, for the issue is not merely political, but one of our very survival.

We must recognize that General Obregón's death exacerbates existing political and administrative problems. These problems arise in large measure from our

---

4. From Gilbert Joseph and Timothy J. Henderson, *The Mexico Reader: History, Culture, Politics* (Durham, NC: Duke University Press, 2003), 421–24. Reprinted by permission.

political and social struggle: that is, they arise from the definitive triumph of the guiding principles of the Revolution, social principles like those expressed in articles 27 and 123 [of the Constitution], which must never be taken away from the people. At the start of the previous administration, we embarked on what may be called the political or governmental phase of the Mexican Revolution, searching with ever-increasing urgency for ways to satisfy political and social concerns and to find means of governing appropriate to this new phase.

All of these considerations define the magnitude of the problem. Yet the very circumstance that Mexico now confronts—namely, that for perhaps the first time in our history there are no "caudillos"—gives us the opportunity to direct our country's politics toward a true institutional life. We shall move, once and for all, from being a country "ruled by one man" to a "nation of institutions and laws."

The unique solemnity of this moment deserves the most disinterested and patriotic reflection. It obliges me to delve not only into the circumstances of this moment, but also to review the characteristics of our political life up until now. It is our duty to fully understand and appreciate the facts which can ensure the country's immediate and future peace, promote its prestige and development, and safeguard the revolutionary conquests that hundreds of thousands of Mexicans have sealed with their blood.

I consider it absolutely essential that I digress from my brief analysis to make a firm and irrevocable declaration, which I pledge upon my honor before the National Congress, before the country, and before all civilized peoples. But first, I must say that perhaps never before have circumstances placed a chief executive in a more propitious situation for returning the country to one-man rule. I have received many suggestions, offers, and even some pressures—all of them cloaked in considerations of patriotism and the national welfare—trying to get me to remain in office. For reasons of morality and personal political creed, and because it is absolutely essential that we change from a "government of caudillos" to a "regime of institutions," I have decided to declare solemnly and with such clarity that my words cannot lend themselves to suspicions and interpretations, that not only will I not seek the prolongation of my mandate by accepting an extension or designation as provisional president, but I will never again on any occasion aspire to the presidency of my country. At the risk of making this declaration needlessly emphatic, I will add that this is not merely an aspiration or desire on my own part, but a positive and immutable fact: never again will an incumbent president of the Mexican Republic return to occupy the presidency. Of course, I have absolutely no intention of abandoning my duties as a citizen, nor do I intend to retire from the life of struggle and responsibility that is the lot of every soldier and of all men born of the Revolution. . . .

I need remind no one of how the caudillos obstructed—perhaps not always deliberately, but always in a logical and natural way—the formation of strong alternative means by which the country might have confronted its internal and external crises. Nor need I remind you how the caudillos obstructed or delayed the peaceful evolution of Mexico into an institutional country, one in which men are what they should be: mere accidents, of no real importance beside the perpetual and august serenity of institutions and laws. . . .

. . . Effective freedom of suffrage must be extended even to groups representing the reaction, including the clerical reaction. . . . The districts where the political or clerical reaction wins the vote will, for many years at least, be outnumbered by those where the progressive social revolutionaries triumph. . . .

I would not be behaving honorably if I did not point out the many dangers that could result from dissension within the revolutionary family. If such dissension should occur, it would be nothing new in the history of Mexico, which has at time abounded in shady, backroom political dealings that brought to power ambitious, unprincipled men who weakened and delayed the final triumph of progress and liberalism in Mexico, surrendering themselves, whether consciously or not, to our eternal enemies.

Document 80. Plan of Los Altos[5]

The Cristero Rebellion continued to spread amid the chaos of the presidential succession and a Yaqui revolt in Sonora, which allowed the rebels to consolidate ground in central Mexico. They gained the services of the former Porfirian general Enrique Gorostieta, who had grown up in a secular family and embraced the cause as a chance to fight a government he despised. With the support of tens of thousands of men and women from Mexico's heartland, the Cristeros attained a fighting strength of 50,000, the size of the Constitutionalist army at the peak of the War of the Factions. In 1928, Gorostieta issued a manifesto on behalf of the Cristero armies.

1.—More than two years ago, the Mexican people, tired of the opprobrious tyranny of Plutarco Elías Calles and his minions, took up arms to reconquer the liberties that those despots had stolen from them, and specifically those of religion and conscience. During this long period, the "Liberators" have covered themselves in glory, and the tyrants have not achieved anything else than to sink deeper into the mud and ignominy by trying to drown in blood the powerful efforts of a people that detests them and is resolved to punish them.

---

5. Román Iglesias González, *Planes políticos, proclamas, manifiestos y otros documentos de la Independencia al México moderno, 1812–1940* (Mexico City: Biblioteca Jurídica, 1998), 941–51. Translated by Jürgen Buchenau.

It is true that final victory has not been obtained, because our oppressors count on many material resources, but it is also true that the struggle has proved to the world that the people have taken up arms against the tyrants not because of a transitory sentiment of wrath and vengeance, but impelled and sustained by the highest ideals. The "Liberators" have spilled their noble blood generously and without reserve: the young, the adult, the old, and even the children and the women have written the most brilliant pages that will grace future generations with glory following our triumph in this bloody struggle against the barbaric Bolshevik dissolution. It will be the remedy for the Americas and perhaps the beginning of a universal cure. . . .

8.—The program that the Liberating Movement has adopted, in accordance with the League and entirely corresponding to my convictions can be summarized in one single word: FREEDOM! Freedom of conscience and worship, freedom of instruction, freedom of association, freedom of labor, freedom of the press: all of the freedoms!

15.—In light of the foregoing, we declare:

I.—Named by genuine national representation, I am assuming the charge of Military Chief of the Liberating Movement. . . .

III.—We confirm the Liberators' disavowal all of the usurping powers, both Federal and at the state level.

IV.—We decree the reestablishment of the Constitution of 1857 WITHOUT THE REFORM LAWS. . . .

V.—The Constitution can be reformed through the proceeding established in its Article 127 or by "plebiscite" or "referendum" so that all citizens, whether armed or not, can manifest their desires and so that the Mexican people can at last have a Constitution that is truly their own, born out of their aspirations and traditions, and that corresponds to popular needs.

VI.—In cases where a "plebiscite" or "referendum" is used, women of age will have the obligation to vote.

VII.—We recognize any and all measures that have been issued up to the present date that aim to recognize the right of working people to form unions, to assert their rights, to defend them and improve their conditions, as long as they are fair. The application of these laws will be effective for all for whom they have been issued, and not for the benefit of favorites.

VIII.—In the area of the distribution of ejidos, the Liberating Government will set up commissions that establish agreements between ejidatarios and landowners and adopt adequate proceedings to ensure that the indemnification due to be paid to the landowners is effective and fair. The redistribution of rural properties will also be continued where it is necessary and useful to the common good, but only in fair and equitable form and pending indemnification. In this fashion, it will be possible to furnish property to the greatest number.

IX.—Our liberating forces will be constituted as a "National Guard," a name that they will use henceforth. The motto of the "National Guard" will be "God, Fatherland, and Liberty."

X.—The Civil Leader of the Liberating Movement will be named by the Directive Committee of the Liga Nacional Defensora de la Libertad Religiosa (National League in Defense of Religious Liberty), after previous consultation to assess the opinion of the National Guard. In the meantime, the Military Chief will recognize, as Supreme Authority, the person who shall be named by agreement between the Directive Committee and the Military Chief.

XI.—The Military Chief possesses all of the powers that may be necessary in the branches of the Treasury and War.

XII.—This plan cannot be modified except by mutual agreement between the Directive Committee of the Liga Nacional Defensora de la Libertad Religiosa and the Military Chief. . . .

XIV.—Upon taking the Capital of the Republic and reestablishing order in the nation, we will proceed with its political reconstruction in conformity with the precepts of the Constitution of 1857.

. . .

GOD, FATHERLAND, AND LIBERTY

LOS ALTOS, Jalisco, October 28, 1928; Feast of Christ the King, E. Gorostieta, Jr.

Document 81. Plan of Hermosillo[6]

The succession question after Obregón's death provided the backdrop for the last serious uprising against the government during the Mexican Revolution: the 1929 Escobar Rebellion. What follows is the official manifesto of the rebels, many of them die-hard Obregón allies who blamed Calles for the assassination of their hero and also believed that Calles would rule like a dictator from behind the scenes. As will become clear, the rebels had political rather than socioeconomic reforms in mind.

ARTICLE 1: The investiture of Citizen Emilio Portes Gil as Provisional President of the Republic is repudiated.

---

6. U.S. Department of State, *Papers Relating to the Foreign Relations of the United States, 1929*, vol. 3, doc. 374 (Washington, D.C.: U.S. Government Printing Office, 1944).

ARTICLE 2: Those members of Congress of the Union who, directly or indirectly, combat or aggressively oppose the present movement shall cease to function as Deputies or Senators.

ARTICLE 3: The members of the Supreme Court of Justice of the Nation who, directly or indirectly, combat or aggressively oppose the present movement, shall cease to hold office.

ARTICLE 4: The Governors, Deputies and Magistrates of the Federal entities who, directly or indirectly, combat or aggressively oppose the present movement, shall cease to function under their respective investitures.

ARTICLE 5: If, at the time this plan triumphs, there be in the Chambers of the Federal Congress a majority of their members who have recognized or sanctioned this movement, measures will be taken opportunely to designate a new Provisional President, in the manner and under the terms prescribed by the Constitution of the Republic.

ARTICLE 6: If, upon the triumph of this movement it be impossible legally to organize the General Congress, the Chief of the movement shall convoke extraordinary elections of Deputies and Senators as soon as possible, and shall dictate the pertinent measures for the complete and prompt reestablishment of Constitutional regime in the country.

ARTICLE 7: In case the Supreme Court of Justice of the Nation be disintegrated, the Provisional President who may he appointed by the Congress shall proceed, opportunely and legally, to the reintegration of said tribunal.

ARTICLE 8: If, with the success of this movement, the powers of some of the Federal entities should disappear because of their having combatted or been hostile to the present plan, the local Congresses, or, in its proper case, the Senate of the Republic, shall dictate, opportunely, the resolutions pertinent to the reintegration of the same.

ARTICLE 9: In case the Federal Congress shall not be reinstated legally upon the success of this plan, the inherent Chief of this movement shall assume charge of the Executive Power of the Union.

ARTICLE 10. During the period of strife, and until the reestablishment of Constitutional rule in the country, the Citizen Chief of this movement shall be charged with reorganizing, by designation of his own, the Provisional Government, for the management and administration of the public affairs of the country.

ARTICLE 11. The Chief of the movement is authorized to make the designations of Provisional Governors and Chiefs of Operations which he may deem expedient for the control and administration of the various Federal entities and territories, until Constitutional rule in the country shall be reestablished.

ARTICLE 12: The Chief of this movement is likewise authorized to dictate all measures which he may deem necessary to safeguard the national interests.

Article 13: The organized forces which shall recognize and support the present movement, and those which during the period of strife shall expressly adhere to this plan and subordinate themselves to the Chief of the same, shall constitute the "Renovating Army of the Revolution."

Article 14: Citizen General of Division Don José Gonzalo Escobar is recognized as Supreme Chief of this movement and of the 'Ejército Renovador de la Revolución.'

Article 15: The Chief of the movement and General in Chief of the 'Ejercito Renovador de la Revolución' shall have all the powers necessary to direct the military campaign in the country and to dictate all measures of a military character which the success of the movement and the interests of the National shall demand.

Hermosillo, Sonora, March 3, 1929.

Document 82. The Socialist ABCs[7]

Several states, especially in the southeast, embarked upon radical revolutionary experiments, earning them the moniker of "laboratories of the revolution." One of the best examples is Tabasco, dominated by the strongman Tomás Garrido Canabal for most of the period 1922–1935. An ardent anticlerical, Garrido sought a genuine cultural revolution that would profoundly change the citizens of his state. He desired to promote atheism, temperance, and collaborative social action, organizing all Tabascans into "resistance leagues" and forming the "red shirts" as a paramilitary force. The following selection appeared in a school primer published by the state press in 1929.

Man is a sociable being.

Anyone who isolates himself is an *egoist*.

Those who want to have everything for themselves, and who try to monopolize land and money in a few hands, impoverish the country and bring general discontent and misery to the majority.

The monopolizers of wealth exploit the workers and are humanity's worst enemies.

The worker needs to alternate between tools and books, between the workshop or field and the school, so that, cultivating his intelligence and forming his sensibilities, he will become a conscious being who thinks, feels, and loves.

The worker who has cultivated his intelligence improves and dignifies both himself and his family.

---

7. Joseph and Henderson, *The Mexico Reader*, 411–17. Reprinted by permission.

The worker's ignorance is very dangerous, for it allows him to be victimized by the exploiters, priests, and alcohol.

Little Proletarian

I call you this because I know that your father is a proletarian and you will be one also.

You lack much, and you and your family work hard for your food.

Although you are still young, you have already begun watering the soil with a sweat of your brow, and your hands are growing course from using heavy tools.

It is good that this is so: although small, you are already manly because as a child, you still enjoy the feeling of being useful. To be useful is to be good for something to do something to get something, and it is the noblest aspiration one can have in life.

To be useful is to be happy.

There are very many proletarian families throughout the world who, despite their hard work, do not have what they need.

The Society of Yesterday

. . . In our society, before the Revolution of 1910, an odious division of classes came into being. There was one class that enjoyed every consideration, and which had support of the government. This was the privileged class.

The victims of the privileged class were the workers of the cities and of the countryside; the latter . . . lived in the saddest conditions you can imagine.

They were exploited without pity, and the greatest fortunes of Tabasco were built upon their excessive labor.

The greedy capitalist packed many tears and sorrows away in their strong treasure chests. . . .

It was within this society . . . that the revolution broke out: the struggle was joined against the regime which protected the state of affairs, and after several years and much blood, tears, and suffering, the revolution triumphed.

With its triumph, the workers freedom was secured, and they abandoned the farms where they had worked as servants for many long years. . . .

The New Society

The current society tries to organize itself without iniquitous exploitation and without shameful servility.

The goal is the dignification of the Mexican family, and we do all we can to achieve that goal.

The principles of solidarity, a spirit of cooperation, and feelings of equality, are inculcated in the school and propagated at civic and cultural meetings.

The leaders of this social transformation seek to organize men into a more just and humane society.

The ideal of the new societies is to derive individual rights from those of the collectivity.

The supreme aspiration is to create governments that respond to man.

Socialism is the system of organization that is the best adapted to reach in these goals, ideals, and aspirations.

The Good Citizen

Worker of the field and city:

If you want to feel the true happiness to which we all aspire, bear in mind your duties. Once these are carried out, you will understand your rights and how to retain them when someone opposes you.

The first duty that nature has imposed upon you, whether you are a son, a husband, or a father, is to provide comfort to those who depend upon you. . . . If you do shoddy work, you will be obliged to take whatever the boss sees fit to pay you, which will never be enough to account for your needs. If your work is done well, you have the right to set the price in accordance with your needs, and you will have enough to live with decency and ease. . . .

Do not ask for a loan, and do not stop eating in order to save money, since savings through debt or the cost of hunger are not savings.

Do good work and economize, and happiness will come to you.

The Plagues of Humanity

Think of how alcohol destroys your system, making you incapable of all human activities which are indispensable for you and your family to live; be aware that if you ruined your body, you enervate and pollute your spirit to the point of allowing it to degenerate into abjection and wretchedness. . . .

Reflect on the brutal scene one sees in the home of the drunkard when, disorderly and demented, he mistreats his tender and long-suffering wife and innocent children with words and deeds. . . .

Campesino, think, reflect, arm yourself with valor and energy, flee from the tavern and from vice, because this depresses and dishonors you and takes away the fruit of your labor. . . .

The False Religions

If you need to have faith in something, have faith in yourself and in your labor. Nothing contributed to the success of an undertaking like perseverance and effort.

No mythical god, no supernatural cause, is capable of granting you the recompense for a job you have not done.

Do not think or hope for aid from gods who live in heaven. The only thing that can make you prosperous is the effort that you make to better your own position.

The only way to achieve welfare is through work. Work that is conscience-guided and always striving toward perfection is what makes us prosper economically and let us enjoy the satisfaction of having finished a job.

Do not have faith and false religions that teach you humility and force you to renounce your rights as a conscious citizen. . . .

Have faith in work as a duty, and this belief will be your best religion.

Document 83. Feminism and Suffrage[8]

Mexico City native Margarita Robles de Mendoza (1896–1954) was a major proponent of women's suffrage. She spent most of the 1920s and 1930s in the United States, but her writings were influential in Mexico, especially because her residence abroad made her immune from reprisals from the government. A graduate of Pomona College, she founded the Unión de Mujeres Americanas (Union of American Women) in 1934 to promote gender equality in the Americas. Robles returned to Mexico in 1938, hoping to see the Cárdenas administration implement women's suffrage. When the reform failed, Robles bitterly criticized the government. It was not until 1953 that women's suffrage became law for presidential elections.

Feminism is the name of the modern movement dedicated to defending women's personal as well as economic, social, and political rights. However, that does not describe all feminist women as necessarily and systematically rabid suffragists. Some might be interested in the economic or social aspect of the movement without concerning themselves with involvement in political issues. Similarly, for an infinite number of talented and highly useful men in society, the world of politics holds no interest at all.

The vote is not the whole of feminism. The vote is sought as a way to achieve economic or social objectives, and never as an obsessive end. Feminists seek suffrage as a concession because they do not regard the denial of the vote to women as reasonable or . . . democratic when many of them are superior in moral, intellectual, and even physical terms to many men who enjoy this privilege. Women who want to exercise this right will do so. Not all men exercise this right, either, if they did, we would not see cases of Nations and States where only two percent of the citizens votes.

Feminism wants a woman's personhood to be respected, and that she be treated as a human being and a responsible adult. It does not seek to knock something down, but to share, participate, and cooperate. . . .

A place for women in the social realm. We only ask for the opportunity to put our abilities into play in the concert of human society. Time and the exercise of those capabilities will show if they are modest or great. . . .

Feminism does not tear women from the home. We are keenly aware that we are different from men. It is precisely for that reason that in all areas of life there might be those who, thinking and feeling as we do, can interpret and understand these "differences." We are therefore delighted to hear musical compositions crafted by women, and we admire paintings and sculptures made by female

---

8. Margarita Robles de Mendoza, *La evolución de la mujer en México* (Mexico City: n.p. 1931), 97–103. Translated by Jürgen Buchenau.

hands. We thus enthusiastically cheer on the female public speaker and adore the poetess and female playwright, because there are flashes of the collective feminine soul in the work of these women, because in them we feel the vibrations of our spirit. It is for that reason as well that we ask that in lawmaking, our criteria be considered as well, rather than only male criteria . . . , because women understand us better. Therefore, we also want juries and judiciaries to include women. Society consists of two elements; why should only one of them . . . receive the satisfaction of its efforts?

Feminism does not endeavor to tear a woman from her home. Rather, it seeks to provide one to the woman who does not have a home, and to condition her to be the creative architect in this sanctuary. Naturally, by home we understand the space that encloses the purest affections, as in a sanctuary, characterized by the unification of high aspirations and the zeal for cooperation among family members, rather than a living space provisioned with . . . material comforts.

Better women will make better mothers. There is no doubt that the woman has not been left satisfied by the different stages through which her agency in the world has progressed. Since the era of the patriarchy, she has occasionally mastered her destiny through power or sexual attraction. But most often, she has been a slave subjected to selfish commands. What she seeks now is neither throne nor chain, but, instead, moral equality. . . .

As a prototype of Mexican feminism, we have looked upon the *soldadera*, precisely because she is the one who has shared the most in her man's life. She has faithfully followed him on his path in a state of sublime primitivism. At his side she has intoned his victory songs and shrieked with pain at his defeats. He has taken her with him everywhere. Wife, friend, comrade, partner: she has been all of those for her man. That is precisely what feminism wants all women to be regardless of their level of culture or social station. Seeking equal rights for men and women equalizes responsibilities as well as participation in matters concerning their life together. . . .

Feminists do not accept the imposition of arbitrary limits for their course in life. As human beings, they believe they have the same right as men to pursue the path that pleases them. Of course, they are willing to suffer the consequences of their actions. They aspire to equality before the law and the treatment by society that they deserve as adults.

Document 84. The Cardenista Agrarian Reform Program[9]

Formulated in the first year of Lázaro Cárdenas's term, the following reflections offer a view into the new government's vision for agriculture. The author of this selection, Dr. Ramón Beteta Quintana, was general director of Mexico's national statistical institute (INEGI), and later, under-secretary of foreign relations. In 1935, Beteta offered these reflections at a binational symposium organized by the University of Virginia. It became clear to all who listened that the Cárdenas administration would give impetus to the land distribution program that had ground to a virtual halt at the height of the Great Depression (1929–1932).

. . . The concentration of land in fewer and fewer hands has been the central factor in the history of Mexico, and the problems that concentration has created the most serious questions confronting the Revolutionary Governments. The *conquistadores* divided the country among themselves with a system of "encomiendas";[10] the war of independence succeeded only in changing the nationality of the exploiters; the Reform movement was able to change solely the name of the owners and to break down the communal holdings; finally, during the Díaz regime the process of concentration was accentuated and by both legal and foul means the rape of the pueblos continued until the end of that dictatorship, 2 percent of the population owned 70 percent of the land, and in some States as much as 98 percent of the rural heads of family were landless. . . .

One may really say that the Agrarian Reform begins in Mexico in 1920. During the Presidency of President Obregón, it got well under way and within the following term, that of General Calles, a steady increase in distribution of the land is to be noted. During the interim Government of Portes Gil, more land was distributed than during the four years of his predecessor, although his term lasted only fourteen months. Then comes the Government of Ortiz Rubia, during which the Agrarian movement slowed down, and it was even in danger of collapse. The provisional Presidency of General Rodríguez, in spite of the fact that many people thought he was rather conservative, was also fruitful in dividing the land.

President Cárdenas, well known for his enthusiasm in regard to the Agrarian Reform has given new stimulus to the movement. In one single day, May 1, 1935, . . . 552,936 hectares of land were distributed to 353 villages and to the benefit of 36,856 heads of families. . . . [The] Agrarian Census taken last April 10 show that there were in Mexico 7,041 *ejidos* . . . benefiting 895,284 heads of families who have

---

9. Ramón Beteta, *Economic and Social Program of Mexico (a Controversy)* (Mexico City: n.p., 1935), 22–28, 44–46.

10. Labor grants given to the conquistadors that allowed them to exploit indigenous labor virtually without limitation.

received 11,741,191 hectares of land, of which 3,735,931 hectares are crop land. The rest is considered pasture or woodland, not suitable for cultivation.

This gives a rough idea of the extent of the Reform, so far as the actual distribution of the land is concerned. One must remember, however, to really understand its significance that Mexico has only 14,517,699 hectares of cultivable land and that according to the Census of 1930, 3,626,278 persons were gainfully employed in agriculture.

It is important in this connection to insist once more upon the necessity of being aware of the fallacy of Mexico's unlimited wealth. In fact, it is the scarcity of arable land that has made the Agrarian Reform so acute. As you know, Mexico is a mountainous country with insufficient rainfall, and therefore a large part of its territory is unfit for agricultural purposes.

That considerable progress has been made, however, is shown not only by the figures given above but also by the tremendous change in the attitude of the people. One cannot judge the agrarian reform in terms of economic factors alone. The Mexican people are the children of their land where they have lived for centuries; where they have multiplied and grown; where they resisted the incursion of the Spaniards, the dryness of the desert, the awe of the mountain and the sterility of the jungle. Attachment to the soil is the central factor in the psychology of our people. Having back their land our native population are again in harmony with nature. . . .

Some of us in Mexico have visualized differently the future of the agricultural economy. We believe that Mexico finds herself in a privileged position to determine her destiny by being a pre-capitalistic state with some of our people even in a pre-pecuniary economy and at the same time by observing the effects of the last crisis of the capitalistic world we think that we should be able to use the advantages of the industrial era without having to suffer from its well-known shortcomings. We think that we should attempt to industrialize Mexico consciously, intelligently avoiding the evils of industrialism, such as urbanism, exploitation of men by men, production for sale instead of production for the satisfaction of human needs, economic insecurity, waste, shabby goods, and the mechanization of the workmen. It's not an impossible dream. We are convinced that the evils of capitalism are not to be found in the application of machinery to the productive process, I'd rather ask a merely legal question: who is the owner of the machinery. We want the land and its necessary equipment to be at the disposal of those who till it, rather than be the means to exploit these men. Some of us believe, furthermore, that profit-making is not the only incentive of human endeavor, but rather a motive that happens to have been chosen and over-developed in the capitalistic regime.

There is nothing fatal in the mistakes of the system, or at least so we hope. We have dreamt of a Mexico of *ejidos* and small industrial communities, electrified, with sanitation in which goods will be produced for the purpose of satisfying the needs of the people; machinery will be employed to relieve men from heavy toil, and not for so-called overproduction. Machine made goods may still be beautiful, for they will be made by the same people whose artistic sense is now expressed by the work of their hands, and there's no reason to believe that the changing of the tools will *per se* make them different. Mechanization meant not the use of machinery; [but instead] the pressure brought to bear on [laborers] to produce at the highest speed the largest amount possible.

In short, we have chosen the *ejido* as the center of our rural economy. Within its limits, land belongs to "him who works it with his hands" as our Indian poet expressed it. Methods of production machinery will be introduced without having to make rugged individualists out of the *ejidatarios* and at the same time without killing the human desire of progress in those communities. Then, and only then, could the national economy be planned, not by directing the conflicting interests of the various individuals, but by conceiving the country as a unit whose needs are to be satisfied by the harmonious working of these villages, agricultural or industrial, in an effort to make the whole country secure and prosperous.

Document 85. Petitioning President Cárdenas[11]

To accentuate his differences from Jefe Máximo Calles, *Cárdenas emphasized that he was a man of the people. His campaign tour included villages and small towns as well as major cities, and he became known as a great listener who cared about his citizens on a personal level. As legend had it, his private secretary once presented him with a stack of official papers as well as a telegram. Each of the papers addressed a major national issue, and Cárdenas referred these matters to a cabinet officer. The telegram came from a campesino of a small village: the author informed the president that his corn had dried up, his burro had died, his sow had been stolen, and his baby was sick. As the story went, Cárdenas ordered the presidential train prepared so he could go to the village at once. The following petition from an indigenous community in Mexico's far north gives a glimpse into popular expectations of Cárdenas.*

Mexico, D.F., May 20, 1937
Citizen President of the Republic
National Palace
Mexico, D.F.
Ernesto Montemayor, member of the Ki ka poo Tribe, with residence in the municipality of M. Múzquiz in the state of Coahuila, asks kindly to be permitted

11. Fondo Presidentes, Lázaro Cárdenas del Río, 502.1/15, Archivo General de la Nación, Mexico City. Translated by Jürgen Buchenau.

to let you know, Mr. President, that I have been commissioned by Captain Pa pi kua no, Chief of the Tribe to which I belong. [I am] to remind you that in September 1936, when you traveled through the north of the country, you offered to the aforementioned Chief of the Ki ka poo Tribe monthly shipments of 3 boxes of ammunition, as well as 3 sewing machines, and that he has only received 2 of the latter. Please give the necessary orders so that we may be sent the remaining sewing machine.

With regard to the ammunition, please send us 1,200 cartridges for the carbine 28.

We also ask for your attention to send the necessary orders to the Agrarian Department to immediately commission the naming of engineers who will undertake the survey (*deslinde*) of our land area.

I send you my thanks, in advance, for your attention to this petition that I am making on behalf of my Chief, Captain Pa pi kua no . . .

The commissioner of the Ki ka poo Tribe

Ernesto Montemayor

Mr. President. We do not have a single centavo. We appeal to your goodness in asking you for your help by paying for the return trip from Mexico to Múzquiz, Coahuila, for 2 people.

Document 86. The Mexican Flag, Capitalists, and the Proletariat[12]

The following document contains excerpts of a speech by Vicente Lombardo Toledano, the leader of the Confederación de Trabajadores Mexicanos (CTM), Mexico's largest labor confederation since the Cárdenas period. In the early 1930s, the CTM had supplanted the Callista CROM, displaying significantly more radical positions including advocacy for a socialist transformation of the economy. In this regard, the CTM of the 1930s far exceeded Cárdenas's willingness to undertake social and economic reforms. A skilled orator, Lombardo Toledano summarized the CTM's position as a partner but also a critic of the Cardenista government. Note the parallels between this speech and the one by the agrarista (since turned conservative) Soto y Gama in Section IV (doc. 38).

In the heat of the period 1910–1935, we . . . ask ourselves once again: what is the Mexican Fatherland? When did it emerge? What is it? Who are its members? How

---

12. Vincente Lombardo Toledano, "La bandera mexicana y el proletariado," February 6, 1936, Memoria Política de México, accessed March 15, 2021, http://www.memoriapo liticademexico.org/Textos/6Revolucion/1936-LTV-bandera.html. Translated by Jürgen Buchenau.

should we defend it? What should we love about it? What should we despise about it? . . . Where is the Fatherland, whose is the Fatherland in Mexico?

We already have the answer: the Monterrey entrepreneurial class raises the tricolor flag and says: "This is the Fatherland; we are Mexicans above all else, and the workers of Mexico are Russians, they are traitors to the Fatherland." (Applause). The Fatherland belongs to Monterrey? What audacity! What cynicism! What sarcasm! . . .

In every nation of the world, there are two fatherlands: that of the exploited and that of the exploiters. The fatherland of the exploiters is always smiling; the fatherland of those who suffer is always full of tears. That is why tonight, in view of the perfidious, mean, false, cynical attitude of the Monterrey business class, the time has come to vindicate what is ours, and to place those so-called patriots in the position they deserve: traitors to the Mexican Fatherland. (Applause).

In Sonora, whom does the fatherland belong to? A group of hacendados, a group of old and new rich; indigenous tribes, eternal cannon fodder; peasants in chains; rapacious priests at the service of the overseer . . . ; brothels in the North; miners eaten by tuberculosis; that is the fatherland of Sonora.

In Baja California, half of the territory of the fatherland belongs to the Yankees. In [Baja California Sur], foreigners also own the mines. Work-related diseases have ruined the miners, miserable people with no possible communication with the Continent. In Chihuahua, the fatherland is the same: mines owned by foreign companies, half-naked Tarahumaras who barely speak Spanish, Creole rustlers who team up with cattle rustlers from the United States. There are many Villista graves, and many graves of anonymous soldiers who can no longer rise up to say that the fatherland is not of Monterrey, but of the hardscrabble land of Chihuahua that punished with rifles, in many battles, those who searched for something to eat in agony. (Applause).

In Coahuila, whose fatherland is it? Who uses it? Who holds it? Who takes advantage of it? Foreign companies own the coal-producing region; old and modern large landowners as well; brothels on the border; ignorance in the fields; people still without ejidos; starvation wages. And in Tamaulipas, the head of a family on the coast receives a nominal salary of one peso, but his wife, his children and his in-laws have to work for that sum of money, and after twenty years of saving part of that miserable wage, he can barely buy a pair of . . . underwear: that is the fatherland in Tamaulipas. And who owns the oil zone? The pariahs of Mexico, the Mexican workers?

And so on, from North to South, all the way to Chiapas: the shame, the mass grave, the torture of those of us who have certain ideas and a certain sense of responsibility; herds of human beasts at the service of an oligarchy of German coffee planters in Soconusco . . . ; blinded by onchocerciasis, painted by the disease that stains the skin, tormented by goiter, which hangs enormous balls from their necks like the shearing of herds; poor and malnourished, because a few tortillas and chiles are not enough to live on.

And let us go up to the region where the air is purest, to the Mexican highlands, so often in everyone's voices: masses that live on the irreplaceable pulque, because if it were not for pulque they would have died of pellagra or any other disease that annihilates men who do not have enough calories to survive.

That is the fatherland in 1935. But the fatherland of the nouveaux riches, of the millionaires, of the old rich is not that fatherland. Their fatherland is brilliant; it has a press, schools, spectacles; it has everything one can possess with money; it has everything that they covet. And in contrast, the other fatherland made up by the immense majority of the people of Mexico—some of whom even have to flee to the United States from time to time to look for food—does not have the right to stand at the side of the one of the millionaires of Monterrey.

For them, the fatherland of the poor is not the fatherland, and they arrogate to themselves the right to represent us. . . . They unfurl the national flag and chant the national anthem in the street as if they were martyrs before the red wave of Moscow. (Applause).

They think that the national flag disgusts us, and that we repudiate it; that we are ungrateful; that we do not love the fatherland. What profound error! What great ignorance! Have these poor people, these poor rich people—or at least their aides—never read the manifesto of Marx or Engels? When has socialism repudiated the fatherland? When has socialism sustained that it is a revolutionary act to destroy the fatherland? Idiots! Ignorant people! Imbeciles! Cowards! (Applause).

(The speaker unfurls the national flag). . . .

This flag does not and should not represent corporations that enrich their managers and defraud their shareholders such as those of Monterrey. (Applause). This flag represents millions of corpses of Indians; rivers of blood in the Revolution of Independence; blood also in torrents in the war until the middle of the last century; more blood in the Reforma; blood . . . in Valle Nacional, in all the political prisons of Mexico; blood in 1910: that of Madero, that of Serdán, that of the Flores Magóns, that of so many anonymous workers and peasants who fought for it. This is blood. It is the flesh of the Mexican masses. It is not a trophy of bandits who exploit the people. (Applause).

We love the red flag. We love the red and black flag. We love all the symbols of the proletariat because they are the sum of all the particular flags stained with the blood of all the proletarians of the world. (Applause). But we are not traitors to the fatherland; we are making a fatherland, building a real fatherland. The question of seven centuries must have an answer: which one? Mexico, a country of well-nourished men; a country of men who read and write, a country of men who can enjoy life; no outcasts, no alcoholics, no syphilitics, no sad people; joyful youth. But the bourgeoisie will not give us joy, nor will it give us the illusion of living. No! Here is our flag, here is the other flag, our flag (he points to the red and black flag that covers the president's table). (Applause).

From today onwards, starting tomorrow, let there be a tricolor banner next to the red flag of the proletariat in every worker's locale. (Applause). Those who have bloodied our country and who have sucked the blood of a defenseless mass for centuries have no right to shelter under this banner that is the blood of their own victims. (Applause)....

Vicente Lombardo Toledano, speech, CTM, February 6, 1936

Document 87. The Expropriation of the Oil Industry[13]

One particular highlight of the Mexican Revolution was the expropriation of the foreign-owned oil industry on March 18, 1938. On that day, the Cárdenas administration acted after years of legal wrangling that had shown that the companies would not abide by Mexican labor legislation. It did so in the awareness that the focus on the U.S. government was in Europe due to the recent annexation of Austria by Nazi Germany. Until today, many Mexicans consider the oil expropriation an iconic event and an excellent example of the ability of a less powerful government to resist foreign imperialism. The following two sources delineate the president's reasoning. The first is the text of the expropriation decree.

Lázaro Cárdenas, Constitutional President of the United Mexican States, in use of the powers granted to the Federal Executive by the Expropriation Law in force; WHEREAS.

It is public knowledge that the oil companies operating in the country expressed their refusal to accept the order by the Federal Conciliation and Arbitration Board on December 18 last to implement new working conditions, notwithstanding the fact that the Supreme Court of Justice of the Nation has recognized its constitutionality. [The companies did not adduce any reasons for said refusal any other than that of an alleged economic inability, which brought as a necessary consequence the application of Section XXI of Article 123 of the General Constitution of the Republic . . . with the result of the termination of the labor contracts derived from the aforementioned award.

WHEREAS.

---

13. Lázaro Cárdenas, "Decreto de la Expropiación Petrolera," March 18, 1938, Memoria Política de México, accessed March 15, 2021, http://www.memoriapoliticademexico.org/Textos/6Revolucion/1938DEP.html. Translated by Jürgen Buchenau.

As an inevitable consequence, this fact implies the total suspension of activities of the oil industry. Under such conditions, it is urgent that the government intervene with adequate measures to prevent the occurrence of serious internal disorders that would make it impossible to satisfy collective needs and the supply of necessary articles of consumption to all population centers, due to the consequent paralysis of the means of transportation and industries. In addition, [authorities must] provide for the defense, conservation, development, and use of the wealth contained in the oil fields, and to adopt measures designed to prevent the possible consummation of property damage to the detriment of the community. I have determined all of these circumstances as sufficient to decree the expropriation of the property destined to oil production.

In view of the foregoing and based on paragraph 2 of Section VI of Article 27 of the Constitution and on Articles 1, Sections V, VII and X, 4, 8, 10 and 20 of the Expropriation Law of November 23, 1936, I have decided to issue the following
DECREE.

Article 1. We declare expropriated for reason of public utility and in favor of the nation, the machinery, installations, buildings, pipelines, refineries, storage tanks, communication routes, tank carts, distribution stations, vessels and all other real and personal property owned by Huasteca Petroleum Company, Sinclair Pierce Oil Company, Mexican Sinclair Petroleum Corporation, Stanford y Compañía, S. en C. Penn Mex Fuel Company, Richmond Petroleum Company de Mexico, California Standard Oil Company of Mexico, Compañía Petrolera el Aguila, S.A., Compañía de Gas y Combustible Imperio, Consolidated Oil Company of Mexico, Compañía Mexicana de Vapores San Antonio, S.A., Sabalo Transportation Company, Clarita, S.A. and Cacalilao, S.A., insofar as the Secretary of the National Economy judges them necessary for the discovery, gathering, conduction, storage, refining, and distribution of the products of the oil industry.

Article 2. The Secretariat of the National Economy, with the intervention of the Secretariat of the Treasury as administrator of the assets of the Nation, shall proceed to the immediate occupation of the assets subject to expropriation. . . .

Article 3. The Ministry of Finance will pay the corresponding indemnification to the expropriated Companies, in accordance with the provisions of Articles 27 of the Constitution and 10 and 20 of the Expropriation Law, in cash and within a term not to exceed 10 years.

The Ministry of Finance will take the funds necessary to make the payments from a yet-to-be-determined percentage of the production of oil and its derivatives from the expropriated properties, the proceeds of which will be deposited in the Treasury of the Federation while the legal procedures are being followed.

Article 4. Notify personally the representatives of the expropriated Companies and publish in the Official Gazette of the Federation.

Given at the Palace of the Executive Power of the Union on the eighteenth day of March of the year one thousand nine hundred and thirty-eight.

Document 88. Cárdenas Addresses the Nation[14]

The second document about the oil question contains excerpts from Cárdenas's address during a massive rally in support of the expropriation on the evening the decree was signed.

To the Nation:

It has been said ad nauseam that the oil industry has brought substantial capital to the country for its promotion and development. This claim is exaggerated. For many years and most of their existence, the oil companies have enjoyed great privileges for their development and expansion; customs and tax exemptions and innumerable prerogatives. Together with the prodigious potential of the oil fields granted to them by the nation, often against public will and law, these elements of privilege represent almost the totality of the true capital that we are talking about.

Potential wealth of the nation; badly paid native labor; tax exemptions; economic privileges and governmental tolerance: these are the factors of the oil industry boom in Mexico.

Let us examine the social work of the companies: how many of the villages near the oil wells have a hospital, a school or a social center, or a sanitary water supply, or an athletic field, or even a power plant fed by the many millions of cubic meters of gas wasted in the wells?

On the other hand, what oil production center does not feature a company police force to safeguard private, selfish and sometimes illegal interests? Whether authorized or not by the Government, these organizations have been accused of numerous outrages, abuses and murders, always for the benefit of the companies.

Who does not know or is unaware of the irritating discrimination characterizing the construction of company camps? Comfort for the foreign personnel; dreariness, misery and insalubrity for the nationals. Refrigeration and protection against insects for the former; indifference and neglect, doctors and medicines only reluctantly provided by the latter; lower wages and rough and exhausting work for ours.

---

14. Lázaro Cárdenas, "Discurso pronunciado por el C. Presidente de la República ante la manifestación de trabajadores organizada el día 23 de marzo de 1938, para significar su respaldo con motivo de la expropiación de la industria petrolera," March 23, 1938, Memoria Política de México, accessed February 21, 2022, https://www.memoriapoliticademexico.org/Textos/6Revolucion/1938MEP.html. Translated by Jürgen Buchenau.

It is true that the ignorance, lies, and weakness of the country's leaders bred the tolerance that the companies have abused. But investors too lacking in the required moral resources to give something in exchange for the wealth they have exploited set the play in motion.

The persistent and undue intervention of the companies in national politics has been another consequence caused by the presence of the oil industry, strongly characterized by its antisocial tendencies, and more damaging than all those listed above.

No one disputes anymore whether it was true or not that the oil companies supported strong factions of rebels in the Huasteca Veracruzana and the Isthmus of Tehuantepec against the constituted Government during the years 1917 to 1920.

Nor is anyone unaware of the fact that . . . the oil companies almost openly encouraged the ambitions of the discontented against the country's regime during later periods and even in the present day, every time taxation, a modification of the privileges they enjoy, or the withdrawal of their customary tolerances has affected their interests.

They have had money for arms and ammunition for rebellion.[15] Money for the unpatriotic press that defends them. Money to enrich their unconditional defenders.

But for the progress of the country, to find a balance by means of fair compensation of work, for the promotion of hygiene where they themselves operate, or for saving from destruction the considerable riches of the natural gases that are united with oil in nature, there is no money, nor economic possibilities, nor the will to extract funds from the volume of their profits.

[The companies believe] that their economic power and pride shields them against the dignity and sovereignty of a nation that has long given them its abundant natural resources and that cannot obtain the satisfaction of the most basic obligations by means of legal measures.

It is therefore unavoidable . . . to decree a definitive and legal measure to put an end to this permanent state of affairs in which the country is struggling, feeling its industrial progress held back by those who have the power to put up obstacles and the dynamic force of all activity in their hands. Rather than using that economic power for high and noble purposes, they frequently abuse it to the extent of endangering the very life of a nation seeking to elevate its people through its own laws, taking advantage of its own resources, and the free direction of its own destinies.

Having thus proposed the only solution to this problem, I ask the entire nation for the moral and material support necessary to carry out a resolution so justified, so important, and so indispensable. . . .

March 23, 1938

---

15. The oil companies had hired mercenaries to keep the revolution away from their property, including the notorious warlord of the Huasteca on the Gulf Coast, Manuel Peláez.

Document 89. Are Mexican Women Free?[16]

The following passage reflects the experience of Verna Carleton de Millán, a U.S. medical professional married to physician Ignacio Millán Maldonado, who served as director of the School of Rural Medicine in the Cárdenas administration. During their time in Mexico City, the Milláns befriended radical artists such as Frida Kahlo and Diego Rivera, and Ignacio Millán helped found the Sociedad de Amigos de la URSS, or Society of Friends of the Soviet Union. Verna Millán's memoir of those years, Mexico Reborn, is deeply sympathetic with Cardenismo but highly critical of the persistence of patriarchy, including among the radicals whom the couple called their friends.

I had only been in Mexico a very short while when I became interested in the feminist movement and woman's problems in general. Generalizations are perilous things, but from the start it seemed to me that Mexican women were much superior in every respect to Mexican men. The men here are momentarily brilliant and enjoy brief spells of power, but there is nothing stable behind it all, and at forty they are fatigued. The Mexicans themselves have noticed this phenomenon; "*Fulano se apagó,*" they say sadly—"So-and-so is all blown out," in the same way a match is extinguished by a breath of air, for the flame of their talent is equally as fragile. . . .

The Mexican woman of today . . . has this enormous burden of race and tradition upon her shoulders; product of a mestizo culture, she is caught in the mesh of not one but two traditions, both equally repressive. The Spaniards brought to Mexico the strict Catholicism that has held women in a subjective, passive role for centuries. On the other hand, the Indian tribes since time immemorial have crushed the spirit of their women beneath ironclad taboos and repressions. Even today, these customs of the Indians remain unchanged, save here and there, in those regions where a rapidly encroaching industrialization has brought about a new concept of life and morals. . . .

The Spanish Conquest was an added burden to the traditional slavery of the Mexican woman. Nowhere in the world have women been more bitterly oppressed than in Spain. The early Spaniards brought their traditions with them; marriage had only one alternative, the convent. Century after century, these precepts were beaten into women's souls until they created a peculiar psychological attitude of utter passivity and abnegation which has been an overwhelming obstacle in the path of the feminist movement. Even the Revolution was not able to make a clean break with the past, and today Mexican women in general are little better off than in the time of Díaz; a great portion of this is due to the fact that they have been suppressed

---

16. From Jürgen Buchenau, *Mexico OtherWise: Modern Mexico in the Eyes of Foreign Observers* (Albuquerque: University of New Mexico Press, 2005), 202–8. Reprinted by permission.

for so long that the mere thought of freedom bewilders them. An entire generation, perhaps two, will have to pass before a wide change becomes possible.

But when anyone takes into consideration the atmosphere that weighs upon the Mexican woman from the moment of her birth, it is a veritable miracle that any of them at all are able to escape its nerve-shattering influence. Within the home, the man reigns supreme, a heritage from the Middle Ages. The daughters are taught absolute obedience not only to their fathers but to their brothers as well. If there is little money in the family, the sons are educated at the expense of the daughters. If the family have money, they refuse to educate their daughters on the ground that they will not need a career after their marriage. Marriage is considered the supreme goal of every woman's life. The mother's marriage may have been a life-long tragedy but she can conceive of no other fate for her daughters, on the theory that any kind of marriage is better than none because at least one thus fulfills the Christian command to multiply. Never have I seen so many tragic marriages as in Mexico. . . .

The Spaniards bequeathed still another tradition to Mexico which is not precisely a guarantee for marital happiness. . . . This tradition is the Spanish one of maintaining two establishments, a large house for the legal wife and children and a little house, *casa chica*, for the mistress and whatever children result from the relationship. Most wives take this as a matter of course; my Anglo-Saxon mind has never quite been able to accept the calm excuse of many Mexican friends who say to me: "I don't care what my husband does outside of the house. He's good to my children and gives me everything I want."

I do not mean by this that all Mexican husbands support these customs. If it were so, I, as well as every other independent foreign woman married to Mexicans, would not have stayed out the first year. Indeed, I touch this subject gently because I am proud that my marriage is considered in Mexico a very successful one; but successful marriages are rare and worthy of attention precisely because these customs exist on all sides and the contrast is therefore ever greater.

A Mexican psychiatrist once expressed the opinion to me that Mexican men have a deeply rooted sexual inferiority complex, and that their incapacity for fidelity, which indicates an incapacity to maintain any consistently stable attitude, is closely related to the necessity they have for fortifying themselves with the number rather than the quality of their love affairs.

. . . Man is the Mexican woman's worst enemy. The very politicians, I soon found out, who drip with tears when they write about motherhood have fought tenaciously, with every weapon in their power, the efforts of organized women to secure the vote and thereby obtain really effective laws to protect maternity, which the country does not possess at present; the very revolutionaries who praise with tremulous emotion the glorious lives of Rosa Luxemburg, Krupskaia and other heroines of the revolutionary movement refuse to let their own wives attend the meetings they address.

"My husband is afraid I'll become infected with his ideas," one woman said to me dryly when I asked her why she had never heard her husband speak in public.

"Mexican husbands are feudal Marxists," another explained, "Marxists outside and feudalists within their homes." . . .

In spite of family opposition and social taboos, women are breaking away from their traditional lives, and when they do they become the most passionate defenders of the feminist movement. I like to tell the story of my friend Carolina as an illustration of what Mexican women can accomplish with courage and faith in themselves. Carolina is the dark-eyed, sensitive daughter of one of Mexico's most outstanding leaders, a man whose name remains in history as one of the most integral talents that the Revolution brought to the fore. Like most Mexican revolutionaries, however, he brought up his daughters in the convent and married them off as soon as they were able to think for themselves. Carolina, at twenty-two, found herself the bride of a man she scarcely knew, because . . . her friendship with him had taken place beneath the watchful eyes of the entire family, and never had she been alone with him a minute. For the next twelve years Carolina scarcely left the house. She lived the traditional life of the Mexican woman, babies and babies and more babies—eight in all and of these three died. Her husband was intent upon his career; a lawyer of considerable prestige, he became a well-known figure in the revolutionary movement and had little time to spend at home. So Carolina, with time on her hands and a keen, actively intelligent mind . . . spent most of her difficult pregnancies with a book. In the course of twelve years she acquired a very solid education by the mere process of reading her husband's entire library devoted to sociology, science, history and literature. One crucial evening she decided to hear her husband lecture, and without warning him she took a seat in the auditorium. In one hour she learned two important facts: her husband whom she had looked up to as a paragon of wisdom was a terrific fake; having actually read the books that he was supposed to have read, she saw with horrible clarity all the flaws and errors of his reasoning; also she learned that the dark-haired little school teacher who hung so attentively on his words was his current mistress and the mother of a baby by him. The next day she moved out of the house and has never been back since.

Now, at thirty-six, Carolina is a social worker and very active in the organization of women. She supports her five children by her own efforts because her husband will neither consent to a divorce nor contribute to the upkeep of the children, a dog-in-the-manger attitude which is, unfortunately, very prevalent. But Carolina, in spite of everything, feels that she is independent at last. This year she began to speak at political meetings, and I shall never forget the radiance in her eyes when she told me that she realized, at last, how much life held for her.

Document 90. Leon Trotsky's Perspective on the
Second Six-Year Plan (1939)[17]

Among the various outsiders' perspectives contained in this collection, the one of the Soviet exile Leon Trotsky stands out as an unusual viewpoint because of the orthodox and internationalist Marxist persuasion of its author. In contrast to Joseph Stalin, who took over the direction of the Soviet Union in 1928 under the aegis of building social- ism in one country, Trotsky—the preeminent orator and organizer of Russia's October Revolution of 1917—desired to advance the proletarian revolution on a worldwide scale. Trotsky arrived in Mexico in January 1937 and befriended Mexican artists and intellectuals such as Frida Kahlo and Diego Rivera. This analysis of the Six-Year Plan of Mexico's ruling party (then called the Partido Revolucionario Mexicano, or PRM) anticipated the party's turn to the right during World War II. Trotsky did not live to see it; he was assassinated by a Stalinist agent in August 1940.

A Program, Not a Plan

We are not dealing here with a "plan" in the true sense of the word. In a soci- ety where private property prevails, it is impossible for the government to direct economic life according to a "plan." The document . . . is a general program for governmental activity and not strictly speaking, a plan. Unfortunately, the authors of the plan do not take into account the limits of governmental activity in a soci- ety where the means of production, including the land, are not nationalised. They have apparently taken the Five Year Plans of the USSR as a model and often use the same phraseology, without taking into account the fundamental differences in social structures. . . .

Agrarian Reform

. . . What is the main question in Mexico today? Agrarian reform, or the *dem- ocratic agrarian revolution*; that is, the life of the peasants is characterised by a massive accumulation of the holdovers of feudal property forms and the relations and traditions of slavery. It is necessary to courageously and definitively liquidate these holdovers from medieval barbarism with the aid of the peasants themselves. The large parasitic or semi-parasitic landed proprietors, the economic and polit- ical domination of the landowners over the peasants, forced agricultural labour, the quasi-patriarchal sharecropping system, which is fundamentally equivalent to

17. "Trotsky on Mexico's Second Six Year Plan," March 14, 1939, Worker's Liberty, accessed February 27, 2021, https://www.workersliberty.org/story/2017-07-26/trotsky -mexicos-second-six-year-plan.

slavery—these are the things that must be definitively liquidated in the shortest possible time. Now, the program does not even call for the completion of this task, which is essential to the democratic revolution, within the next six years; but at the same time it does call for the complete collectivisation of the common lands in the same period of time. This is complete inconsistency, which can lead to the most dire consequences, economic, social, and political.

Complete Collectivisation

A. Collectivisation means the replacement of small-scale rural agriculture by large-scale agriculture. This change is only advantageous if highly developed technology adequate to the tasks of large-scale agriculture exists. This means that the proposed rate of collectivisation should be adapted to the development of industry, of production of farm machinery, fertilizer etc.

B. But technology alone is not sufficient. The peasants themselves must accept collectivisation, that is, they must understand the advantages on the basis of their own experience or that of others.

C. Finally, the human material, or at least a large part of it, must be educated and prepared for the economic and technical management of the common lands.

The plan . . . calls for the creation of a sufficient number of schools, especially agricultural schools. If we allow that such schools will be established in sufficient number during the next six years, it is clear that the necessary personnel will not be ready till quite some time later. Collectivising ignorance and misery by means of state compulsion would not mean advancing agriculture, but would rather inevitably lead to forcing the peasants into the camp of reaction.

The agrarian revolution must be completed within six years in order for the country to be in a position to advance toward the goal of collectivisation on this foundation, very carefully, without compulsion, and with a very sympathetic attitude towards the peasantry.

The Example of the USSR

The USSR went through not only a bourgeois democratic revolution, but a proletarian revolution as well. The Russian peasants, although very poor, were not as poor as the Mexican peasants. Soviet industry was considerably more developed. Nevertheless, after the nationalisation of the land, i.e. the complete agrarian democratic revolution, for many long years the collectivised sector of agriculture formed only a tiny percentage of the agricultural economy in relation to the individual peasant economy. It is true that twelve years after the abolition of the latifundia, etc., the ruling bureaucracy passed over to "complete collectivisation" for reasons that we do not need to go into here. The results are well known. Agricultural production fell off by half, the peasants revolted, tens of millions died as the result of terrible famines. The bureaucracy was forced to partially re-establish private agriculture. Nationalised industry had to produce hundreds of thousands of tractors and farm machines for the kolkhozes to begin making progress. Imitating these methods in Mexico would mean heading for disaster. It is necessary to complete the democratic revolution by giving the land, all the land to the peasants. On the basis of this established conquest the peasants must be given an unlimited period to reflect, compare, experiment, with different methods of agriculture. They must be aided, technically and financially, but not compelled. In short, it is necessary to finish the work of Emiliano Zapata and not to superimpose on him the methods of Joseph Stalin. . . .

The Industrialisation of the Country

In this area the program becomes extremely vague and abstract. In order to collectivise the common lands in six years an enormous outlay for the production of farm machinery, fertiliser, railroads, and industry in general would be necessary. And all of this immediately, because a certain technological development, at least on an elementary level, should precede collectivisation, and not follow it. Where will the necessary means come from? The plan is silent on this point except for a few sentences about the advantages of domestic loans over foreign loans. But the country is poor. It needs foreign capital. This thorny problem is treated only to the extent that the program does not insist on the cancellation of the foreign debt and that is all.

It is true that the realisation of the democratic agrarian revolution, i.e., handing over all the arable land to the peasantry, would increase the capacity of the domestic market in a relatively short time; but despite all that, the rate of industrialisation would be very slow. Considerable international capital is seeking areas of investment at the present time, even where only a modest (but sure) return is possible. Turning one's back on foreign capital and speaking of collectivisation and industrialisation is mere intoxication with words. . . .

State Capitalism

The authors of the program wish to completely construct state capitalism within a period of six years. But nationalising existing enterprises is one thing; creating new ones with limited means on virgin soil is another.

History knows only one example of an industry created under state supervision— the USSR. But, a) a socialist revolution was necessary; b) the industrial heritage of the past played an important role; c) the public debt was cancelled (1.5 billion pesos a year).

Despite all these advantages the industrial reconstruction of the country was begun with the granting of concessions. Lenin accorded great importance to these concessions for the economic development of the country and for the technical and administrative education of Soviet personnel. There has been no socialist revolution in Mexico. The international situation does not even allow for the cancellation of the public debt. The country we repeat is poor. Under such conditions it would be almost suicidal to close the doors to foreign capital. To construct state capitalism, capital is necessary.

Leon Trotsky, March 14, 1939

Document 91. Plan Almazanista[18]

In 1940, Mexicans readied for another contested presidential succession. Unlike in 1934, when left-wing movements pushed for social change, conservative factions were ascendant in the late 1930s, particularly the "Union Nacional Sinarquista" that had grown out of the Cristero movement and the "Partido Revolucionario Anti-Comunista" under the leadership of Calles's old allies. Opposition to Cárdenas's handpicked candidate, General Manuel Avila Camacho, coalesced around General Juan Andreu Almazán (1891–1965). Almazán boasted one of the most erratic careers of the revolution, fighting on behalf of several of the opposing factions at one time or another. He backed Obregón in 1920 and went on to become one of Mexico's wealthiest citizens with investments in construction, mining, real estate, and other areas. He served as President Pascual Ortiz Rubio's communications minister and later as zone commander before announcing his candidacy for president in 1939. In July 1940, Avila Camacho triumphed easily amid allegations of fraud. The following is the Almazanista manifesto, crafted a few months after the election. Another massive rebellion never materialized, showing that the revolutionary state had finally consolidated its power after thirty years.

Yautepec, Morelos, September 22, 1940

The Substitute Constitutional President, General Héctor F. López, to his fellow citizens:

On a temporary basis, I have established here the seat of the Executive Power of the Federation . . . in substitution of the functionary who failed to honor the solemn oath he swore to guard and uphold the Constitution. As my first act, I will inform my fellow citizens . . . of the norms and principles that will guide the proceedings of the Substitute President.

The government over which I preside arose from the most genuine and indisputable expression of the people's will. In order to fulfill their mandate, it is

---

18. González, *Planes políticos, proclamas, manifiestos y otros documentos,* 990–92. Translated by Jürgen Buchenau.

indispensable to direct the nation along a truly liberal, advanced and progressive path, from which it has departed. My brief role will be unswervingly dedicated to enforcing the mandate of the people that the usurpers have attempted to supplant.

Without any commitment whatsoever to reactionaries within or without, and regardless of the color imprinted upon them by the totalitarian Hitler-Stalin-Mussolini triumvirate, I will endeavor to raise the standard of living of all Mexicans . . . without any distinction, in spiritual, moral, and material terms, giving special attention to the destitute. Those have been the ones most exploited and oppressed by a political [rhetoric] that—with sarcastic cruelty—proclaims that they are the targets of special predilection to achieve the goal of a proletarian republic.

Our program, in political and social terms, will continue to be the Constitution of 1917.

Sincerely democratic [and headed by] an old soldier of Maderismo, the administration over which I preside will defend with zeal and devotion the rights and freedoms of man and our democratic institutions that are imminently imperiled by the agents of the totalitarian triumvirate whom we will sweep from our Fatherland without any compassion or tolerant exceptions. The free men of the world need to fight them tenaciously and inflexibly. . . .

The troubling and difficult reality of Mexico brings together the most terrible hunger, as a direct product of a government of the unprepared and imitators of totalitarian designs. It cannot and should not serve to cover up or justify electoral fraud, the most apparent and cynical injury to the sovereignty of the people. On the contrary, to tolerate . . . the continuity of the only Party (totalitarian party) and of the "Six-Year Plans" (communist plans) that have produced that distressing reality would mean working for the consummation of national disaster.

Those who rebel against the government today are not the only ones who have sought to wrap themselves in the sacred mantle of the Fatherland. All usurpers of Mexico allege that the Fatherland they dare to personify stands above what they call "political passion."

[The government] has forged the minds of children and youth in the hard mold of Marxist communism. It has attacked the inviolability of conscience and moral unity of the family. It has exercised illegal despotism and extended persecution and political assassination from one corner of the republic to another, with the only end of imposing a successor. It has turned the soil of our young and our old into an international dumping ground, attracting and welcoming political-social outcasts, destabilizing agents of foreign governments. After all of this anti-patriotic labor, [the government] has the audacity and arrogance to occupy the venerated stage of Father Hidalgo to ask for the union of all Mexicans and for appeasement, which would be nothing less than complicity in the usurpation and cowardly abandonment of democracy.

Such union and appeasement cannot exist because they do not exist in the souls. If democracy is really the link and banner of liberty raised in the Western Hemisphere; if the union of American republics, reiterated in the Havana conference, serves to "preserve in them Christian civilization" to defend our families, our households, and our bodily and spiritual liberty—everything that ennobles and dignifies human beings and defends them through the free determination of the popular will—then our first obligation is and will be to defend and preserve the democratic institutions of Mexico that are currently ignored and defiled.

In order to defeat the totalitarian menace with the symbol of democracy on an international basis, it is indispensable that every American republic achieve interior victory by means of the abnegation and bravery of its sons, guided by that same symbol.

For Mexico to become an active and efficient member of the alliance for the defense of democracy in the Americas rather than a perturbing element as one of the figurehead governments of foreign dictators, it is a most urgent imperative for all Mexicans to restore the reign of national sovereignty, which resides essentially and originally in the people, as manifested in the elections of July 7. It is necessary to install the Legislative and Executive powers designated by that same people, in full exercise of their functions. The democratic union of the Americas would be a myth without the existence of democracy in each one of the republics.

At this moment, our mission is to defend and restore democracy in Mexico. If the calamity of a fratricidal war should occur in the process of defending it, the culpability will not be with those who represent and sustain the legally elected public powers, but those who attack those powers in violation of the sovereignty of the people.

To fulfill this high civic mission, I call upon the Mexican people, all of the free men and women who have resolved to make their civic rights respected, to prevent the consummation of electoral fraud and usurpation with the means that each of us has at their disposal, adding their efforts to those of this government. I am confident that each and every one of you will fulfill your duty, and I am sure that freedom, order and social justice will reign in Mexico thanks to our sacrifice and abnegations, accompanied by the sympathy of the democratic peoples.

Suggested English-Language Readings

Azuela, Mariano. *The Underdogs: Pictures and Scenes from the Present Revolution—A Translation of Mariano Azuela's Los de abajo, with Related Texts.* Translated by Gustavo Pellón. Indianapolis, IN: Hackett Publishing, 2006.

Boyer, Christopher. *Becoming Campesinos: Politics, Identity and Agrarian Struggle in Postrevolutionary Michoacán.* Stanford, CA: Stanford University Press, 2003.

Brenner, Anita, and George R. Leighton. *The Wind That Swept Mexico.* New York: Harper, 1943.

Buchenau, Jürgen. *Plutarco Elías Calles and the Mexican Revolution.* Lanham, MD: Rowman and Littlefield, 2007.

Cumberland, Charles C. *Mexican Revolution: The Constitutionalist Years.* Austin: University of Texas Press, 1972.

Dulles, John W. F. *Yesterday in Mexico: A Chronicle of the Revolution, 1919–1936.* Austin: University of Texas Press, 1961.

Garner, Paul. *Porfirio Díaz.* London: Longman, 2001.

Gonzales, Michael J. *The Mexican Revolution, 1910–1940.* Albuquerque: University of New Mexico Press, 2002.

Hall, Linda. *Alvaro Obregón: Power and Revolution in Mexico, 1911–1920.* College Station: Texas A&M University Press, 1981.

Hart, Paul. *Zapata: Mexico's Social Revolutionary.* Oxford: Oxford University Press, 2017.

Henderson, Timothy J. *The Worm in the Wheat: Rosalie Evans and Agrarian Struggle in the Puebla-Tlaxcala Valley of Mexico, 1906–1927.* Durham, NC: Duke University Press, 1998.

Joseph, Gilbert M., and Daniel Nugent, eds. *Everyday Forms of State Formation: Revolution and the Negotiation of Rule in Mexico.* Durham, NC: Duke University Press, 1994.

Joseph, Gilbert M., and Jürgen Buchenau. *Mexico's Once and Future Revolution: Social Upheaval and the Challenge of Rule since the Late Nineteenth Century.* Durham, NC: Duke University Press, 2013.

Katz, Friedrich. *The Life and Times of Pancho Villa*. Stanford, CA: Stanford University Press, 1998.

Kiddle, Amelia M., and María L. O. Muñoz, eds. *Populism in Twentieth-Century Mexico: The Presidencies of Lázaro Cárdenas and Luis Echeverría*. Tucson: University of Arizona Press, 2010.

Knight, Alan. *The Mexican Revolution*. 2 vols. Cambridge: Cambridge University Press, 1986.

———. "Cardenismo: Juggernaut or Jalopy." *Journal of Latin American Studies* 24 (1994): 73–107.

Meyer, Jean. *The Cristero Rebellion: The Mexican People between Church and State, 1926–1929*. Translated by Richard Southern. Cambridge: Cambridge University Press, 1976.

Meyer, Lorenzo. *Mexico and the United States in the Oil Controversy, 1917–1942*. Translated by Lidia Lozano. Austin: University of Texas Press, 1972.

Meyer, Michael. *Huerta: A Political Portrait*. Lincoln: University of Nebraska Press, 1972.

Mitchell, Stephanie, and Patience A. Schell. *The Women's Revolution in Mexico, 1910–1953*. Lanham, MD: Rowman and Littlefield, 2007.

Olcott, Jocelyn. *Revolutionary Women in Postrevolutionary Mexico*. Durham, NC: Duke University Press, 2005.

Osten, Sarah. *The Mexican Revolution's Wake: The Making of a Political System*. Cambridge: Cambridge University Press, 2018.

Smith, Stephanie J. *Gender and the Mexican Revolution: Yucatán Women and the Realities of Patriarchy*. Chapel Hill: University of North Carolina Press, 2009.

Vaughan, Mary Kay, Gabriela Cano, and Jocelyn Olcott, eds. *Sex in Revolution: Gender, Politics, and Power in Modern Mexico*. Durham, NC: Duke University Press, 2006.

Womack, John. *Zapata and the Mexican Revolution*. New York: Knopf, 1968.

INDEX